The Portugal Traveler

Great Sights and Hidden Treasures

by

Barbara Radcliffe Rogers

and Stillman Rogers

Mills & Sanderson, Publishers

Bedford, Massachusetts

LIBRARY OF CONGRESS

Library of Congress Cataloging-in-Publication Data

Rogers, Barbara Radcliffe.
    The Portugal traveler : great sights and hidden treasures / Barbara Radcliffe Rogers and Stillman Rogers.
        p. cm.
    Includes index.
    ISBN 0-938179-19-5 : $9.95
    1. Portugal -- Description and travel -- 1981 -- Guide-books.
I. Rogers, Stillman, 1939-   . II. Title.
DP516.R64 1988
914.69'0444--dc 19
                                                        89-3173
                                                        CIP

Printed and bound in the United States of America

Printed and maunfactured by Thomson-Shore, Inc., Dexter, MI.
Cover photograph by Stillman Rogers.
Cover design by Lyrl Ahern.
Photo of authors on back cover by Al Karevy.

To Julie, whom we can still see playing in the cobbled streets of the Alfama and guarding the ramparts of Marvão in the morning fog. For all of us, Portugal will always be the magic place of her childhood.

Other Books by Barbara Radcliffe Rogers

Yankee Home Crafts, Yankee Books, 1979

Old Fashioned Family Christmas, Yankee Books, 1981

Encyclopedia of Everlasting, Weidenfeld & Nicolson, 1988

The Christmas Catalog (revised edition), Price, Stern and Sloan, 1988

Acknowledgements

Although two people may be the authors of a book, it is nearly always with the help and support of many other people. We would especially like to thank a few of them. First, our friend and advisor, Tony Madeira in Lisbon. It was at Tony's suggestion that we sought out many of the fascinating corners we might otherwise have missed, including the lovely private guest homes of the Minho.

Dr. Olivo Sousa of the Portuguese Tourist Office in New York helped in many ways, especially by arranging lodging and telling us about the brand new Hotel Dom Luis in Coimbra. Ed Hunter of TWA found us seats at the very last minute during a busy travel season, and introduced us to Jacques le Couls as he was about to leave Boston to become the manager of the Hotel Meridien in Porto. We are grateful to both of them.

Evelyn Heywood, of Evelyn Heywood Associates provided us with valuable material and offered suggestions which made our work easier.

Although we can't list them separately because we don't know their names, our heartfelt thanks goes to the helpful people who staff the tourist offices in cities and towns all over Portugal. They have, over the years, solved our problems, found us lodging and given us advise and information on local attractions. With them go all those wonderful people — the priest in Aveiro, the altar ladies in Bragança, and the countless others who took the time to show us the treasures of their native place. It is these people that make Portugal such a delight for the traveler.

And to our family — Dee, Julie and Lura — who keep things running while we travel (when they are not traveling with us) and who have helped in countless ways to make this book a reality, our biggest thanks of all.

Table of Contents

Dear Reader: Why Portugal?

How fascinating it would be, I thought while traveling through the French countryside, if I could have seen this a hundred years ago. What an experience it would have been to live in Verona in the century before I did, to revel in the Octoberfest or waltz in Vienna in the waning years of the nineteenth century. What was market day like then in Saanen or in Bergen?

Old copies of National Geographic and the great authors of the Grand Tour era were my only clue. It was a world that didn't exist any longer — or not in Europe at least. The local customs and dress that varied from town to town are homogenized now; the weekly market has too often given way to supermarkets. In Central America, Peru or Ecuador, perhaps, but no more in Europe would we find the pre-industrial world, except in a few tiny isolated or carefully preserved places. The wars and the common market have changed it all.

Then we strayed from the Grand Tour path — not to just a different town or mountain peak, but to Portugal. Forgotten in its corner, lumped with Spain in the mind of travelers and tour operators, unexploited in peace, unimportant in war, unsung in books and unseen by even the well-traveled, it has lived its own tumultuous life, threatened by the sea on two sides and by Spain on the other two.

Since the final days of the early explorers, it hasn't even been a stopping off place for west bound travelers. Only the British and the Spanish saw much of it. The Spanish weren't welcome and left, and the British kept it a close secret. Today's traveler finds English spoken with British usage, and Spanish hardly spoken at all.

It was a backwater, not on anyone's way, not flashy or expensive enough to become an international playground, despite its mild climate and beautiful beaches, too unstable in economy to attract foreign investment.

Don't misunderstand — it is not a primitive place without the amenities of comfortable, even luxurious, travel. Few hotels can boast of the grandeur or luxury of the Pousada Rainha Isabel, few restaurants the cuisine of Queluz's Cozinha Velha. Fine wine, beautiful resorts, magnificent palaces, gardens, grand and profoundly moving shrines both religous and historic, elegant shops, meticulous handwork — all the things that travelers need and seek — are there in abundance, and enjoyed by those who return there year after year.

But in the terms of the hordes who have seen Venice or Nice, or Amsterdam, most of Portugal is undiscovered. Lisbon and the Algarve are its best known sights, but they are only a taste — the appetizer. Tiny walled towns cling to craggy hill tops and overlook the Spanish border with mistrust, startling white villages stud the southern shore, women await the return of the brightly painted fishing boats on the beaches of Nazaré each day, Prince Henry the Navigator still haunts the lonely windswept point of Sagres, and village markets are the high point of the week in towns all over the country.

The people, despite their unspeakable language, are friendly, eager to meet and help the stranger, proud of their treasures and heritage and unjaded in their role as hosts. The cities are safe and clean, the small towns rich in local folklore and regional traditions, all intensely human. Political unrest is past and the economy keeps prices a travel bargain.

While there is much to see and do there, Portugal is still small enough to be manageable. A two-week trip allows time to see nearly all the country, although, of course, not its every possible attraction. A month allows a leisurely pace, with time to bask in the sun, stay a few extra days here or there, and seek the nooks and crannies with ease. In a week, the casual tourist can see a good deal of the central area and still have time left for Lisbon.

Its history, too, is of manageable proportions and in a very little time the visitor, or reader, will feel that the kings and queens, both the saints and the sinners, are real people. There is a humanity to Portugal's story, and to the way they tell it even today, that is touching and personal. You, too, can believe that King Pedro will arise at the resurrection to meet his tragic Inez, and feel a presence at Fátima that leaves you silent all the way to Tomar.

With no time there at all, the armchair traveler will enjoy it too, and find a link with our own history not often explored past fourth grade social studies classes. However explored, the experience of Portugal is a glimpse into Europe of the last century, and into the hearts of a forgotten people. Their unasssuming hospitality will charm, their ways often amuse, their treasures dazzle, and their landscape impress you. Most important of all, you will enjoy your stay, and always treasure the hope of returning.

Introduction

Getting There and Getting Around

Whoever said "Getting there is half the fun" doesn't travel much. The business of transporting body and baggage from home to destination can be aggravating, boring and time consuming — eating up time you'd rather spend where you're going. We've been in and out of Lisbon via nearly every route and airline available and we're ready to name names.

The easiest routing, least hassle and most accommodating airline on the route is TWA. Here are a few of the reasons. The transatlantic portions of all direct flights begin in New York. By flying TWA from your nearest gateway city (and they fly everywhere) you fly right into JFK and directly to the terminal from which you will leave for Lisbon. Avoiding a terminal change in New York is a major plus.

If you fly the same airline straight through, your luggage is far more likely to arrive with you. TWA's baggage record is excellent, and it is a comfort to know that your baggage will arrive in Lisbon, not Nairobi. But the most important single factor is that when you return to the United States, all baggage has to be claimed and taken through customs. This usually leaves you toting it all over JFK (have you ever tried to find a porter there?) to your connecting flight. But TWA passengers simply hand their inspected luggage to the waiting TWA representatives who transfer it to your next flight.

All the things you expect (and sometimes get) from an airline are there, too, but this bit of pampering alone is enough to convince us. It also helps to have an English speaking staff handling your questions, reconfirmation and changes in schedule.

TWA offers some excellent ground package plans which can save you a lot of escudos in lodging and car rental. For example, in 1989 an eight-day package which includes six nights in the top class pousadas in Setúbal, Estremoz, Evora, Sagres and Palmela, plus unlimited mileage rental car is $469 per person ($566 in high season). A fifteen-day itinerary into the north and Alentejo with two days in Lisbon is $862 per person. TWA also arranges special rates for their passengers at some of Portugal's best private hotels including the Meridien in Porto, the Estoril Palace and the Setais Palace in Sintra.

One more note on transatlantic flights: Ambassador Class is well worth the extra cost for its significantly wider seats and increased leg-room on an all-night flight. There is a higher ratio of flight attendants and Ambassador Class passengers pre-board with First Class so there is extra time (and space) to get hand baggage and coats stowed before the aisles become crowded. TWA's toll-free number is 800/221-2000.

Lisbon's airport is a pleasure to use. It is small, easy to find your way in, and has good, inexpensive food service.

Getting around in Portugal is easiest by car. There is, however, frequent train service to the attractions around Lisbon, making a day trip to Sintra or Óbidos quite easy — especially if you're living at the Avenida Palace right next to Rossio Station. Train connections to other cities are noted in the *At A Glance* sections throughout the book.

Rental cars are easily available through all major companies, but we recommend Rupauto in Lisbon. They are prompt, nice to deal with, speak fluent English, are reasonably priced and their cars are in top condition. Be sure to make car reservations in advance of your trip: have your travel agent telex them at 62033 Rupaut P. Their Lisbon telephone number is 01/77 80 86.

You will find standard transmission helpful on mountain roads, but if you insist on automatic, be sure to specify that when you reserve. Standard also uses less fuel, a consideration in Europe, where gasoline is so expensive. Service stations in Portugal keep full hours and many are open 24 hours a day. In the far north or mountain areas, always leave a city with a full tank, since towns are few and far.

With Common Market membership came the VAT — a steep tax on everything. Since your car rental is a major budget item, be sure to ask for VAT rebate forms. Take these to the tax desk at the airport, located just past the passport control station, where they will refund your tax.

If you plan to take your rented car into Spain, you will need to tell them in advance so there will be a special stamp on your car papers. Be sure to check for it when you get the car. Your car will be delivered to your hotel — ask the concierge to call when you are ready.

How to Use This Book as You Travel

Forget what the librarian told you when you got your first library card; it is O.K. to write in books, as long as you own them. Especially in travel books, since they become both a planner for each day's itinerary and a record of where you've been. Use a red pencil — and a blue and a green one if several people are sharing the trip. Underscore the places that sound best, and use the margins for a notebook.

While we're suggesting heresies, here's another. It is O.K. to photocopy it, too. Throughout the book you will find specially marked *At a Glance* sections that give the nuts-and-bolts information on each area. This includes the telephone numbers and addresses of hotels, the restaurants, the times and dates and details that the armchair traveler doesn't need to plow through, but which you will need on the spot. Before you leave, photocopy these pages for the areas you will be visiting. Each day, carry in your pocket the pages for the area you are in. That way the details you need will be at your fingertips and you can keep the book in the car for reference. Copy the menu guide, too. That's much more discreet in a restaurant than hauling out an entire book when you read a menu.

If your copy center is a law-abiding place which will not reproduce copyrighted material, show them this page: this is our official permission to copy any and all of the *At a Glance* pages for your personal use.

One other tip: the greatest boon to travelers since the hair-dryer is the Scotch Post-it note pad by 3M. We carry several 2 by 3 inch pads on every trip. They are perfect for marking the pages you need to refer to each day. They stick to the page, so they don't fall out as bookmarks do, and they peel off without damage when you are through with them. Each evening over our glass of port we map out a general plan for the next day and mark the pages we will need to refer to. For even quicker reference we note the name of the town or attraction on the loose end of the note so we can tell them apart.

Now that we've told you how to abuse this book, let us tell you a little about what is left. A travel book cannot possibly be all things to all readers. It can, as most do, describe the major sights and the places closest to the beaten path, leaving out a multitude of less known (and less crowded) gems. But to include all the wonderful places in Portugal would require a volume that would not be either useful or portable while traveling. And so we have made our choices.

Perhaps we have not always chosen the finest example, or the largest or the oldest or the easiest to find. But the choices have not been arbitrary, and we have mentioned as many of the others as we could, in hopes that the traveler who reads this will track some of them down and discover their particular delights as well.

We have chosen to talk at greater length about those places that have impressed us the most or that are generally considered to be the highlights. When the two criteria did not coincide, we have discussed both. After — or maybe even before — you have visited these places, we hope you will strike out on your own, following a blue sign with the monument symbol at some forgotten crossroad just to see what is there.

You may never find it — although road signs and town markers are excellent in Portugal, the monument signs often leave one to flip a coin at the next fork in the road — but you will certainly find something interesting. For there are no boring corners of this country, and no dull landscapes. So take time as you travel between the "important" sights, to wander the backroads and byways and find your own Portugal.

Speaking or Not Speaking Portuguese

No one really trusts a travel writer who speaks the language. "That's easy for *you* to say," is the reaction, "but how will I get around?" Quite easily in Portugal.

The language is not an easy one. Unlike Spanish or Italian, words aren't pronounced exactly as they look. Like French, there is a distinct nasal lift at the ends of some words, but, unlike French, every letter is pronounced. The *ñ* and *ll* sounds of Spanish are indicated by an *h* following the *n* or *l*, as in senhora (senyora) and Batalha (Batalya). *S* sounds are a bit slushy at the end of a word, so adeus is "adiush."

But you won't learn that from reading about it. The best plan, if you just don't feel comfortable without the language, is to get the records or tapes and listen to them for a few weeks before the trip.

That is Tim's method, and in two weeks he is not fluent, but can ask and understand directions. I do nothing but use "point and grunt," along with faint remnants of a year of college French (much more useful here than our Spanish) and a phrase book, and I get around comfortably.

Every tourist office has someone who speaks English, as do most hotels and all pousadas. In the border towns, Spanish is spoken, but elsewhere it is not popular. In an emergency, you can count on the Portuguese to find someone who speaks English who will help. Most restaurants have translated menus, and in little places that don't, they'll take you to the kitchen to show you what is available or bring it out for you to see.

Learn the polite phrases of greeting, apology and request, and everyone will be delighted that you have gone to so much trouble. If you don't understand a price, ask them to write it — and if you don't recognize the coins, someone will simply pick the right ones out of your hand. Best yet, they will never make you feel stupid in the process.

The most important thing to remember is the nature of the Portuguese people. Hospitable to their toes, they really try to understand and be understood. They will engage in pantomime, lead you by the hand, draw little maps, and try every other language they know. Above all, they will not leave you lost, hungry, with a disabled car or without lodging. Someone will understand your problem and everyone will help solve it. So relax about their unspeakable language, where puxe is pronounced "push" and means pull.

The Menu: Your Most Important Travel Document

Portuguese food, traditionally, is neither fussy nor "fancy." It is moderately seasoned, uses the freshest of ingredients and is plentiful. Someone once wrote a glib little book about Portugal with the word "garlic" in the title, and, ever since, writers have cautioned about the garlic. We have been puzzled by this constant warning in guidebooks, as have our friends who travel there. It may have once been true, but in the years since we've been going there, we haven't found even noticeable traces of garlic except in one soup where it is commonly used. In fact, we've commented from time to time that a little garlic would have been an improvement. This shows how myths get started and hang on.

Fish is fresh and always delicious. It is also always listed separately on the menu. If you aren't sure what kind of fish you might like — and there are varieties that we don't have here — the waiter will usually offer to go to the kitchen and bring back a platter of samples so you can tell the nature of it before ordering.

Bacalhau is salted cod, and a national standby. We think it appears by law on every menu, like ice cream at Harvard. The salt is soaked out and it is then cooked in an astonishing variety of ways — all of them good. But it has a distinctive texture, different from fresh fish.

Meat is usually pork or veal, sometimes kid. Chicken is usually there, too, but it is not the ubiquitous menu padder that it is most places. Liver, even if you are not fond of it, is excellent and unlike liver anywhere in the world (except Venice where it is equally delicious).

Desserts are sweet, but fruit is also offered. Vegetables are rare, except for potatoes, which are freshly fried to perfection or boiled. Salads are ordered separately. Inexpensive and safe to eat, these are usually a plate of sliced tomatoes in a vinegar and oil dressing. Coffee is strong and we've never had a bad wine, whether we chose a pitcher from the cask or a bottle from the cellar.

The Menu Terms found in Appendix II will help you through the menu, although most places have (roughly) translated ones. We always read through these for the wonderful expressions we find. We have collected such gems as "dreaded veal cutlet," "balls of codfish" and the most appetizing of all, en brochette translated to "beef with spit." Eat up!

Restaurants are often hidden behind or above bars, adegas and cafes. The only clue may be the menu posted on the door or in the window. It is perfectly acceptable behavior to stand there and read these and to browse around before choosing a restaurant. Sometimes a waiter will see you squinting to read one and bring you a copy to read in better light. If you decide not to eat there, he's not offended.

In choosing a place to eat, follow your nose. If savory scents pervade the dining room or the street, follow them inside. But if the smell isn't appetizing to you, the food won't be either. *Don't* slavishly track down all the places we mention and miss the adventure of finding your own. These are the ones we've stumbled into or had recommended to us and have been happy with, but don't be shy about coming upon your own finds. As with lodging, you will get at least what you pay for, and often a good deal more. We have never had a bad meal in Portugal. We've had some very plain ones, and some beef that tended toward tough (but who needs beef when there is such excellent veal?) but we have never left hungry or unhappy with our dinner.

Don't forget to bring a copy of the Menu Terms located in Appendix II at the back of this book!

The Lodging Riddle

No one has ever been able to explain to us all the subtle distinctions of the official classifications of lodgings in Portugal. There are hotels, which may be elegant bastions of fine service or be quite small and plain. They are rated by stars, based on a formula which is not always directly related to their comfort or attraction to a traveler.

There are pousadas, government-run inns, often in remote areas where lodging has been scarce, and often in old castles or convents. These are in three price ranges which vary significantly depending on the time of year. We have not listed all nine of the possible prices for each pousada, simply the high and low for a double room. Singles are less, suites more. The high season is July 1 through September 30, low is November 1 through March 31. High season for the islands is during the winter. Middle season is between the two, both spring and fall — probably Portugal's best travel seasons. Pousada reservations are made through Enatur in Lisbon (telex 13609 Enatur P, telephone 01/ 88 12 21, in the U.S., call 212/ 686-9213).

Estralagems are in the same price range as pousadas and similar in style, but privately owned. Albergarias are inns — often in the smaller towns and family-run. They are priced below the estralagems — usually. Then there are residéncias and pensãos, the pensions of Europe, which can be anything. The star ratings don't tell you much, so you simply have to ask to see a room. These often have restaurants, but meals except breakfast are not included in the rate.

Quite recently a new type of lodging has cropped up which is very attractive to the traveler who enjoys meeting people and longs to peek inside their homes. Especially prevalent in the north, guest homes are often in elegant villas, quintas, manors, estates and town houses. Reservations must be made in advance. We have listed a number of these, but you can get an up-to-date list and make bookings through TURIHAB, Praça da República, 4990 Ponte de Lima, Portugal (058/942-355, telex 32618 PTPL) for guest homes in the northwest or through Turismo de Habitacão, Rua Alexandre Herculano 51-3.0, 1200 in Lisbon (01/ 68 17 13). These are classed according to type as "Casas Rusticas" which are farms or rural homes, "Solares" which are estates, sometimes small palaces, and "Casas Antigas" which are homes of some historic interest. Prices vary greatly, but solares are the most expensive and casas rusticas the least. Enquire at the Portugues National Tourist Office in New York, which sometimes has a list of these.

All cities and most towns of any size have a tourist office (Turismo) which will help you find lodging. These are very helpful and friendly and have information on other places in the region as well. Although you are likely to have no trouble finding rooms from night to night in the off season, if you travel in the high season, it is wise to reserve in advance. The pousadas in major tourist destinations — Palmela, Estremoz, Marvão and Evora — are more likely to be full. How much of your lodging you reserve in advance depends on how adaptable and flexible you are. It is always wise to reserve your Lisbon lodging well ahead.

Please Take the Children

There are few places in the world so perfect for traveling with children as Portugal. There are fantasy palaces such as Pena and Bucaço, castle ramparts to walk, ruins to climb in, boxwood gardens to get lost in. Most of all, the Portuguese love children and will do anything to please them.

Throughout, you will read of our adventures with Julie, our daughter who opened so many doors for us. People would literally stop us on the street to ask if they could show her some hidden treasure. Waiters presented her with gifts and took great delight in bringing her special goodies. Wherever we went, other children were fascinated by her blond hair and little camera, and she got some wonderful pictures we never could have taken.

Hotels will roll in cots at a very small extra charge and restaurants will bring half servings if asked. Children go everywhere at night, so no one thinks it strange to see them in restaurants at 10 p.m. They will soon discover the delicious Sumol fruit drinks and be glad to join you in a cafe stop. Because everyone looks out for children, you will find yourself comfortable in letting a child go alone to the TV rooms of hotels, and, of course, anywhere in the pousadas.

Gardens

The public and private gardens of Portugal are among the finest in the world and the traveler will find them everywhere without searching them out. Dooryards, windowsills and public parks are filled with flowers, there are several outstanding botanical gardens and the spring wild flowers are glorious.

Portugal's climate has blessed her with the richest natural flora of Europe. In Peneda Gerês National Park grow species of wildflowers native only to that small area, and, in the spring, the wild flowers literally turn the mountainsides yellow and pink. The altitude in this region varies so abruptly that within a few miles of each other are both subtropical and Alpine flowers.

In April the high country of the Alentejo and Algarve are carpeted in purple, gold, red and white, with chrysanthemums, poppies, gum-cistus and matricarias, while in the north the roadsides bloom with wild narcissus. The moors are yellow with broom in the summer and pink with heather in the fall.

The Serra da Arrabida on the Setúbal peninsula, just south of Lisbon, is a 2,000 foot limestone ridge whose summit divides the floral region like a fence. On the north slope grow peonies and bluebells, while to the south of the crest grow the heaths, wild lavender, blue gentian, an occasional rare wild tulip, poppies and gaiety of others. From mid-March into early summer there is a constant variety of bloom.

The best time for wild flowers in the Algarve is in February and March, and on into early April. Roadsides are bordered by roses and iris, while gladioli, anemones, tulips and tiny hyacinths grow as field flowers.

As though nature's own gardens weren't enough, there are cultivated gardens of all types. In Lisbon, the finest of these is at the Palace of Fronteira, where topiary and formal beds are set in walls covered by azulejos. Two botanical gardens, one at Belém near the monastery, and the other just off the Avenida da Liberdade, are filled with rare exotics.

At the zoo are formal rose beds — in fact the zoo is set amid lovely gardens. In the Parque Eduardo VII is the Estufa Fria, where a slatted roof protects over an acre of flowering plants.

In Sintra are Monserrate and the botanical gardens of Pena Palace, as well as the eighteenth century palace gardens at Queluz. Coimbra, farther north, has a terraced botanical garden and Castelo Branco has a most unusual formal garden with box hedges bordering brilliant flowers, punctuated by statuary and orange trees. Nearly every city has at least one public garden filled with beds solid with color — the traveler comes upon these quite unexpectedly even in very modest towns.

Many of the private quintas have gardens which are open to the public, the most notable of which are at Mateus, near Vila Real and N.S. do Carmo at Estremoz. The former Convent of S. Marinha da Costa near Guimarães, now a pousada, is set in an outstanding eighteenth century garden.

Why so Many Churches ?

A casual flip through this book might lead the reader to ask why there are so many churches and monasteries. The answer is simple. In Portugal, the churches and monasteries are the art galleries, museums and historic sites. The talents of the finest artists and architects of Portugal's golden age went into building these. When something good happened — a battle won, a royal heir born — a monastery was built in thanksgiving. When the hour was grim, vows were made to build one if the outcome were favorable. Two of Portugal's greatest travel destinations are monasteries that were built to honor vows made on the eve of battle.

Monasteries were royal homes as well; widowed queens and unmarried princesses retired to them, kings and queens were frequent guests. Abbots were men of great wealth and power and it showed in their churches. Kings bestowed gifts of magnificent chapels or cloisters upon favored monasteries and convents. Almost every artistic expression was made to God, or through His holy orders.

Churches were (and are) the focal point of village life; festivals all revolved around the church calendar and local residents followed the lead of royalty in offering thanks and petitions in the form of elaborate gifts to the church. Hospitals were established by the church and so arose the Misericordias in nearly every city of any size, each with its own church richly decorated in the baroque style.

Gold was cheap — it came by the boatload from Brazil. Rare woods arrived from Goa, Brazil and other colonies, ready for artists to carve and inlay. Marble was a local building stone, so plentiful in some areas that it was used for doorsteps and window frames on the humblest homes. The abundance of these riches drew Europe's best craftsmen to Portugal.

There are palaces and stately homes as well, scattered throughout the land, but most of the magnificent sights are in the churches.

"Restorations"

You will hear us lament the damage done to churches, monasteries and other buildings in the name of restoration. Portugal has, in the last 150 years, destroyed more of its art treasures than two world wars destroyed in most of the rest of Europe. The Ancient Monuments Commission has directed the destruction of priceless altars, carved choir stalls, statuary, azulejos and even structural features, in the name of "purification." With the dissolution of the holy orders in 1836, the government became owners of all the monasteries and their properties. Somewhere they acquired the notion that all these buildings should be stripped of any ornamentation added since the completion of the original structure, as though a church were a loaf of bread which, once baked, is finished.

Churches, more even than homes, are living things which grow and change and continue to be decorated and embellished with the finest works of each age. Since many of the greatest Portuguese churches were begun when the Romanesque style was current, the Commission set about making every structure under its control "pure" Romanesque. They stripped the frescoes, smashed out the azulejos and literally burned the carved choir stalls.

They have slowed down considerably, after a century of outcry by art historians, travelers and writers, but even into the past two decades the notion and the destruction have continued. To make it worse, they have spent their limited resources on this and failed to take the essential measures to protect and preserve other properties under their care, allowing some to fall into complete ruin.

Church Names

Santa, Santo and São, all Portuguese words for "saint," have been shortened to S. for easier reading except where the name is that of a city or island. Likewise, N.S. has been used for Nossa Senhora (Our Lady). These shortened forms, along with Sta. and Sto. are commonly used on signs in Portugal. The Igreja Matriz, or Mother Church, is the parish church, the Misericordia was originally attached to a hospital. The Cathedral is always called the Sé.

Architectural and church terms, as well as a floor-plan of a typical church, can be found in Appendix III — The Anatomy of a Church.

The Protocol of Churches

The Portuguese are justly proud of their churches and are pleased to show them to visitors. If the door is unlocked walk right in. Feel free to look all around, but keep voices low, especially if there are people at prayer. It is all right to go into the chancel to see things more closely, or to look for a light switch. Even for non-Catholics, it is considered polite to at least nod toward the high altar when crossing in front of it.

Since the finest treasures of many churches are their sacristies, it is important to seek these out. It is not rude to try a closed door when looking for the sacristy, although we always open it just a little first and peek inside, asking permission if there is anyone inside. Even just before and just after Mass when the priest is busy robing, they usually welcome visitors.

If you enter a small church with Mass in progress, it is probably best to just look around from the door. In a larger church, you can usually slip inconspicuously along a side aisle or into a rear pew from which you can observe the church unnoticed. It is an important courtesy to show that you respect it as a place of worship.

Saturday is a good time to find churches open, as the "altar guild" ladies prepare all the flowers for Sunday. If one of these ladies shows you around, it is polite to give her 100 escudos "for the church" (por l'igreja). If a sacristan takes you around or has to be summoned to open the church, the same sum is usually offered when you leave.

If a church is locked, ask anyone nearby who has the key. If necessary point to your car keys and to the church door, and they'll understand and send you off to the house of the sacristan — or go find him for you. Once you've been through this routine a time or two, it becomes second nature — and very often leads to interesting adventures.

Have You Met Manueline?

Just as you think you have baroque and rococo straight, let us introduce you to an architectural style that is peculiar to Portugal. Born of the age of discoveries, when the riches of three continents were arriving by the boatload, the sea played an even greater part in life than usual. The Manueline style draws heavily on these maritime themes.

Columns twist like great cables, coral branches frame windows, knotted ropes form groining for vaulted ceilings, tree trunks are supporting pillars. There are anchors and chains, sails, fishing floats, barnacles, mariners' knots, even octopus tentacles. They are combined in a fantastic, flamboyant style decorating portals and windows set against wide open expanses of walls — like the flat surface of the sea broken by a craggy, surf-sprayed islet.

The relief is deeply carved to catch the intense light and cast deep shadows. While all this frothy, busy design would seem to place it in the rococo class or in baroque, with its use of blank spaces, it is actually a Gothic style, with heavy overtones of North Africa and the Orient.

The portal and Chapter House window at Tomar, the Convent Church of Jesus in Setúbal, the unfinished chapels at Batalha, the Palace at Bucaço and churches scattered throughout central and southern Portugal provide fine examples of this distinctive style.

PORTUGAL

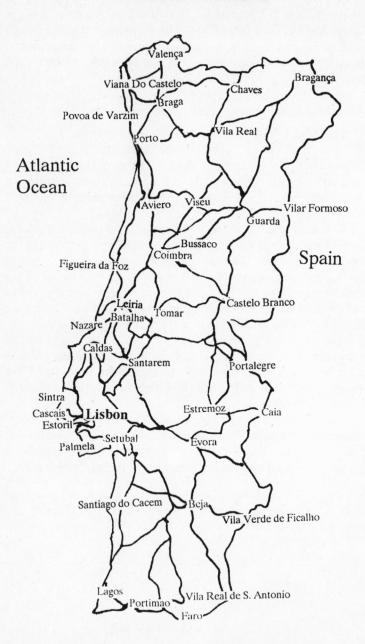

Valença
Viana Do Castelo
Braga
Povoa de Varzim
Porto
Chaves
Bragança
Vila Real

Atlantic
Ocean

Aviero
Viseu
Vilar Formoso
Guarda
Bussaco
Coimbra
Figueira da Foz

Spain

Leiria
Batalha
Tomar
Castelo Branco
Nazare
Caldas
Santarem
Portalegre

Sintra
Cascais
Estoril
Lisbon
Estremoz
Caia
Palmela
Setubal
Evora

Santiago do Cacem
Beja
Vila Verde de Ficalho

Lagos
Portimao
Vila Real de S. Antonio
Faro

Lisbon(Lisboa)

Despite the internationalizing influences at work in any capital city, Lisbon is still very Portuguese. Even after leveling by an earthquake and tidal wave in 1755, and a fire in 1988 that destroyed entire blocks of the architecturally rich Chiado, Lisbon still doesn't look like other cities.

It sits on hills, with broad avenues and tiny twisting streets broken by belvederes and little squares called largos. This terraced effect leaves the facades of many of its churches open and visible from a distance. Above the Alfama rises Castelo S. Jorge, immediately giving an air of ancient grandeur to the city below. After the earthquake, the Marquês de Pombal — a man of iron will, but great vision — set about building a beautiful, well organized city that would have enough housing. "I want attics on top of attics," he is said to have ordered his architects.

The result is a beautiful city, harmonious but never boring, where tangles of narrow lanes rise out of grand squares connected by broad avenues. Just when it might become pompous, delightful relief comes from a block of houses all covered in blue azulejos, or a trolley-car funicular, or a little largo with a fountain or the ships of the great Tagus anchored below a grand square.

The easiest way to deal with Lisbon is to break it into its neighborhoods, as the Lisboans themselves do. Our divisions may not follow the "technical" geographical lines, we have followed the natural terrain and local usage.

The Rossio sits in the center of it all — a giant square whose official name is the Praça Dom Pedro. With the exception of Belém and a few attractions near the university, nearly everything to see is within walking distance of this square. This is why we suggest making it "home" while staying in Lisbon.

From the Rossio to the Tagus (Tejo) runs a grid of straight, level streets, ending at the Praça do Comércio, which overlooks the river. The line from the Rossio to the Praça do Comércio runs almost exactly north-south, with the river running east to west.

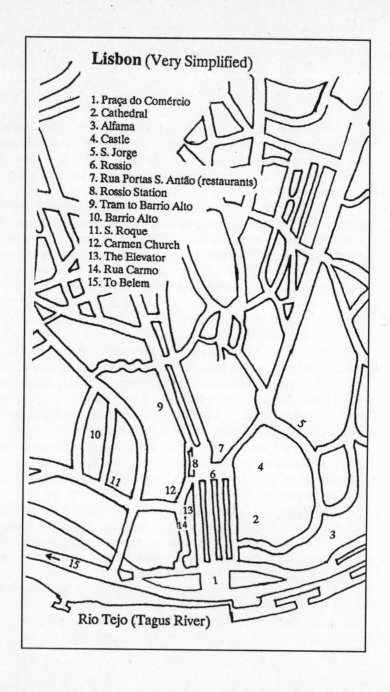

Lisbon (Very Simplified)

1. Praça do Comércio
2. Cathedral
3. Alfama
4. Castle
5. S. Jorge
6. Rossio
7. Rua Portas S. Antão (restaurants)
8. Rossio Station
9. Tram to Barrio Alto
10. Barrio Alto
11. S. Roque
12. Carmen Church
13. The Elevator
14. Rua Carmo
15. To Belem

Rio Tejo (Tagus River)

The Rossio is overlooked by the Castelo S. Jorge to the east, behind which lies the Alfama. On the west it is overlooked by the Bairro Alto, meaning high neighborhood. Along the edge of this hill in a crescent shape is the Chiado, an unofficial name that doesn't appear on maps. The area from the Rossio to the river is the Bairro Baixa, or low neighborhood. To the west along the river, for quite a distance, is Belém.

Finding your way is complicated by the fact that, except for the Bairro Baixa, there is hardly a straight flat street in Lisbon, but the hills also provide landmarks and the belvederes stand as beacons from which the visitor can immediately take his bearings.

First, the Rossio. The square itself is large, with two fountains, lined with eighteenth century buildings. The absurdly out-of-place Rossio Station — termed neo-Manueline in architecture, but looking much like a World's Fair pavilion or a multi-storied harem — stands just off it, with horseshoe-shaped doorways and its facade newly cleaned to a cream color. Trains to Sintra and Alcobaça leave from here, and inside there is an escalator for quick access to the Bairro Alto above.

Hanging over the west side of the Rossio, even more noticeable at night, when it is flood-lit in a ghostly green and seems to float above the square, is the apse of the ruined Carmo church. Just in front of it is a wonderfully ornate elevator connecting the Baixa and the Alto with a confection of iron grillwork. It is Lisbon's answer to the Eiffel tower, but there is some discussion over whether he actually designed it. The elevator is entered a block south of the Rossio, from a walking street full of shops and cafes, in the center of Lisbon's best shopping district.

Beyond, facing the river, the Praça do Comércio is entered through a monumental baroque arch. In the center of the square stands a statue of José I, the king who gave such broad authority to the Marquês de Pombal. This was, before the earthquake, the terrace of the Royal Palace and is still called Terreiro de Paço on some maps and by some Lisboans.

The Praça has other royal associations. It was from here that Catherine of Bragança sailed to become Queen of England (she came back after Charles II's untimely dispatch). It was also here that King Carlos and the crown prince were assassinated just as they ascended into the royal carriage. For all practical purposes, the monarchy died with them in this square as quickly as the great royal palace itself fell in the earthquake.

The Chiado runs along the edge of the flat area from the Comércio to the Rossio, bounded by buildings whose backs hold up the Bairro Alto. The map names of the streets are Carmo and Garret, ending in the Largo do Chiado.

The area, always known locally as the best of Lisbon's shopping streets, made world headlines in 1988 when a fire swept through several blocks of it, fanned by the natural updrafts of Lisbon's hills. Now the Rua do Carmo is blocked off just past the elevator, and months later, Lisboans still stand on the arch at its top, looking down into the tangle of steel and stone, muttering "no credo" — I don't believe it.

Gone are the shops, the restaurants and the fashionable cafes, but, fortunately, most of the fine facades with their stone carved architectural details can and will be saved and returned to the way they looked when the area was rebuilt after the earthquake.

To consider the earthquake, the visitor really should ascend the elevator and follow the little street along the gray walls of the Carmo church to its entrance on the largo. Inside, its magnificent nave stands open to the sky. It was All Saints Day, 1755, just as the faithful had gathered for the morning Mass, when the earthquake struck in three separate shocks. Buildings crumbled into rubble and the vaulted roof of Carmo collapsed into the crowded nave.

In addition to those who died in the quake, others were washed away by the tidal wave that followed, and much of what remained of the city was burned in fires started by fabric and wood falling into lighted candles in the churches. The city and the country were paralyzed, and the king, never an administrator, gave de Carvalho (later the Marquês de Pombal) even greater authority. To his credit, Pombal built a beautiful city, with elegant buildings, broad avenues and gracious open squares. Despite his despotic rule, Pombal is still honored today for bringing Portugal out of disaster and into the modern world.

A street leading up from the opposite corner of Largo do Carmo leads into another square with a church at the far corner. S. Roque is atypical of Portuguese churches, and a gem. The nave is short for its width, unbroken by arches or heavy columns, so it appears more light and open and square. Its lines are clean and straight, its main altar uncluttered. The four founders of the Jesuits are represented, but there is little other statuary. What really sets

S. Roque apart is its deep-set side chapels. Unusual reliquaries fill the Chapel of the Assumption — polychrome wooden busts with glass windows. On the left, N.S. de Pietá is done in gold intaglio, with a balustrade carved from wood brought from India. The highlight is the blue and gold Capela S. João, made in Italy of lapis lazuli, agate and marble, with a mosaic "painting."

The ceiling, although flat, is painted in trompe l'oeil to simulate vaulting and add visual height. The sacristy is lined in blue and yellow azulejos. A reminder here about sacristies, in case you skipped the Introduction. If there is no obvious door off the chancel, or if it is locked, ask someone if you can see the sacristy. Adjacent to S. Roque is a very fine treasury of ecclesiastic art in the former convent buildings.

Beyond is a belvedere overlooking the city, and a funny little trolley-car funicular leading down to the Praça dos Restaurádores.

Overlooking the Rossio from the east, like a great gold crown over the city at night, is Castelo S. Jorge. The steep streets surrounding it, including the famed Alfama quarter behind it, are the most charming in Lisbon, and the oldest. This is almost the only area to survive the earthquake.

Rua Magdalena runs along the lower edge of this hill, reached from a street leading out the southeast corner of the Rossio. A right turn onto Magdalena leads past a set of stairs that go almost directly to the base of the castle. Straight on toward the river making a left turn onto Rua S. Antonio da Sé, leads to the Cathedral. Ask for the "Sé" (pronounced "say") when seeking directions to any cathedral.

The Romanesque facade may look a little formidable up close and by daylight, but it is quite elegant lighted at night and seen from the opposite hill, standing out in its largo. Inside, the nave is also Romanesque, lightened by a Renaissance chancel. Behind the high altar are several good Gothic tombs, but to the faithful, the highlight of this church is the font where S. Anthony was baptized, along with centuries of Lisbon babies since. While Padua may claim him, the saint was born in a house right in front of the Sé (a chapel stands there now) and took his holy orders at Coimbra.

The street ascends to a belvedere and garden called the Miradouro de S. Luzia with fine views over the Tagus. Above is the Espirito Santo Foundation, a school of antique decorative arts where the students are taught the nearly lost skills of leather bookbinding, gold leaf decoration, woodcarving, and fine restoration. From here come the craftsmen who are able to restore and maintain the artistic treasures of Portugal.

The Alfama is a maze of narrow, steep streets, closely lined with homes, some covered in tile, others stucco, most with balconies, trailing pots of flowers, and strings of laundry. The street is an extension of the homes that line it, where commerce, social life and domestic activity all blend. When the terrain becomes too steep, the streets turn into stairs and when too steep even for these, it ends in a belvedere overlooking the gardens and rooftops below. Views out over the Tagus open up and are gone in a few steps. Along the lower edge runs the Rua S. Pedro, with shops, restaurants, cafes and street merchants, including the colorful varinhas selling fresh fish.

To reach the castle from any point here, just head uphill, and eventually a gate will loom above. The favorite time to arrive at the castle is just before sunset, as the Lisboans do, to watch the sun drop behind the hill into Belém. As it falls, it bathes the castle in a rich glow, and stands the trees which line its outer walls out in black silhouette against the orange sky. The Tagus below turns a misty pale blue.

S. Jorge's history is almost the history of the city itself, first built by the Visigoths, then the Moors, then the Portuguese, it retains bits of all in its ten towers and connecting walls. Inside the outer wall is a complete medieval town.

Not far beyond the Alfama and also at the crest of a hill is Igreja S. Vincente, with fine azulejos in its cloister. Its main interest is in its former refectory, which is now the royal pantheon of the Bragança line. While the tombs themselves are not especially interesting, the names tell us a great deal about Portugal — not just the history, but its character as well.

The Braganças were the last dynasty to rule Portugal. They were not always wise or efficient rulers and they faced the rising tides of republicanism that swept across Europe, but they were loyal, and, in the end, respected. The first Bragança, João IV, is here, along with his daughter Catherine, once Queen of England. But most interesting are the last. The assassinated King Carlos and Crown Prince Luiz Philipe one would expect, but beside them rest Luiz's brother Manuel II, last king of Portugal, who fled into exile in England in 1910, rather than throw Portugal into civil war by defending his crown. After his death in 1932, he was brought home to rest in royal honor, and later so was his widow. He left his considerable fortune to Portugal.

Through an arch beside the church is the Campo da S. Clara, where there is a Feira de Ladra, a flea market, every Tuesday and Saturday.

In contrast to the Alfama and Bairro Alto, crowded onto their hillsides, Belém is flat and broad with space to spare. Although a long distance, it is on a straight trolley line from the Alfama and Praça do Comércio, a good chance to ride these elegant old street-cars with their interior wood varnished like an old pullman car.

Belém stretches along the river at the point where the great explorers sailed; Vasco da Gama left from its shore to sail around Africa to India. There is a modern monument to the explorers, in the shape of a caravel prow.

The enormous <u>monastery of Jerónimos</u> dominates the center of <u>Belém</u>, considered the finest example of Manueline architecture. Its carved doorway leads into a nave, rising to incredible height upon slender columns that seem even more fragile because of the intricate stone carving that covers them. The sacristy ceiling is supported by a single central column in the shape of a palm tree, unique, but consistent with the Manueline use of exotic themes taken from the travels of the explorers.

The cloister crowns Jerónimos — a graceful, double-storied arcade with each window carved in a lacework of stone, and each in a different pattern. In the garth is a garden which completes its design and draws it together as a carpet does a room. It is a triumph of this late Gothic style peculiar to Portugal.

The museums of Belém are among the most interesting as well as the most informative for the traveler, of any in Portugal. We normally don't spend much time describing museums, but these are exceptional.

Belém The first is more like a royal cavalcade than a museum, the <u>Museu Nacional dos Coches — Coach Museum</u> — which rivals even the splendid one in Vienna. Set in the elegant halls of the former royal riding school is a dazzling collection of royal coaches from the seventeenth to the nineteenth centuries. The gala state carriages of the eighteenth century are like high altars, so covered are they with baroque swirls and ornaments.

Here we meet more of the royal family: #24 is the coach of the scheming Queen Carlota Joaquina, wife of João VI, whom she loathed, and #22 is the coach of King José I whose statue stands in Praça do Comércio. In a smaller chamber, look for the little Coche do Meninhos de Palhava, "worthless children, " illegitimate sons of João V, half brothers of José I. These children wander sadly along the raveled edges of history, and we shall meet them again, exiled in a remote and lonely monastery. It's a lovely little carriage, and the crown on top is symbolically askew.

The next, the Museu de Marinha, shows a glorious seafaring past, with mementos of the years of sea power and empire, when the world's bravest and best equipped adventurers and explorers sailed under the red cross of Prince Henry the Navigator. There are models of the ships and treasures from the voyages as well as a fully equipped royal barge!

The Museu de Arte Popular assembles the finest examples of historic and contemporary Portuguese folk arts, arranged to give perspectives on the history and everyday life, as well as the artistic heritage of provincial Portugal.

The Manueline tower beyond is the Torre de Belém, which used to stand in the water but has been beached by the changing course of the Tagus. It is not open to the public.

The Museu Etnológico contains artifacts from the many Roman and pre-Roman sites throughout Portugal, its chief interest to visitors who will be traveling to these. In addition, it has fine ethnographic collections from the former colonies in Africa and Asia.

There are many other interesting things to see and do in Lisbon. It has a delightful zoo set in flower gardens and a botanical garden with a cool house to protect delicate plants from the heat (amusing to those of us from the northern climates who have the opposite problems with our gardens). The Gulbenkian Foundation on Avenida de Berna near the university has an eclectic collection from Greek, Roman, Egyptian and other ancient civilizations as well as later painting, sculpture, furniture and assorted art treasures.

A particularly fine church, designed by the architect of Mafra, is Madre de Deus, which sits above the Tagus past S. Apolonia Railway Station. It is done in gilded baroque wood carving, set above azulejos, and has a fine small sacristy and nuns' choir. Attached is a tile museum, where there are outstanding examples of this art so integral to Portuguese church and domestic decoration. There are azulejos here from all centuries and styles.

Beyond its "sights" Lisbon is one of the world's pleasantest cities to be in, and one of its safest. The residents of Lisbon, like those of the rest of Portugal are hospitable almost to a fault. If they fear you do not understand a direction, they will take you there themselves, and often also to a favorite place you didn't know about. They love Lisbon and they want you to love it too.

Lisbon At A Glance

Capital city and main airport for arriving visitors.

LODGING: *Hotels are plentiful in Lisbon and the quality is good. Since there are so many we feel we can afford to be choosy; here are our criteria: 1) Location — we like to stay in the center where we can walk everywhere day or night, but we want a place that is easy to get to by car. 2) Service — since there always seems to be business to attend to in Lisbon, such as car rental, air reservations, things to be sent, messages to be delivered, tickets and reservations to be confirmed, we like a hotel with a concierge that's a combination of nanny and executive secretary. 3) Charm — we are staying in one of the world's loveliest and most gracious cities and we like our home there to reflect that. 4) Cost — we like to get what we pay for, whatever the price range. 5) Comfort — we like good beds, spotless rooms, big bathtubs, a desk and a place to sit with a glass of port in the evening.*

The hotel we've found that fits all those best is the Avenida Palace (01/360-152, telex 12815), an elegant building overlooking the Rossio. We can drive there along wide boulevards without ever encountering a one-way street, leave our car in the little courtyard, and walk anywhere.

It is from the era of the grand hotels, with a marble lobby, chandeliers, antiques and a grand staircase, but its rooms have modern marble baths. They also have plenty of space, huge closets, and comfortable furniture in the classic style. It is a $4 taxi ride from the airport. Spacious doubles cost about $85, which includes a full sausage and eggs breakfast.

For those who prefer the glow of modern sophisticated architecture and style, and don't mind having to take taxis, the new Meridien (01/ 690 900, telex 64315), just off Edward VIII Park, north of the center of Lisbon, is the best choice. It is marbled and mirrored, the rooms are handsome and crisp, and the service is excellent. Doubles run *between $120 and $150. Our choice is to enjoy this atmosphere later in the trip, at the Meridien in Porto, where there isn't a hotel like the Avenida Palace.*

For charm in an older part of the city, and a fine view, top grades go to the small Albergaria da Senhora do Monte (01/862 846), in the Gracia district behind the Alfama. A bit difficult to get to by car, and a long walk from the center, but a delightful lodging, each room is individually decorated, with little balconies overlooking the city. Doubles are in the $50 range.

Possibly the best bargain among good comfortable hotels in Lisbon is the Hotel da Torre (01/636 262), right beside the Jerónimos monastery in Belém. For those who enjoy, as we do, settling into a neighborhood on a longer stay, this corner in Belém is perfect. It is quiet, but there are restaurants and cafes just down the street. Museums are minutes away and the trolley to the Baixa and Alfama runs almost past the door. Plain and modest, but especially good for families, the Torre has several suites with small singles attached to doubles; Julie always loved having her own little room here when she was small. Rates are in the $35 range.

FOOD: *Since we think any chef does best with the local cuisine, we won't tell you where to find a great Chinese restaurant in Lisbon (if there is one). Restaurants tend to group in areas where you can browse before choosing by reading the menus posted in front. We shall suggest our own favorites, as well as areas in which to "shop." Our taste runs to smaller, more personal restaurants, not big flashy ones, so bear that in mind.*

In the Alfama we like the tiny A Tasquinha, where along with the regular well-varied menu there are daily specials of regional dishes often hard to find in Lisbon. On Wednesday, for example, they serve the Trasomonte bean and sausage dish, Feijoada. Any night the mixed grill (Espatadas) is good as are the veal scallops in Madeira. It's hard to spend over $10 apiece here. Just above the Miradouro da S. Luzia, it's on Largo do Contador Mor, at its narrow end.

On the same largo, with gleaming crystal and white linens (the Tasquinha is provincial in decor) is L'Arliquin, with a very good, very international and fairly expensive menu.

In the Bairro Alto, there are restaurants everywhere. For an unsurpassed view of the castle lit up at night, we like Quinta, almost under the flying buttresses of Carmo church, at the top of the elevator. Their sardines narrowly missed the ultimate grilling, since this building *was at the very edge of the Chiado fire. The sardines are delicious, as is the sausage-stuffed squid. Full dinners with dessert are about $10 each.*

Local friends often take us to lunch at the Baralto on Rua Diariade (newspaper street) where their Escabeche de Carapão is an excellent first course to share. Full meal for two with wine is under $10.

When shopping for restaurants here in the evening, we avoid the highly advertised fado places, opting for the smaller ones such as Don Quixote on the street just uphill out of Largo de Carma. Fado, a soulful singing, usually begins about 11, so the time to go for dinner is about 9:30 or 10. Or you can eat elsewhere and go just for wine and the show.

There are probably more restaurants per linear foot on the first two blocks of Rua Portas S. Antão than any other street in Lisbon. Just off the Restaurádores, which adjoins the Rossio to the north, a block from the Avenida Palace Hotel, is a street filled with restaurants and menu-reading prospective diners each night. Restaurants are in all price ranges. At the top is the Solmar, known for its seafood as well as wild boar, pheasant and venison; dinner here will cost about $20 each. In a little terrace between this street and the Restaurádores is Arameiro, with outdoor tables and a pleasant dining room. While chicken is their specialty, we've also had good veal and shellfish dishes there, never paying over $10 each.

Those staying in Belém, or visiting the museums there, can find several well-established restaurants on Rua Belém, right by the monastery. Caseiro is a good value with great food in the $10 range, and S. Jerónimo is just a little more expensive. Caseiro's trout is especially good and we made this our restaurant-to-come-home-to, eating there several times during one long stay. When at last we were about to leave Lisbon, the waiters gave Julie a little pottery vase as a goodbye gift, a story we tell to underline the pleasures of settling into a neighborhood.

We ended our long days often with a stop at a little cafe near the corner, and one night Julie asked for a pastry they were out of. She'd become such a regular customer by then that the owner sent a waiter up the street to another cafe to get her the pastry.

SHOPPING: The major shopping streets are those leading south from Rossio toward the river and along Ruas Carmo and Garrett. A portion of Carmo is closed because of the fire, but there are good shops at either end, including a bookstore. There are antique shops on Rua *do Alecrim, Rua de S. José, and Rua S. Bento. Santa Anna, the major source of azulejos, is also on Rua do Alecrim, in the Chiado, Quintão on Rua Ivens is the place to buy Arraiolos carpets and the shop at the Popular Art Museum in Belém has small handcrafts from the provinces. There is an artisinato at Rua Castilho 61, which will not only ship your purchases from there but from other shops as well. Fine embroideries from Madeira, for those who are not going to the islands, are at Casa Regional da Ilha Verde on Rua Paiva de Andrade.*

There is a grocery store, a good place to find small gifts as well as picnic supplies, on Rua 1 Decembre 81, near the base of Rua Carmo just off the Rossio. In case of emergency, the shops in the Rossio Station are open late in the evening.

FESTIVALS: *June 12 is the feast of S. Anthony, patron saint of Portugal and Lisbon. Look for bonfires, fireworks, and general merrymaking. The bullfight season is from April to October, usually on Sunday and Thursday afternoons at the new bullring on the way to the airport. The best way to get a schedule and tickets is to ask that magical and omniscient man, your concierge.*

IF TIME IS SHORT: *See Jerónimos monastery in Belém, Castelo S. Jorge, and take a walk in the Alfama, dividing whatever time is left among those sites that appeal to your own interests.*

Setúbal and Palmela

Only in the old quarter of Setúbal, with its narrow winding streets, does any of its ancient charm remain, for it is now a modern industrial city. But to those interested in tracing the development of the Manueline, that architectural style peculiar to Portugal, the Igreja do Jesus is an important stop.

The church, constructed in the last years of the fifteenth century, of local marble, is the earliest example of Manueline building. The twisting pillars are of colored marble and seem too delicate to support the vaulting above. Unfortunately, "restoration" here was so heavy handed, removing all of the carved and gilded work, that the church now appears to be nothing but a scrubbed shell. This makes its peculiar balcony-like high altar appear even stranger, but one can at least see the beginnings of the style that was to culminate in Jerónimos and Batalha.

It is worth asking to see the cloister and the nun's choir, now used as a chapel, with good gold rococo work, although it is sometimes not possible to gain entry. The Chapel of Senhor do Bomfim is an even better example of gilded rococo woodwork, which covers the main and side altars. Although very small, the chapel also offers a fine paneled ceiling, and azulejo panels. It is open 3-6 every afternoon, or enquire at the house next door for the key. Bomfim is off the park Campo Bomfim about three blocks from the waterfront and from the Igreja de Jesus.

There is a good view from the castle where the Pousada de S. Filipe is located.

About 15 km north of Setúbal on the road up the Serra toward Vila Nogueira lies the Quinta de Bacalhoa, hidden behind a thick hedge. One of Portugal's oldest houses, it was built in the late 1400's as a small palace for the Infanta Beatrice (the one for whom the swan room at Sintra was decorated). Gardens and a pavilion were added early in the sixteenth century, including the earliest date tile picture panel in Portugal. The house is not open to the public, but the garden with box hedges and orange trees is open 1-5 p.m. (except Sundays). Farther on, Vila Nogueira Azeitão is

27

an attractive town with fine houses and a good carved fountain. There is a market there on the first Sunday of the month.

Near Setúbal as the crow flies, but some distance by road, is the Troia Promontory, a long sandy spit with a Roman town, half submerged at the point. A few years ago one could poke about its ruins, mostly covered by sand on their lonely spit with only the sea birds for company. Now the whole area is being made into a tourist complex and the ruins have just recently been sealed off. Before making the boat trip, it would be wise to see if access to the Troia Promontory is open.

Sesimbra, like Setúbal, has little of its old sections left, but these are in the area descending to the beach, a warren of steep streets with laundry and fish drying along the housefronts and songbirds in cages outside the windows. The harbor is under a cliff, a short distance from the town, its fleet of painted boats usually the most active in the mid morning or late afternoon when the catch is sold. In the evening the nets are untangled and spread in the streets to dry.

The Moorish castle, much restored, offers a good view of the coast. About 10 km west of the castle is Cape Espichel with its lighthouse and pilgrimage chapel, which is the scene of a Romaria on August 15 and a fisherman's pilgrimage on the last Sunday in September.

The northernmost road between Setúbal and Sesimbra goes right along the top of the Serra da Arribida, a spectacular drive with the ocean and coast almost directly below. The slopes of the Serra are covered with wildflowers, one of the finest displays of native flora on the continent (see Introduction, p. 9), at their height in March and April, but with something in bloom most of the season. There is a cave, Lapa de S. Margarida, on the lower road.

The strategic location of Palmela's Moorish fortress made its possession essential to the control of the peninsula south of the Tagus, and Portugal's first king, Alfonso Henrique, quickly secured it. Unfortunately, this outstanding example of Mediterranean architecture was seriously damaged in the 1755 earthquake which left the monastery and castle walls in such a tumble that much of it was used to rebuild the town just below.

More fortunately, the decision was made to restore the monastery as the Pousada do Castelo de Palmela and the result is not only a fine restoration but one of the loveliest of the pousadas as well. It preserves the look and feel of the original cloister with the cells turned into guest rooms and the refectory, its pulpit still intact, into the dining room.

It is thought that the Moors built on the site of a Celtic settlement from the third century B.C. and a Roman road has been discovered behind the castle. About 3 km west a megalithic necropolis was discovered, so the history of Palmela is an old and continuing one, its remnants reflecting nearly every stage in the history of Iberia itself.

South Of The Tagus At A Glance

Setúbal, Sesimbra and Palmela are each about 40 km south of Lisbon, reached by the gigantic new bridge over the Tagus. There are also buses from Lisbon.

LODGING: In terms of quality, this small area has a largess of riches. Two pousadas and an outstanding private quinta head the list. The Pousada S. Filipe (65/ 238 44) in the castle at Setúbal offers nice rooms, antique furnishings and an excellent dining room with a panoramic view. Be sure to request a room with a view. It is upstaged, however, by neighboring Palmela's pousada (01/ 235 1226), described above.

Near Vila Fresca de Azeitão is one of Portugal's first quintas to open its doors to guests, the sixteenth century baronial mansion of Quinta das Torres. Surrounded by farmland, well-kept gardens and a pool (even a swan) with a stone gazebo surrounded by water, the main house is lovely, although beginning to show its age a bit. Rooms are furnished with antiques, some have balconies and all have private baths. A double room is about $50 and the lovely suite is only a few dollars more.

FOOD: Local specialties include fish of all varieties, fresh and well-prepared, as well as Azeitão's ewe's milk cheese. On weekdays 9-11:30 and 2-5 in Nogueira de Azeitão, the producers of Lancers as well as much better red and white wines give tours and wine tastings. Since this is a resort area, restaurants are very easy to find.

Quinta das Torres serves an outstanding meal in their azulejo-walled dining room at about $15 each and the Ribamarin in Sesimbra is reliable, although a good deal more expensive than many of the small restaurants that you will find just by walking around a little. In Setúbal, the Rio Azul is near the pousada and O Beco is on the Lago da Misericordia.

SHOPPING: *Is ordinary here, with no particular specialties. There is a market the first Sunday of each month at Vila Nogueira Azeitão.*

IF TIME IS SHORT: *Skip this area entirely, or make it an overnight stop on leaving or returning to Lisbon.*

Cascais and Estoril

Popular seaside resorts have an atmosphere that transcends nationality, and Lisbon's coast is especially international in character. But the jet set in Estoril is more likely to be exiled nobility, and there is a distinctly old world character even to its shiny new facilities. Cascais is considered a bit more chic and less matronly with its smart shops and profusion of bars and restaurants.

Portugal's own royal court favored Cascais, still an active fishing port, where anyone will tell you with certainty that America was discovered by their own Alfonso Sanches in 1482. After watching them haul and set heavy nets we decided not to pursue an argument.

The pleasures of these resorts are the expected ones — the beach, the shops, the cafes and in summer, the Sunday bullfights in Cascais. The fishing and pleasure boat harbor at Cascais is overlooked by a sea wall from which one can easily spend hours watching boats come and go. Unfortunately an unsightly building project at the far end of the harbor has spoiled the view somewhat for photographers, but there's plenty of local color here and at the fish auction.

Blessed by good weather even when nearby Lisbon is wrapped in clouds, the bougainvillaea blooms in winter in these towns. A nice little museum and English language library is housed in a fine old home right on the coast road just north of the fortress, displaying some of the finds from the neolithic tombs at Alapraia.

Shortly past the museum is Boca do Inferno, which translates to Mouth of Hell, a natural arch in the ocean cliffs where the crashing waves create a foaming cauldron. Across the road are stalls where you may buy ceramics, leather goods and other locally made items. Beyond is Cabo da Roca with its tall lighthouse, westernmost point on the continent of Europe, but it appears like the end of the earth when viewed at night from Ericeira, its beacon flashing far off, beyond the crashing waves at our feet.

Lisbon's Coast At A Glance

Estoril and Cascais are both resort towns which can be reached by train from Lisbon's Cais do Sodre. Estoril is 24 km west of Lisbon and Cascais is 28 km. A direct road leads from Praça do Pombal and a coast road from Belém. The latter passes a series of coastal forts, most almost toylike in their size and architecture, built by João IV to protect the coast.

LODGING: If you watch a lot of old movies, or just love pre-war luxury, you won't be able to resist the Palacio in Estoril (01/ 268 04 00). Exiled royalty, spies of the World War II era and wealthy refugees all stayed here, where the jewelry they managed to carry out with them in their flight was accepted in payment. The jewels worn here are still real and a double room in season costs about $130. Guest rooms are well-located for fine sea views and landscapes and well-furnished and have desks and marble baths.

In Cascais, the Hotel Baia (01/28-10-33), although not the town's most lavish, is certainly the best located, with balconies overlooking the fishing harbor and a lively sidewalk cafe in its front yard. Doubles are from $60 to $80 in summer. In the other end of town past the fort is the Estralagem do Farol (01/ 28-01-73) built for a count about a century ago. It is a good place for families, since there are nearly always other children there. Rooms are $50 to $65 in high season. You will need a car. As with all oceanfront hotels in Portugal, rates at these hotels drop dramatically out of season.

FOOD: Each of the listed hotels serves meals, and restaurants are so plentiful and fast changing here that visitors will have better luck "shopping" for one on their own. There is fado at Kopus Bar.

SHOPPING: Both towns have a full assortment of shops and there are sidewalk stalls set up at the beaches and at Boca do Inferno. The latter is a good place to buy small terra cotta pieces quite inexpensively. Estoril has a summer craft fair and market days in Cascais are Wednesday and Saturday.

IF TIME IS SHORT: Skip this area and go straight to Sintra.

Sintra

People fall in love with Sintra and never leave. It has been rhapsodized by poets, doted on by English eccentrics, embellished by Portuguese royalty and overrun by bus loads of tourists to the point where any little city might well lose its head, even its character. While hardly unspoiled, Sintra has remained charming in an expensive sort of way.

Its climate is lovely, a sea breeze fanning it in summer, but warm and sheltered in the winter. Here grow an amazing variety of exotic plants, brought from all over the world. Its gardens, from the plummeting tropical forests of Monserrate to the back yard rose gardens viewed through fences, are spectacular.

It was the darling of the royal family and they built two palaces here and another not far away at Queluz. On its hillsides, hiding behind walls and fantastic gates, are quintas of the very rich. Nothing is level for more than a few steps, everything built just above or just below its neighbor on its steep slopes, pinnacles and ravines.

There is here a fairy tale sense of unreality, as though they were waiting for the monarchy to return. The center of the town is dominated by the National Palace, its two tall chimneys looking more like the silhouette of an English oast-house than a royal residence. From down in the ravine there juts a fanciful turret and on a facing hillside there is a building, its stone facade so carved, convoluted, fluted and turreted that it must be seen from a distance — up close it would overwhelm. Above this, there hang the ruined walls of a Moorish castle and Pena Palace.

Like everything else in Sintra, the National Palace is in a number of styles, from Manueline to Mudejar. Portuguese kings were never restrained by the notion that a palace had to be one style or another, and the result has been a style of its own — sort of exuberant eclectic. They built their homes like most of us furnish ours, a bit of this and a bit of that, based on what they liked.

The facade of the palace gives little hint of its rich embellishments. The azulejos are stunning, especially in the Moorish dining room. They range from the fifteenth to the eighteenth century and include rich Moorish bas relief designs, faience and polychrome.

Most of the ceilings are painted, the best known (although not the best executed) being the Sala de Pegas, in which magpies, each bearing the red rose of Lancaster and the inscription "por bem" (for the best). The story goes that Phillipa of Lancaster, Queen of João I, happened upon him just as he was embracing one of her ladies in waiting. Never perplexed, he passed off the incident as inconsequential, quoting the "por bem" of the royal motto.

The queen wisely agreed and the matter would have been forgotten except for the persistent chatter of the ladies in waiting. Tired of it, the king had them portrayed as a flock of magpies, bearing his rebuke and the story into posterity. Here, in a juicy slice of court gossip turned around, we meet a very human João and Phillipa, whom we shall meet more formally later in our travels.

Another ceiling is painted in graceful swans, presumed to be a gesture of King Manuel to his daughter Beatrice who loved swans. The most impressive is in the armory, its tremendous dome painted in swirls and arabesques as a setting for the royal crests and those of the sixteenth century's noblest families.

Although the Palace is built on the remains of a Moorish one, its Mudejar effects are overtones, not undertones. They were added by Manuel the Fortunate who had traveled in Spain and had admired the Moorish style with its water-filled patios, rounded arches and arabesques. He employed artisans from North Africa to give his palace its Moorish style and imported dancers to entertain his court (and his majesty).

Its hard to take Pena Palace seriously, and one shouldn't try. It looks like a caricature of itself, designed by Walt Disney. If it were a piece of needlework it would be termed a sampler, for there is nearly every style known to Portugal here — except perhaps Romanesque. The relationship between England's Prince Albert and Portugal's consort Ferdinand (they were cousins) is clear here, but Ferdinand's folly makes Balmoral look like a conservative London club.

There is nothing of earth shattering importance here, but no visitor should miss it for its sheer fun. Much as Queen Amelia left it when she fled to Mafra and thence to English exile in 1910, it maintains its original furniture and decoration.

Here, more even than in strung-together royal apartments elsewhere, we are conscious of the appalling lack of privacy that royal families endured. Nowhere is there a hallway, only bedrooms reached one through the other, which must have created a steady line of traffic. Pena's small bedrooms seem to emphasize this public nature of monarchy. It's hard to imagine a king and queen engaged in pillow talk — or anything else — here.

For all of its Victorian excesses set upon Germanic Wittlesbach style, Pena is delightful. One room is done in cement to simulate wood, another in porcelain furniture, another in papier-mâché. There is no place for the eye to rest. Children love it, and no wonder: it has everything a child ever dreamed of in a fairy tale castle, from moat to crenellations and turrets.

The only remnant of the ruined Jeronomite monastery upon which it was built is a chapel with a lovely little cloister, so light and feminine that it reminds one more of a lady's garden than a place of monastic contemplation. The carved altarpiece in the chapel is also exquisite.

Below, and forming the foreground for the views over the hills and fields below to the sea, is Pena Park. Pools, rare trees, camellias, a Japanese bridge, formal gardens, and exotic plants from all over the world fill this botanical treasury which rivals Monserrate. Near Pena, overhanging Sintra, is the ruined Moorish castle from whose walls are good views of the entire area spread below.

We toyed at Monserrate with the proper "guidebook" language for describing the house itself; "pink Moorish confection," "stone carved frippery," "Mudejar Victorian conceit" were some suggestions. The saving grace of this building is its size, for it is quite small, although when viewed from the vale below it appears much larger.

There is a portico all around with Moorish/Gothic arches looking down into the lower gardens. One can peer inside through the four glass doors, but its interior is in a bad way, broken statuary, crumbling stonework and wiring left hanging from the ceiling when the chandeliers and all of the furniture were sold at auction in the 1940s. It is possible to look the entire length of the main floor, from the ornate vestibule with its ceiling carved in a tracery of leaves, through the salons lit by the domes above them, along the rows of pink marble columns whose arches are set in a tracery inside Gothic arches echoing the exterior.

The building, while interesting is not the main attraction. Its builder, Sir Francis Cook, assembled here one of the world's finest botanical gardens, with thousands of plant species set in a deep moist ravine, creating almost a rain forest in the humid atmosphere. Although these gardens are beginning to show serious signs of neglect, they are still unlike any other and a place for botanists, Sunday gardeners or those who simply appreciate lovely things to wander in at leisure. Tropical trees and flowers blend with European favorites in a landscape that, while appearing wild and natural, is far from random or accidental. From its creeping ground covers to the majestic palms and conifers, most planted in the nineteenth century, it is, for all its recent neglect, a collection unparalleled in Europe.

There is always a sadness at seeing once grand places crumble away. Ruins are one thing; a twelfth century castle whose walls have been in pieces for several centuries isn't so disturbing. They served their purpose and are now historic relics and curiosities, links with the past. But to see a home, a church, or a garden, once lovingly planned by visionaries who believed in their dreams and carefully created by artists who cared about their work, deteriorate and die through sheer neglect is a betrayal. And I always close the door or gate regretfully, glad to have seen what was left but wondering what, if anything, will be left when I return. Baedeker, in his 1898 edition, speaks of a Monserrate we can only imagine, giant ferns in the gorge, its turf in "English-like" perfection.

The hazards of Sintra are several for the traveler. Quite apart from the danger of falling in love with it and never leaving, by no means an unpleasant fate, the problem is that there is so much to see and do there, that one is torn between visiting all of the sights and simply enjoying the town. For one thing, it is temptingly near Lisbon and easy to reach in a day trip. Just seeing the top sights can fill the day, leaving no time to browse in the shops, sit in a cafe or stroll the narrow streets peeking into people's gardens.

It may not be the "glorious Eden" Byron portrayed, but it is certainly worth a stopover of a day or so, especially since one of its sights is also one of the country's loveliest hotels. The Seteais Palace was built in the late eighteenth century by the Dutch consul in Lisbon and has been beautifully preserved and restored. Its public rooms, with their marble floors, high ceilings and painted walls are furnished with fine antiques and oriental carpets.

The Palace's name has for centuries been sullied by the erroneous idea spread by Byron in "Childe Harold" that this was the site of the signing of the infamous treaty that allowed French troops to leave Portugal unharmed and to take their booty with them. A fine way for Byron to thank his hosts as he worked on the poem in their garden! From its terrace there is a fine view over the sea and from beneath its arch, Pena Palace is silhouetted on its hilltop right overhead.

On the way to Sintra from Lisbon is Queluz. Perhaps Portugal's most perfect Palace, Queluz is built in a single style, on a single level and spread out among its gardens to provide a sense of space and light. It is a gem of eighteenth century baroque, very well restored and maintained. Such is its charm and livability that the Portuguese government houses visiting heads of state here.

The rooms are decorated with painted walls and ceilings, as well as azulejos; some of the painted scenes, such as those in the queen's dressing room, are delightful, showing children playing dress-up with adult finery. The formal gardens are, like the palace, light and graceful, with some unusual sphinx statuary. Below a flight of stairs, is a canal lined with azulejos of boating scenes.

The kitchen is now a very fine restaurant serving traditional Portuguese specialities in a splendid atmosphere. Open for lunch and for dinner every day, the Cozinha Velha (01/ 95-02-32) is an experience to savor. The Palace itself closes Tuesdays and between 1 and 2 for lunch. It is accessible by train from Lisbon's Rossio Station.

Sintra At A Glance

Divided into three towns at different levels with São Pedro de Sintra at the top of the hill and Santa Maria in the middle, Sintra itself sits at the lowest level. It is 28 km from Lisbon and a 45 minute train ride from the Rossio Station.

LODGING: Top choice not only for its grandeur, but for the luxury of its lodging, is the Seteais Palace (01/ 923-3200), where a double room is about $150.

The Hotel Central (01/ 923-8863) is an old favorite, not fancy, but very personal and well furnished. Its location is a plus for those arriving without cars since it is right in the center of town facing the National Palace.

The tourist office, which is open from 9 a.m. to 8 p.m. without a noon break, can make last-minute lodging arrangements.

FOOD: Sintra has so many good restaurants that finding one will not be difficult.

SHOPPING: *Sintra is filled with shops, some simply souvenir vendors, but many of which offer fine examples of Portuguese craftsmanship. Caves de Turismo, under the tourist office, has an excellent selection of handwork displayed by region, and offers the best prices in town. Casa Branca carries a wide range of embroidery and the Bazar Central, right across from the National Palace, has an entire show room full of Arraiolas carpets (priced by the square foot, with a 6 x 8 rug at about $1,300.)*

For lovely embroidered baby clothes, lingerie and linens don't miss Alfazema in São Pedro da Sintra. This shop is a joy to enter, with the owner's handmade potpourris and sachets displayed with very fine white-on-white embroidered clothing and accessories. Next door are several antique shops where you won't find bargains, but will find a fascinating collection of old cooking utensils, furniture and fine examples of the unusual carved ox yokes from the north. (These start at about $250.)

On the second and fourth Sundays of each month there is a big market in São Pedro, where there are many crafts for sale as well as everyday items and produce. There is a Romaria at Janas, 15 minutes from Sintra, on August 17, where there is also a pre-Roman chapel.

IF TIME IS SHORT: *Don't miss Sintra. Concentrate on the National Palace and Pena Palace (which can be combined with Queluz in one busy day), and if gardens are a special interest, see Pena Park and Monserrate. When planning, remember that Pena is closed on Mondays, Queluz on Tuesdays, and the National Palace on Wednesdays. But neither of the two in Sintra closes during the noon hours. Tours take a half hour to 45 minutes each.*

Mafra

The great hulk of the Monastery/Palace of Mafra doesn't just dominate the main square, as the one at Alcobaça: it dominates the whole town. Even from miles away a backward look still shows the palace on the crest of its plateau. During the Peninsular War it housed seven British regiments, presumably with room to spare.

The main reason for seeing Mafra — the inside, that is, since you can't help seeing the outside — is its library. Ranked with Coimbra's, although it is quite different, it is definitely worth seeing. The catch is that you cannot just see the library. Only after a tour of nearly an hour and a half, up and down long flights of stairs, along miles of corridors, is one at last taken into one roped-off corner of the great room. By then, if interest hasn't waned, the impact is at least dulled.

Having led with my opinion (which Tim does not share), let me back-track a bit, since there are some bright spots on the tour. The guides are certainly not among these. Grim, bored and lifeless they can make even the interesting parts dull. And the visitor interested in knowing more than the memorized spiel in Portuguese is doomed to disappointment. A question put to these robotic creatures simply brings instant replay. For amusement, I tried this a few times just to see if he'd miss a word. He didn't.

I found myself wishing for Mark Twain and the good Doctor as traveling companions. What fun these Innocents Abroad would have had with these Furgesons from Mafra!

During this interminable tour, visitors are led through all the royal apartments, of which only a few catch the attention. Among these is the light and surprisingly delicate room in which Manuel II spent his last night in Portugal before leaving for exile in England. Its cream walls are frescoed in a small almost wispy border, and on the adjoining dressing room walls are beautiful frescoes of native wildlife. There is nothing ponderous or pompous in this suite; a fine ivory carving simply adds to its fragile air. Although there is nothing here of Manuel except history, there is a poignancy and a sense of its having been a living place, which is absent throughout the rest of the palace.

Of these royal rooms, only the dining room rouses a smile, for its Balmoral style is completely out of character. Entire chairs, table legs, chandeliers are all made of stag horn and upholstered in deerskin. Great stuffed heads hang on the walls, including wild boar, their tongues hanging out as if ready to eat everything spread on the dining table below — and the dinner guests as well. It is easy to miss among all this some very small azulejo hunting scenes. The chairs look too uncomfortable for royalty, as if they belonged in the cell of a penitent monk instead.

There is a royal apothecary, a ward of cells lined in azulejos, the plaster molds for the statuary, a small kitchen, and a room for penitent monks whose bed has a human skull mounted on the tester. There are some fine vestments and a florid throne room with trompe l'oeil panels and hung heavily with dark red tapestries which pale the light frescoes. The whole room jars with the rest of the palace, which for all its lack of human touch is tasteful and light.

The library, when at last it is reached, is impressive. Here the guide's memorized speech included its only English — the dimensions of the room, which is over 200 feet in length. Its lovely barrel ceiling was never covered in gold as was intended, and its white plaster makes the room seem even taller and lighter.

Unlike Coimbra, visitors here are kept behind ropes at one end and cannot see the fine carvings of the gallery, the little window alcoves or the flat central dome with its rayed sun. Nor can one stand in its midst and enjoy its full effect. Having climbed so many steps, trod so many corridors and listened to so much droning, it seems a cheat to simply peek into what is certainly one of the country's greatest rooms (where photography is forbidden).

The basilica is not part of the tour, and it is certainly worth seeing. Tall and narrow, full of marble grandeur and elegance, it is more Italian than Portuguese in style, and quite different from other churches of this country.

The marble work is exceptional, especially the floor, but a wide and crude wooden platform with a table has been erected to provide the now-mandated freestanding altar, and it has been set right in the great rotunda, covering the focal point of the design in the floor. The bold inlay pattern culminates only here, drawing the entire interior into a beautifully harmonious whole, which has been shattered needlessly. There is plenty of room for this temporary altar in the chancel, which is where the parish churches throughout Portugal have put them.

Mafra's architect was a German goldsmith who had been a protege of the Jesuits in Rome. How he came to be awarded this plum of a royal commission to build one of the largest palaces in Europe is still unknown. There have been many suppositions, the most likely of which is that King João did not anticipate such a grandiose building when he first commissioned it.

After three years of marriage there was still no heir, possibly because the pious king who had right of entry to the convents was too busy siring illegitimate offspring by nuns. A prominent Franciscan friar said that if the king would agree to build a monastery at Mafra, an heir would be born. (He apparently didn't mention swearing off nuns.) The king proclaimed his permission to build a convent to house 13 friars and presto, a princess, and soon thereafter a son.

By the time of the monastery's consecration, 13 friars had grown to 300, plus 150 lay and novitiate brothers and a royal summer palace as well. The talented goldsmith proved a gifted architect and the entire country pitched in to complete the structure. Money was no object, since vast riches were pouring in by the shipload from Brazil.

Right behind Mafra Palace lies an enclosed park, filled with wildlife and once the hunting preserve of King Carlos. The turn to its entrance is marked "Gradil" and leaves the Ericeira road to the right. The gate will likely be closed, but there is a bell. The road inside leads to a funny little hunting museum and a fine collection of coaches, carts and carriages. It doesn't rival the Coach Museum in Belém, but is nonetheless interesting.

The countryside around Mafra is dotted with windmills, some working, some with only the huge empty skeletons of their arms, others simply round stone buildings set crumbling on hillcrests. A good view of several of these, as well as a long look back at Mafra is just off the Ericeira road before it drops into town. The turn is marked "Lapa de Sera," and a few hundred yards along it is a series of windmills, their empty arms outstretched over the sea and the rolling countryside.

Mafra At A Glance
Monastery town, 19 km north of Lisbon. May be reached by bus from Lisbon or Sintra. Monastery closed Tuesday.

LODGING: *The only choice is the Albergaria Castelão (61/526 96) on Avenida 25 Abril right in the center of the village. Although it is a good hotel, we would opt for the Turismo in nearby Ericeira, a more active and interesting town in the evening.*

FOOD: *Fish and shellfish are the specialties here, as well as the "trouxas" of Malveira, a sweet pastry. The dining room and adega of the Estralagem are both good, but our choice is Tocada a Raposa, which is down the narrow street beside the BNU bank, just around the first corner to the right. Try their Bacalau a Tocada Raposa, with thinly sliced presunto (the Portuguese version of proscuito) folded inside before frying. A full meal with wine is about $5 each in this attractive well-decorated restaurant.*

SHOPPING: *There is a very good shop, the artisinato, right on the main square, with handmade products and other gifts from all over Portugal. They have a good selection of fashionable fishermen-knit sweaters, Arraiolos carpets and woven rugs, as well as smaller items. Sobreiro, on the Ericeira road, is known for its pottery, and Livramente, a bit north off the Torres Vedras road, is famous for its wood inlay work, mostly furniture. Both are good stops for those interested in crafts. Malveira, right on the main rail line from Lisbon, has a Thursday market.*

IF TIME IS SHORT: *See at least the exterior of the palace, since it is one of the major architectural works of Portugal, and the interior of the magnificent church in the center.*

Ericeira

One winter afternoon some years ago, we drove into Ericeira looking for lodging. Surely in a beach town we would have our choice. We did not. The Hotel Turismo, the policeman assured us, was the only place open. Year 'round tourism hadn't caught on in this little-known resort yet. The search for lodging may not always follow the course one has charted, and so it was with Ericeira.

But we were freshly out of Lisbon and it was getting late. We'd already driven the steep cobbled streets in search of a "pensão" sign and there was none, so the Turismo it was to be. I walked through its porticoed entrance into a grand, dark and empty lobby. It exuded the aura of decaying grandeur — the maritime version of grand old hotels everywhere. It needed only the tatty old dowagers sipping their tea. But there was no-one, not even behind the long desk with the bell on it. I rang and waited.

I rang again and waited again. From far away came voices, then a pleasant-faced lady in an apron appeared. Oh, she told me apologetically, it is not our season and we are — how I say — changing our structure and have no hot water. Our services, they are limited and the elevator, it is being made new. This grand dame of a hotel was a bit indisposed, it seemed.

And the rate for no hot water, I suggested, would be a bit less? A long sigh. Yes, she supposed it was only right: a 2,000 escudo room for 1,500. I hesitated, still not quick at conversion. With breakfast, she added after a moment.

And how about my little girl — a bed for her could perhaps be brought in? Long pause. She sighed again and then brightened. There was one of sufficient size with a balcony overlooking the garden and the ocean with the setting sun. There was poetry in the place, if no elevator.

We drank our port on the balcony and watched the sun drop into the sea (a rare treat we easterners always enjoy) and the lights blink on along the pale blue scoop of the coast as far as Cabo da Roca. The lighthouse there blinked its steady pattern, marking the westernmost point on the continent of Europe. The waves began as far-off swells and moved in steady sweeps toward the rocks to

43

crest in a seething froth that made us at last understand the patterns of Manueline. The sky stayed pink and the shore became a deeper blue through a second glass of port, and we went to dinner.

Ericeira, for all its being described as a seaside resort, is really more of a fishing village with a beach and grand hotel attached. Much of its beach trade comes by train for the day from Lisbon. So when it is not their season, as the lady phrased it, it looks not like Ogunquit, Maine, all boarded up, but like the fishing village it is.

The fishing harbor is a stretch of beach under a cliff, and the boats are drawn up side by side on the sand. Above are the white walls and red roofs of the town, highlighted by the bright blue of their trim. There is a little chapel overlooking, whose name means Our Lady of Pleasant Journeys. We thought of Manuel II, the last king, whose final view of his native land was Ericeira disappearing into the mists, the little chapel bidding him a pleasant journey, if such could be found in exile.

If the weather is at all pleasant, the promenade occupies the town until quite late in the evening. There is little traffic and people walk in the streets, stopping at La Paloma or another cafe to watch the world go by. Tourists may seek entertainment at their hotel or the flashier places, but it is here on the corner that the locals settle in. The coffee machine sparkles and hisses forth steam and the tables are always full. But space will be found somewhere and chairs offered from other tables to accommodate one more group. Ages in this cafe-bar range from babies asleep on shoulders to ancient fishermen, their hands gnarled by age and icy seas. Children wander about under foot and under tables, stepped over and befriended by everyone. The waiter comes only when summoned and some families are clearly here for the evening.

Later, in our hotel, we found a group assembled in the deep plush of the overstuffed sofas in a parlor, watching a folk festival on television. There were dancers, singers and traditional instruments — a sort of variety show. We were invited to join them, and we sank into one of the sofas and looked around. There was the lady in the apron and three others, plus two elderly gentlemen and a middle-aged couple.

They all applauded a ballet as though it had been performed on the big round table in our midst, and as everyone commented their approval, I realized that one of the ladies was the chambermaid who had brought the towels and Julie's bed.

Our room was at the very end of the wing, the long corridor dark until we found the light switch. It was still, except for the ocean below and it seemed as though we were in the long-closed wing of some great palace, alone without our retinue. We went out onto the balcony. One other light burned in that great wing spread along the edge of the sea, and it shone from the room right next to ours. Only two parties of guests in the hotel, and we were neighbors in the dark end of nowhere.

The sea broke against the wall beyond the garden in a constant hum now, more like wind in the trees than beating waves. The moon was high and we could watch the swells form way out beyond the point and move in, shimmering silver, to break first against the wall below us, then on the crescent cove of beach just beyond.

In the morning there was no hot water, but there were two white peacocks in the garden below, and we ate breakfast from the thinnest of china in a sun-filled room overlooking the sea. Each of us had our own china pot, one of coffee, one of tea and one of rich brown chocolate. The lady with the apron brought these and a mound of breakfast pastries wrapped in an immaculate starched white linen napkin. The hotel was closed, but all was in order in the kitchen.

We were glad we hadn't known of the estralagem in town, or we would not have stayed in isolated grandeur, with our balcony and red velvet drapes, and the enormous tub without hot water to fill it, received in splendor to share the ballet with chambermaids.

We've been back to the Turismo since, now that it has been "made new." And we still like it, with its garden and pool and balconies all overlooking the sea. The staff is a bit more formal, but just as friendly as they were that first night we met the Turismo with her make-up askew and not quite ready to receive. We like her both ways.

Ericeira At A Glance

Fishing and beach town, 50 km from Lisbon, 22 from Sintra, 11 from Mafra. May be reached by train from Lisbon.

LODGING: It is best to reserve ahead in the beach season, since these towns near Lisbon are popular. The Hotel Turismo's (61/63545) rates are $25 for a double in the winter to $55 in the high season. The mid-seasons in the spring and fall are delightful here, with the weather warm enough for swimming and no crowds. With its pool, it is a good *hotel for families with children. There are also two very expensive estralagems, the Morais (61/62611) and the Pedro-o-Pescador (61/62504).*

FOOD: *Poco, on Rua Mendes Leal is the best independent restaurant in town, not large, but with a varied menu, in the $10 range. O Lavagante is less expensive, has very good food and a homey atmosphere. The Turismo offers an elegant dining room with a fixed-price continental menu.*

IF TIME IS SHORT: *There is nothing here you must see or do — it is just a very pleasant stopover town.*

Torres Vedras

Known more for the defensive lines that took its name, than for its own attractions, Torres Vedras is set in a rich wine growing area. It has a ruined castle and a reconstructed fort which is of particular interest to those who care about defensive fortifications. Much of the line of redoubts and batteries of the Torres Vedras line can still be traced from here to the Tagus and, just as Wellington had envisioned, it saved Lisbon from Massena's troops. These lines were so formidable that the French, with remarkable wisdom, didn't even attempt to take them, camping instead in the scorched land from which Wellington had moved every living (or edible) thing. After five months the half-starved French army retreated to Spain.

The city itself is not filled with attractions, but the surrounding area has some fascinating places. Primary among these is the iron age hill fort, Castro de Zambujal. It is most easily reached via the bridge from the barrio of S. Antonio, or, traveling from Ericeira, from a road to the right just before the town sign for "Gibraltar." There is a yellow arrow-shaped sign marking the turn. At the fork past the village a road leads uphill to the left, ending near a set of stone farm buildings by the ruins of Castro de Zambujal.

Zambujal was built, evidently by eastern Mediterranean people who may have come in search of metals. Carbon dating shows the beginnings of the fort to have been about 2,500 B.C. making it one of Portugal's oldest. Subsequent building and artifacts indicate that it was not abandoned until some 800 years later. It is still possible to trace the three sets of defensive lines and to find the round buildings.

Although much of the stone had been removed to build surrounding farms, the site remains impressive. Overgrown with wild-herbs, the air grows heady with mint as one climbs about the stones. Holly and thistle, rue, thyme, yarrow and dill grow between the stones. The stones are pitted and pocked and covered with yellow and white lichens. The walls are in bits and pieces, some hard to trace, some taller than ourselves.

Artifacts show that the early settlers were adept at making pottery and that they raised meat and grains for food. When abandoned at what archaeologists think may have been as late as 1700 B.C., Zambujal was a sizeable and complex group of structures designed for defense and habitation. But artifacts don't tell the real story of these Mediterranean adventurers; how long it took them to make their journey, or where they went from here, or who they built these walls of stone against. The few tools in the Municipal Museum and this tumbling mass of stones are all that is left of what is thought to be one of Iberia's oldest and most complex fortified prehistoric settlements.

Below are the vineyards and beyond them more grape-covered hillsides receding in layers and fading in the late afternoon haze to pale blue mountains at the horizon.

Purcifal, south of Torres Vedras, is worth driving off the main road to see for its fine eighteenth century houses and grillwork and for the church of the same period built of stone left over from Mafra. Behind its huge facade the interior is of pink and white marble set off by a dark wood retable.

Further south at Enxara do Bispo, there is a prehistoric burial site with a large circular tomb thought to be eleventh century B.C. At Varajoto, just 5 km from Torres Vedras off the Ericeira road is the enormous fifteenth century convent of S. Antonio, an early Franciscan friary which is again an active monastery. Its entrance sits below the level of the largo, reached by a double set of stairs lined in azulejos. The fine Gothic cloister and small church are usually closed. A good time to see them would be just before or just after the daily 8 a.m. Masses or the 10 a.m. Mass on Sunday and Saint Days.

The ceiling to the unlocked vestibule is Mudejar and there is a little chapel, just to the left as you enter, done in pale blue stone and gold with very nice azulejos. Outside once again, we started up the double stairs, this time facing a wall of azulejos that had been behind us as we entered. Instead of a scene or pattern, the wall was a jumble of leaves and noses and pieces of scroll and fingers and bits of flowing robes and flowers — it had been repaired with azulejos recovered from other damaged pieces, a charming miscellany, all set neatly together without any pattern, like a jigsaw puzzle put together all wrong.

Torres Vedras At A Glance

Wine growing town 52 km north of Lisbon; accessible by train but since most of its points of interest lie well outside of town, a car is advisable.

LODGING: There is no hotel, but it is close enough to Mafra, Ericeira, and even Óbidos, that lodging is not a problem. There is a tourist kiosk in the center of town.

FOOD: Pasteis de feijão is a regional sweet (try the Cafe Imperio for these) and the various caldeiradas are at their best in this area when seafood is plentiful. Barrete Preto on Rua Paiva Andrade serves regional specialties.

FESTIVALS: Purcifal has a fair the fourth Sunday in August.

SHOPPING: Latoaria Ramos carries regional handcrafts, but we'd advise waiting for Óbidos.

IF TIME IS SHORT: Skip past this area unless you are interested in prehistoric sites, in which case see Zambujal only. **NOTE:** In the untried category, near Torres Vedras is Hespanhol, the estate of the Perestrello family, inhabited by them since 1393. Columbus is said to have lived there after his marriage to a Perestrello daughter in 1498. While the manor house is not open for tours, its great hall and patio, gardens and winery are the scene of historical reenactments and performances of folk culture. Buses transport guests from Lisbon hotels for an evening of wining, dining, fado, dancing and craft demonstrations in historic settings. We haven't been, since we aren't personally fond of staged events and we think that $65 per person for 2½ hours there (plus nearly 2 hours of bus rides) is a bit pricey. Call their Lisbon agent at 01/3284-56 or ask your concierge.

Óbidos and Caldas da Rainha

While Nazaré is the most photographed, Óbidos is the most described town in Portugal. The very notion that an entire white town, neatly wrapped in golden walls and tied in wisteria ribbon, was presented to queens as a wedding gift is irresistible. But had it not been a royal gift, it would still rate far more than a passing notice.

The whole town is white, and sits within a wall. The road enters through an elaborate, tiled gate-house and immediately encounters a blank wall! These sudden sharp turns within the town gates once provided effective defense and now serve to slow entering traffic to a pace appropriate to the narrow streets.

Whitewashed houses line the way and wisteria vines are espaliered at random along the walls, heavy with purple flowers and heady oriental perfume. Because of all the white, everything is more brilliant here, and the huge pots of red geraniums and orange nasturtiums seem brighter than elsewhere.

Where the streets rise or fall with the land, the bottom edge of each house is painted in a straight line with the wedge below painted in a darker color, so the houses appear straight and geometrical, like neat white boxes. Upper story windows or hilltop belvederes look out on red tile roofs and green trees accented by the gleaming white of the walls.

There is room to park in the square or at the far end of town past the castle, then enjoy Óbidos on foot, following little stairways and narrow alleys to discover surprising vistas and perfect tiny gardens. Steps ascend to the battlements where walking the walls gives intimate views down into the town and vistas across the rolling countryside.

The interior walls of the church of S. Maria are covered in magnificent swirling blue azulejos, and its wooden ceiling is painted in a most unusual style, with Moorish faces and floral fancies. Nearby is a small museum with paintings, outstanding polychrome sculptures, and some fascinating folk art oddments, such as parish records decorated in a fractur-like painting almost too precise to have been executed in brush.

There is also a collection of items from the Peninsular War, most notably a relief map of the Lines of Torres Vedras, constructed under the command of Wellington to protect Lisbon from French invasion in 1810.

History in Portugal takes on a very personal quality, quite unlike that of any other country. Its queens, kings, heroes, saints, villains and visionaries all become strangely real, as if you had known them in life, as you meet them again and again. After only a few days in Portugal, their names become familiar, the little stories about them become windows on their personalities.

The good King Dinis and his Queen Isabel of Aragon are among the first friends. You meet them in Óbidos as they ride past, and she admires its gleaming walls and hill setting. Very much in love, the king made the grand gesture that was to become royal tradition. He gave her the town, and subsequent kings also presented it to their brides. Perhaps it is the poetic nature of the Portuguese that makes these vignettes as much a part of history as the battles and the lines of succession. Whatever the cause, it makes Portugal more enjoyable, and you can be sure that you will meet this royal couple again.

The morning market in Caldas da Rainha, 5 km north, is one of our favorite events in Portugal. The Praça de República is filled with farmers and fishwives, bakers and butchers selling everything from tantalizing fresh bread to the biggest cabbages that we've ever seen. It's what Tim calls a ten roll town where there's a good picture everywhere we turn. Craggy-faced farmers, women old far beyond their years with the loveliest fine faces, groups warming their rough hands over a pot of steaming Caldo Verde, live chickens and rabbits, bright carrots, golden onions, red tomatoes and bouquets of kale — Kodak stockholders rejoice whenever we enter town.

There is more of the spirit of a place in its morning market than in its adegas, for here is the business of life in progress. Commerce and society mingle and blend in a very earthy and colorful mix. Set in a town so stately and with a royal history, it saves Caldas from its spa chic.

The aching Queen Leonor stopped her travels en route to Batalha in order to bathe in the sulphuric waters beside the road. She returned and stayed and built the hospital and church there in 1486, selling the jewels given her by her late husband João II. In the nineteenth century it became *The* Spa and during World War II it was temporary home to a lot of refugees, as Portugal took in countless of those fleeing from central Europe.

Apart from the market and the lovely peaceful Spa Park, there is little to see except the church of N.S. do Populo, the same one built by Queen Leonor. It has a rare Manueline tower and fine sixteenth and seventeenth century azulejos in blue and yellow.

Óbidos And Caldas At A Glance

Perfectly preserved walled town and spa town, 5 km apart and 100 km north of Lisbon. Access by train from Rossio Station.

LODGING: In Óbidos, the Pousada do Castelo (62/951-05) is one of the smallest and most elegant of the pousada network, so reservations are essential. It is inside the castle, furnished with antiques, and has fine views from its windows. Double rooms are from $70 to $110, depending on the season. For a bit over half the price, you can join European guests at the Estralagem do Convento (62/952-17) on Rua Dom João Ornelas, a converted convent where a double will cost about $45. At the same price, you can stay inside the walls, on the narrow stone-paved main street, in an old private home converted to an inn. The Albergaria S. Isabel (62/951-15) is on Rua Direta, and our favorite location. On the road out of town is the inexpensive Pensão Martim de Freitas (62/951-85), with doubles at about $30.

In Caldas, the Hotel Malhoa is, according to accounts of friends, clean and pleasant, with a pool and doubles at $35 – $40.

FOOD: The pousada serves local specialties to guests as well as non-guests at $18 – $23 a person. Just down the street is one of our favorite restaurants in Portugal, Alcaide, with a tea room and bar as well as the upstairs dining room overlooking the town and valley. The Sopa Camarão is excellent, and with a wedge of local cheese and a serving of their specialty, Torta de Almedoa (almond tart) it's a satisfying and inexpensive lunch. For a full meal, try the rabbit with a bottle of Josel wine. In Cortico, 4 km from Caldas, the Pensão Portugal serves good Portuguese specialties, in a plain dining room.

SHOPPING: Óbidos is one of the best places to shop in Portugal, even for handwork which is the specialty of other areas. Prices, even on the embroideries of the north, are comparable to those in the place of origin, and there is a fine selection here. The major local crafts are weaving and ceramics. Look for the weaver's studios where you will see the big looms working. Pottery and ceramic character figures are locally made as well as the distinctive ceramic dishes of Caldas da Rainha. This is a ceramic town where you will see ceramics decorating houses and public parks. Its best known work is the dreadful, garish green soup tureen shaped like a crinkly Savoy cabbage. These are so unspeakably ugly that they invade one's memory, almost like a homely mutt, so that upon seeing them in subsequent trips one becomes nostalgic about them. Be careful or you will find yourself trying to figure out how to pack one (as we did).

IF TIME IS SHORT: Óbidos is a showplace and its entire preserved village is a national monument. But it is still alive for all its careful tending, and a highlight of Portugal. See it at least on a day trip out of Lisbon. Pass through Caldas, stopping in the main square if there is a market.

Alcobaça

Try to arrive in Alcobaça late in the afternoon so that your first view of the monastery's facade is bathed in the rich warm glow of the lowered sun. It is a different place in the morning, when it is backlit and gray in shade, and in memory the two scenes remain almost as different places.

The monastery doesn't dominate the square; it is the square. Everything is spread around its wide stairs like seats around an orchestra pit. Baroque and massive as it is, it lacks the ominous overhanging presence of so many grand facades in small towns. Perhaps because of the spacious square around it, it is more of a friendly backdrop for the daily life of the town.

A good place from which to contemplate it, at any time of day or evening, is a table across the square. As you sit in the late afternoon and sip your coffee or wine, the monastery will grow a deeper shade of gold, almost orange, and bathe the entire square in its rosy reflection.

The monastery deserves an unhurried inspection. It is one of the architectural treasures of Iberia, but more than that, it is a place to linger and enjoy, and to meet some of the historical friends who will accompany you throughout Portugal.

As you enter the long stark nave, the plain clustered columns stand so close that they appear to enclose rather than frame the nave. In this severe setting, stripped of all its later ornament, it is hard to believe that in the Middle Ages this was one of Europe's richest and most powerful monasteries, and its abbot one of Portugal's most esteemed personages.

It is easier to imagine the hundreds of Cistercian brothers who celebrated the Mass around the clock and to hear the echoes of their voices in this silent place.

An even more poignant echo arises at the transept end of the long nave, where Ines de Castro and Dom Pedro I lie foot to foot carved in marble so fine it seems translucent. Their story is a favorite of the romantic Portuguese — as tragic and dramatic as the fado itself.

Ines was lady-in-waiting to the Infanta Constanza of Castile to whom Dom Pedro, then prince, was married. The king, Alphonso II, had Ines exiled, but after the Infanta died in childbirth, Ines returned and they were secretly married (or so he later claimed). The king, afraid of the Spanish influence of Ines's powerful family, arranged for her murder by a group of courtiers. The logic of his fear escapes us, since he had married Pedro off to a Spanish princess in the first place.

Heartbroken, Pedro bided his time until he ascended the throne. He then had Ines's body exhumed and crowned (the guides love to tell of this grisly scene, which has doubtless grown better with each telling), then brought in ceremonious procession to Alcobaça and buried in this tomb which he himself designed. The strange little half-human creatures that support the sarcophagus are reputed to be her slayers. Pedro's subtitle, The Cruel, doubtless stems from his vengeance upon the slayers he later caught, for it was terrible, if not swift (another tale the guides delight in telling).

He designed his own matching tomb and positioned it so that as they rose on the Day of Judgement, their first sight would be of each other. Some of the delicate artistry of Ines's tomb was damaged by French soldiers who sacked the monastery in 1810.

Be sure to walk around the tombs to see the carved detail, especially the foot end of hers, where the dead are shown lifting the lids of their tombs at The Judgement. History and legend have preserved (or invented) every gory detail of the story, but lost the name of the artist who created these magnificent stone memorials, on which you may still occasionally see a nosegay of wilting flowers.

The cloister, with its green maze garden framed in delicate Manueline pillars, is a welcome relief from both the cold austerity of the nave and the cold tombs of the transept. Enter it from the north aisle and walk all the way around, as did the monks and King Dinis, patron of the abbey. He brought a literary flavor to life here, keeping scores of monks busy translating ecclesiastical works. There is a lovely little well house on the northwest corner, a fine place to compose poetry as the king often did. Local girls rub the water from this well on their cheeks to hasten marriage.

Off the cloister, to the northeast, is the impressive kitchen through which a stream of water from the Alcoa River is routed. Whether this was for fishing or dishwashing, or a bit of both, is uncertain, but it is a feature common to several Cistercian abbeys.

The center of the immense room is dominated by a roasting pit of at least six-ox capacity, rising into a chimney. The left-hand wall is lined with deep stone sinks, above which carved animal heads spew water from eighteenth century brass spigots set in their noses. The kitchen descends in a series of levels with huge marble tables. The tiles that cover the whole room are of an opalescent glaze, with a blue and white border at the edge of the chimney.

Next door, the refectory also rises in layers, with a pillared stone arcade and little niches where monks prayed as their higher orders ate.

Off the southwest corner of the cloister is the Salados Reis, its walls lined with azulejo scenes of the founding of Alcobaça. Portugal's first king, Alphonse Henriques, had persuaded foreign crusaders bound for the Holy Land to stop and assist him in his efforts to wrest well-defended Santarém from Moorish grasp. Shortly before the battle, his Christian conscience made him doubt the righteousness of his diversion of those in holy pursuit, and he vowed that if he could be victorious at Santarém, he would build a monastery dedicated to S. Bernard.

The tiles show the rest of the story — S. Bernard and his monks praying during the battle, the king laying the first stone, etc. Above these are statues of the kings of the Avis line, except for three which were destroyed in the 1755 earthquake. At the end are the sad, empty pedestals waiting for the rest of the Avis, but the line died out when Sebastian, too young to sire an heir, went off to Africa where he was killed. The room is usually kept closed, as though waiting for the Avis to return, but it is not locked and you can walk right in.

The monastery at Alcobaça, like many churches in Portugal, has many surprises and few guides. There are none of the handy little guidebooks that every town in Italy has for its art treasures. Perhaps this is because there was no mass of literature left or inspired by the Grand Tour that swept across the rest of Europe. We don't complain, since this has left Portugal singularly unspoiled.

But behind closed doors there are often surprising rewards. When there is someone to ask, we do. When there is not, we try the door. That's how we found the beautiful little Chapel of the Holy Sacrament. What would be the fourth chapel on the south side of the ambulatory (behind the chancel) is instead an ornate Manueline doorway framed by stone trees rooted to the floor, branches intertwining to form the arch. It was closed, but experience told us that through it there should be a sacristy, which is often the most beautiful part of a Portuguese church.

We opened it and were in a of vestibule with two closed doors. The left one led to the sacristy as we had expected, a small domed room full of interesting reliquaries. The door to the right hid a chapel with a good painted ceiling. After the vastness of the rest of the abbey, this silent place was peacefully intimate, like a parish church. We sat for a moment, then tiptoed out and closed the door.

For all the power and wealth of Alcobaça and its abbot, the monks took their work seriously from the moment of their arrival in the twelfth century. They drained the marshes around the abbey, clearing the land and planting olive and fruit trees. To this day the region is known for the best fruit in Portugal, especially for its peaches. You can sample these in season at the market stalls which spring up in the square each day. On Monday the entire square is filled with a full-scale market.

Alcobaça At A Glance

Monastery and market town, 125 km north of Lisbon, with access by train from Rossio Station.

LODGING: The Hotel S. Maria (62/ 432 95) is located just above the plaza, some of its rooms overlooking the monastery. Doubles are $30 to $40, depending on size and location .

FOOD: Cafe Trindade, off the square to the left of the monastery is the place for dinner, lunch or coffee or wine in between. The cafe is in the tree-shaded square across a street which the waiters must navigate to bring your wine. It's worth it for the show on a market day. The dining room is attractive and their Frango na Pucara is splendid, with roast rabbit a close second. It is closed Saturdays in the slow season, and like many, doesn't serve dinner until 8 p.m.

SHOPPING: The local blue faience which nearly overwhelms you here, has far more appeal taken singly and at home. It is easy to dismiss it as gaudy when you see so much of it. Remember, however, that these are fragile and awkward to carry on an airplane. If you will not be in Caldas da Rainha, this is also the best place to buy the fanciful vegetable-shaped dishes. Look here for the small fabric-covered boxes with wool-embroidered designs, some of the few available examples of that traditional Portuguese embroidery style. These are easy to pack and make good containers for smaller fragile items.

IF TIME IS SHORT: The monastery is one of Portugal's outstanding sights.

Nazaré

Nazaré is perhaps the most photographed town in Portugal. The long strand of beach, with surf-beaten cliffs rising dramatically at the end and the houses climbing the mountain behind it, would be photogenic alone. But add a foreground full of bright painted fishing boats, their narrow carved prows curling in graceful lines against the pink stucco of the buildings facing the beach, and it's a cover story every time.

Like Alcobaça, it is most beautiful late in the day, when the sun catches the buildings full face and makes deep shadows of every wrinkle in the sand. Bathed in this pink glow, with long surreal shadows, fishermen unload the catch and haul in the boats. Not long ago the boats were pulled to shore by teams of oxen, but noisy tractors have replaced them, their tires leaving a crisscross pattern carved in the sand.

Against this backdrop is played a rich pageant, as the fishermen, most of them dressed in traditional red plaid shirts create a lively ballet in center stage, with playing children and barking dogs underfoot. The women help unload the fish, lay them out to dry, or wait for the right boat to come in.

The older ones, wrapping their black shawls more closely against the evening breeze, sit alone, or in motionless knots of two or three. The sun makes a shaded furrow of each crease on their faces. These are stoic faces, used to waiting and peering into the setting sun for the sight of the prow of a familiar boat. The people of Nazaré are reputed to be descended from the Phoenicians, and their long narrow noses are unlike the usual Portuguese faces.

These women have waited on this same beach all their lives — for their fathers, their brothers, their husbands and their sons — in the evening sun, and in the howling storms that send the surf flying against the houses across the street. In their faces, eyes squinting against the sun, is the history of Nazaré, and their stoic immobility is like an anchor to the constant activity around them.

Nazaré is a pleasant town even at the midday, when the children come home from school, and the old men gather in the cafes that line the beachfront buildings. It is a good time to settle in for a leisurely lunch if the weather is fine. The seafood, of course, is superb, and the view unmatched.

The only time to avoid Nazaré, in fact, is in the heat of summer, when it becomes one of the few places in Portugal that is overrun by tourists — most of them from Lisbon. The beach is awash with sunbathers and you may spend hours just looking for a parking place, unless you have reservations in one of the few hotels that provide them.

There are no real "musts" on the Nazaré itinerary — the beach, the boats, the fish, and the people are the sights here. If you choose, as we do, to spend a few quiet days, ride the funicular up to the Sitio, which is the residential area on the top of the cliff. Or you can climb up by a steep stone path.

The church is lovely, with azulejos of the New Testament, and a gold altar, as well as some fine sculptures. At the top of the cliff is an eighteenth century chapel built to commemorate a twelfth century event. A young nobleman chasing a stag in a heavy mist rode perilously close to the sheer cliff, when the Virgin Mary appeared to show him the edge. In thanks he built the original Chapel of Memory, which was replaced by the present one.

Nazaré At A Glance

Fishing and beach town, 82 miles north of Lisbon, 9 from Alcobaça. The nearest train station is Valado, from which take a local bus. In season, plan to stay in Alcobaça, or reserve in advance.

LODGING: Hotel da Nazaré (Largo Alfonso Zuguete, 62/ 513-11) is a short walk from the beach. This modern hotel may jar your senses after the timeless beach scenes, but offers sea view balconies, picture windows, a good dining room and parking. Doubles are from $35 to $40. Hotel Praia (39 Ave. Vieira Guimarães, 62/ 514-23), also modern, is near the market and beach and offers parking. Double rooms in these two range from $40 to $55. Our choice, however, is the Pensão Ribamar (9 Rua Gomes Freire, 62/ 461-58) for warmth and charm as well as beachfront location and balconies overlooking the main street and beach. The spotless rooms are more typically Portuguese, and less Miami-Danish-modern. Candelit dinners are rich in local specialties and worth a stop even if you aren't staying. For a stay of a few days, opt for the full-pension plan which gives lodging for two and all meals for under $90.

FOOD: *Good local dishes featuring seafood are available here in the $6 - 10 range for a complete meal. Along with the Ribamar (try the roast kid if you are tired of fish), the Mar Bravo, also located along the beach, offers seafood and the national standby, grilled pork. You are more likely to meet a lively local crowd here.*

SHOPPING: *Shops along the seafront show white sweaters and knit hats as well as the red plaid fishermen's shirts. There is embroidery here also, but you will see better if you are headed farther north.*

IF TIME IS SHORT: *At least drive through Nazaré and spend a few minutes along its beach, or come here in the evening after you are settled in your Alcobaça hotel.*

Batalha

The approach to Batalha is a strange one, for the road crests a rise and curves down upon the pinnacles and spires of a very large church in a very small town. Clusters of new houses cover the slope behind it, giving an air of incongruity and hardly any place from which to photograph the abbey.

Once in the tidy little town, the logical entrance to the abbey is from the side by the statue of Nuno Alvarez. But it is better to walk around to the left and enter through the front of the building. The first view will then be from the end of the long nave, down the rows of stark columns, ending in a triumphant upward thrust of vaulting. At the far end is the chancel, its stained glass windows providing the only decoration.

The first reaction is of surprise, since the plain smooth lines are not what the fru-fru of the exterior leads one to expect. The nave is a place of repose for the eye, a chance to relax between the masses of carved pinnacles and buttresses outside and the architectural and artistic gems that are to come.

To the right of the entrance is the first of these, the Founder's Chapel. If it is locked, the guard sits about halfway down the other side of the nave with the key. He will come and unlock it, a very inefficient system, but a very Portuguese one. He will not stand there rattling his keys, but will wait patiently and quietly.

The pillars and ceiling vaulting give the room the appearance of being round; it rises to a central dome whose arches meet at medallions of carved white stone, so fine they look like huge paper snowflakes. Under the dome lies the founder, João I, and his English wife, Phillipa of Lancaster. Portugal's most devoted and remarkable royal couple, they are shown in their youth, carved in stone, wearing cathedral-spire crowns, hand in hand for eternity, The sun streams in through the stained glass windows above and around them, not at all mausoleum-like, but a beautiful and bright place to await the Resurrection.

It is not only a fitting tomb for them, but it is right for them to be surrounded as they are by their children. In a day when most royal families were torn by rivalries and jealousies, this one was close-knit, remaining so even after the death of the parents. It is somehow startling to find Prince Henry the Navigator resting in such splendid luxury. He would, I think, be more comfortable awaiting Judgement in a plain tomb on his windswept point at Sagres, looking eternally out into the unknown.

It was João I whose vows at the nearby Battle of Aljubarota promised this church to the Virgin Mary if she would intervene to give him victory over the well-manned and heavily armed Castilian army of Juan I. Both sought the Portuguese throne and each had a claim, but with Juan's came Spanish rule. This was in 1385, and the surprising victory gave Portugal nearly 200 years of independence from Spain, as well as a magnificent abbey.

Like Rome, Batalha wasn't built in a day, or even in a century, its construction lasting from 1388 through the third quarter of the sixteenth century, when King João III left it unfinished to move his masons and resources to Belém to work on his own monastery there. Batalha was the work of several architects and spanned two periods — the Flamboyant and the Manueline. João's new bride favored the Perpendicular Gothic, which accounts for the haunting sense of English cathedral about the nave. Happily, all are based on Gothic structural patterns and blend in harmony.

Nowhere is the use of Manueline against Gothic seen so beautifully as in the Royal Cloister, entered from the north side of the nave. The graceful arches rise smooth and clean, each filled by a tracery of carved stone supported by delicate columns decorated in the shell and coral patterns of Manueline. The simple boxwood garden shows off the delicate tracery around it and at the far end a fountain sits in its own carved stone gazebo. These lavabos are characteristic of Manueline cloisters, and are a perfect place to stop and view the courtyard.

Off the corridor on the side opposite the lavabo is the Chapter House, an architectural triumph easily lost in the array of carved stone outside. Here a magnificent square vault rises without support, or so it seems, to a dome far above. The story is told that no one dared to enter it after the construction supports were removed, until the architect himself slept a night under it. Today it houses the Tomb of the Unknown Soldier, a simple stone monument with a lacy wrought-iron spire, topped by a lamp perpetually lit. The guard is a single soldier in fatigues and beret, and the only light is from a high stained glass window.

Across the cloister is the Museum of the Unknown Soldier, with medals and gifts presented by visiting dignitaries. There is a laurel wreath with a simple card, "Buckingham Palace" engraved at the top, and "Elizabeth R" and "Phillip" in dark bold handwriting. The ties between England and Portugal that began with João and Phillipa are centuries old and the friendship has endured.

Beyond, the Alfonso V Cloister is a smaller, plainer one and a door on the opposite side leads outside. Follow the building around to the right to the Unfinished Chapels (Capelas Imperfeitas), entered through a little porch just at the rear of the main structure. There may or may not be a guard, and he may or may not offer to show the way — the guardians of these government owned shrines, as we've noted before, are strangely indifferent.

No matter how many descriptions I have read or how many times I have seen these chapels, I enter each time unprepared. They are taller, more intricate, more ornate and more unreal than I had imagined or remembered. The golden honey-ochre of the weathered limestone is rich in the bright sun, making the sky appear a deeper blue against them. Swirling stone vines entwine the outer pillars that separate the seven chapels and, having no support beyond the last block, end abruptly.

King Duarte, son of João I, had envisioned this as a royal pantheon where members of the Avis line would be reunited, and each succeeding Avis monarch continued the work until Manuel, after erecting the buttresses and the magnificent doorway of tatted stone, more lace than sculpture, put his workers to honoring his own vows to the Virgin of Belém. Since the late sixteenth century, the doorway has led to a magnificent empty octagon, its carved pillars soaring to a dome of sky. Fortunately, the Portuguese climate is kind and the delicate stone lace shows little sign of its centuries of neglect.

Batalha At A Glance

The abbey, 120 km north of Lisbon is best reached by car, although there is a train as far as Valado and a bus from there.

LODGING: The new Pousada do M. Alfonso Dominiques (44/ 962 60), within sight of the abbey, offers 19 rooms, with doubles $50 in low season and $80 in high. The Motel S. Jorge, on the main road, has 10 rooms and a pool at about half the rate. Most visitors stay in nearby Nazaré or Alcobaça.

   FOOD: *The pousada offers excellent meals at between $13 and $18 and there is a cafe and restaurant in the group of buildings beside the abbey.*
   IF TIME IS SHORT: *Don't miss Batalha.*

Fátima and Tomar

There isn't much to describe at Fátima; its attraction is not so much what one sees there as what one senses has happened there. Except during the pilgrimages (the 13th of each month from May to October) it is a spread-out, sleepy town that doesn't look like it would have enough life to house and feed all those pilgrims.

There is a white basilica sitting on the far side of an enormous paved square; a tiny chapel sits to the left. Everything is white and very empty and it is hard to picture that huge area filled with people. But six times a year it is, and they spill out onto the streets and buildings beyond.

The story of the Visitation there is a well known one. In 1917, on May 13, the Virgin appeared to three children in the middle of a barren countryside near the tiny village of Aljustrel. Each succeeding month that year she came, and so did the children, despite government threats against their lives. They stuck to their story, and the word spread. On October 13, over 50,000 people came with them to the field, from all over the world, many of them skeptics and atheists. The press came to record the fact that nothing really happened there.

Afterward, they all described the same scene, the sun suddenly bursting through the storm thickened sky and appearing to lunge out of the sky toward the earth. Only the children saw the Virgin, but everyone else saw enough of the phenomenon to spread Fátima's fame throughout the world.

It is not a beautiful place: the basilica is simple, the little chapel plain, the landscape barren. But there is a transcendental beauty to Fátima, a sense of presence or of an important happening. We left strangely touched and silent.

The nature, temperament and history of the Knights Templar are all evident in the Convento de Cristo at Tomar, and a familiarity with the order is helpful in understanding their temple.

It was a religious order of knights, with its own rules, its own confessors, its own requirements and its own tremendous wealth. Originally under the Patriarch of Jerusalem, they guarded the routes and protected the pilgrims bound for the Holy City.

Unlike other religious orders they were not limited to the elite — or to the pious. They were a haven for the excommunicated, and they lived by their own rules, which included confessing only to priests of their own order, who were the equal of bishops in their authority to grant absolution. There were different levels of membership and only the highest required vows of chastity. But this motley bunch grew to a highly disciplined fighting force, capable of fighting off the Moors, and an increasingly wealthy and powerful one.

When the King of France ran out of money, he convinced the Pope that these Templars were more powerful than they were pious, and with the encouragement of other European monarchs greedy for wealth, the Pope dissolved the order and turned their property over to the kings of the countries in which the property lay.

Portuguese loyalties lay deeper, and King Dinis was a fair man who hadn't forgotten that the Templars had driven the Moors from his own cities. He officially dissolved them as ordered, but instead of plundering their properties, he applied to the Pope for permission to found a new Order of Christ. The Pope agreed and they were chartered "for the defense of the faith and the discomfort of the Moors" and placed forever under the royal authority of the crown of Portugal. The word spread quickly that all former Templars would be welcome, and the estates of the Templars were placed in the care of the Order of Christ.

A century later, Prince Henry the Navigator became the Grand Master and the order began to serve the crown by sending their ships with red crosses emblazoned on their sails, farther and farther into the unknown seas. Henry used their wealth to explore Africa and the seas to the south and west. Templars were in turn granted patrimony over the lands of their discovery and they became even richer.

It is against this historic tapestry that Tomar rose. It represents nearly every style of architecture of the twelfth through the seventeenth centuries, and combines them well. Everyone connected with the Templars had a hand here, each king adding his signature.

The richly carved and almost lacy Manueline portal of the Temple is without doubt the finest in Portugal, surpassing even the portal at Jerónimos. It seems almost too frilly for a military order, but as we shall see inside, these Knights had a flair for the beautiful which was not in that age considered at odds with a macho image.

Inside it reflects not only their taste for the beautiful, but the influence of the Holy Land where they began. The church is sixteen-sided, with its high altar in the center, surrounded by eight pillars, very tall and narrow and exceedingly graceful.

Much later, Manuel I added painting and frescoes, as well as polychrome statues in the niches. It was then, too, that the long Manueline nave and the coro alto were added, enlarging the small church and turning it into a chancel at the end of the nave. Some of the finest choir stalls ever made were commissioned and set in place.

Although Tomar and the Templars had withstood the Moors, its militarism was diluted and made into a strictly monastic order by João III, and Tomar soon fell to the French troops who occupied and sacked it. They burned the great choir stalls for cooking fires, and smashed the statuary and stonework they couldn't burn.

Only barely re-occupied before the dissolution of the holy orders in 1834, Manuel's great nave was again sacked, this time by government restorers who stripped it bare (completely disregarding the fact that it had been ornamented at the time of its construction) and leaving it a shell. How the magnificent original church with its frescoes and painted stone work, decorated long after its construction, escaped these plunderers, no one knows, but they give us a clue to the splendors with which these fighting men of God surrounded themselves.

To the Chapter House behind the nave, on the outside, Manuel also added a window which has been condemned and admired ever since. Whether it is the ultimate triumph of Manueline or an absurd caricature of it, it is the one thing everyone remembers about Tomar. Like the work of a seafaring stonecutter gone mad, it is a tangle of all the symbols of the sea and the explorations rolled into one. It is a catalogue of Portuguese sea power set in stone — not only the twisted ropes and the coral and seaweed, but the fishing floats and octopus tentacles as well, mixed with symbols of the faith and royalty.

Far more restrained than this later monument, Prince Henry's Cloister, reflects his own high bred simplicity. His Claustro do Cemitério, off the high altar, is the smallest of them, in perfect Gothic style with graceful arches and fine carving. João III added the final royal mark, with the dormitories and the great double-storied cloister. It is almost mathematical in its Palladian symmetry, and it adds the final chapter of this volume on architecture.

While the conventual buildings dominate the town, they do not dominate it physically, standing above, but a bit set back behind the trees. The town is a pleasant, open one built along a river. It was never enclosed by castle walls, so it could spread along the banks amid parks and squares.

Three kilometers from town is the Aqueduct of Pegões, built in the 1500s to carry water to the hilltop monastery. It is still intact, its arches spanning a wide valley.

Between Tomar and Fátima is Vila Nova de Ourem, a very attractive walled town with a restored castle. It has some fine houses and within the walls the newest of these is eighteenth century. The area southwest of Fátima is honeycombed with caves, the closest of which, at S. Mamede, is reached from the road to Batalha. Farther south, near Mira de Aire are the Grutas de Alvados and S. Antonio. All have interesting rock formations, but the Alvados Caves have a very unusual lake inside them and the fossilized remains of an ancient deer.

Southwest of Tomar is the larger city of Abrantes, with an arcaded castle overlooking the Tagus. Its Misericordia church on Largo Motta Ferraz has good eighteenth century woodwork and azulejos in its Casa Definitorio. Just below the castle is the old section of town, with narrow streets and flower decorated houses.

Standing on an island in the river, just west of Abrantes is Almoural Castle, reached by a road just past the military base at Tancos. The present castle is twelfth century, with nine towers. A boat may be rented to take visitors across the river to it, but the castle, which has absolutely no history of encounter, is closed.

Fátima And Tomar At A Glance

Tomar is a river town, 172 km north of Lisbon; Fátima is 34 km west of Tomar.

LODGING: The Hotel Dos Templarios (49/ 321 21) is a modern, attractive place set along the river. Doubles are between $40 and $50.

The Pousada de S. Pedro (49/ 381 59), at Castelo de Bode, 13 km south of Tomar on the Abrantes road, overlooks an enormous dam. Were it not for the Pousada S. Catarina in Miranda do Douro, we would note that this is the best pousada by a dam site, but we'll refrain. Its 16 rooms are in a moderately new building, with doubles from $40 to $60, depending on the season.

In Fátima, the four star Estralagem Dom Gonçalo (49/ 9 72 62) is our choice, set in a garden at the edge of town. Double rooms are

$35 – $40. There are several other hotels, none of which will be full except at pilgrimage times, when they all will be. Near the 13th of any month between May and October, it is best to plan to see this area from a base elsewhere. Although not very close, the Hotel Turismo (41/ 212 61) in Abrantes is quite comfortable, in the $40 range.

FOOD: *Neither Tomar nor Fátima is filled with restaurants, except those in the hotels, which are all perfectly good. Look on the menu in this area for Lebrada (rabbit) and Ovas de Sauel (shad roe).*

In Fátima, the Retiro do Caçadores serves local specialties under $10 and Grelha is slightly higher. In Tomar, it is hard to pay more than $5 for a dinner at the Nun Alvares. The Dos Templarios, although very good is a bit overpriced.

SHOPPING: *Tomar is known for its gold filigree work, especially little Templar ships with crosses on their sails.*

FESTIVALS: *On odd numbered years, during the first week in June, is the Festa dos Tabuleiros, marked by young girls in procession, carrying enormous columns of bread and flowers on their heads. The columns are as tall as the girls and weigh over 30 pounds. The girls carrying them never look very happy, but everyone else has a good time and it is very colorful. Like many of these, this festival is variable, and sometimes they skip a year, so check with the Portuguese National Tourist Office in New York, before planning a trip around this.*

IF TIME IS SHORT: *Pass briefly through Fátima and see the Convento de Cristo at Tomar, especially the church, cloisters and Chapter House window.*

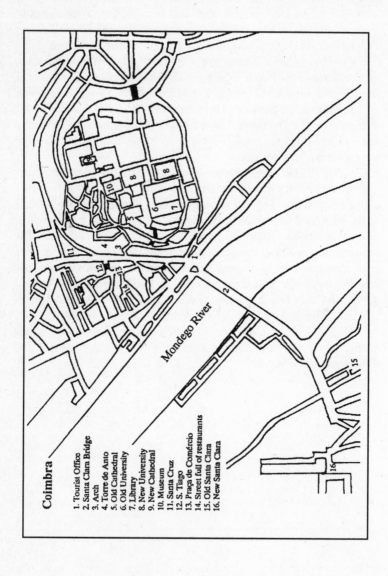

Coimbra

1. Tourist Office
2. Santa Clara Bridge
3. Arch
4. Torre de Anto
5. Old Cathedral
6. Old University
7. Library
8. New University
9. New Cathedral
10. Museum
11. Santa Cruz
12. S. Tiago
13. Praça de Comércio
14. Street full of restaurants
15. Old Santa Clara
16. New Santa Clara

Mondego River

Coimbra

Coimbra is a hard city to describe; its memory tumbles back as a series of impressions — steep winding streets, windows full of delicious pastries, the smell of rich coffee, the lonely grace of the half-submerged S. Clara, the golden swirls of baroque, the strains of fado sung by a tenor, gray stones, endless stairs, deep green gardens. If it's hard to sort it out in retrospect, it's just as hard while there.

We finally learned two rules of getting around in Coimbra: go on foot and don't try to follow streets on a map. It's easiest if you think of the town as a series of levels and squares. At the top is the University of Coimbra. Below it, to the right as you face the river, is the old cathedral, the Sé Velha. The steep streets that drop down from the University all seem to lead there.

Stairs below that lead through an impressive arched gate in the old walls to a street whose name changes halfway — the main street of this third level, and about the only straight one in the old city. More stairs lead down to the Praça do Comércio. A left through it, or a left on the main street above it, both lead to the river-front plaza and the bridge. Almost any street leads into one of these eventually.

This area along the river is about as far as a car should go. There are public parking lots near the bridge, and the main attractions are within walking (or climbing) distance.

To make a circular tour, saving the steepest part for the downhill half, go uphill to the right across the square from the bridge, along Couraça de Lisboa, turning left at the large square and following Rua S. Pedro to the great plaza surrounded by the new, box-like, university buildings. At the other end of this is a gate through which everyone hurries, probably to escape the sight of the enormous and hideous Soviet-style statues in the square.

We were standing in the little enclosure inside this gate, when a man in an upper window of the porticoed building to our right hailed us. He pointed to the stairs below him which we then climbed. Inside he greeted us as though we were distinguished guests of the University. He was afraid that we would just take the little girl to the library, and she would miss this, he told us.

He led us to the Sala dos Capelos where doctoral candidates are examined and degrees conferred. He indicated in turn where the faculty sits around the edges, the director (president) in front, and the candidates on benches in the center. The room is at once ornate and simple — its lines long and unbroken, its colors strong, its wooden ceiling entirely painted. He described how the ceremony proceeded, with marshals carrying the spears and maces, kept in an adjoining chamber in an impressive rack. The ceiling of that room, although low, is painted with allegorical figures which appear in perfect proportion despite their nearness. From the far side of the gallery, windows can be opened for a fine view down on the University and the old Sé.

The library, Coimbra's magnum opus to which we were headed when he hailed us, stands in the far corner of the square, not a large building. When its great wooden door swung open in response to our ring, we stepped in and stopped short. For all we had read about it we were unprepared for just how big, how lovely and how impressive it was.

Divided into three rooms, each almost a perfect cube, connected by high arches, surmounted by a crown, the doorways line up in perfect perspective to frame the portrait of King João V, its founder, at the far end. Above, beside and all around are books, their leather bindings row upon row, gallery upon gallery.

The effect is that the books, like the portrait, are framed in gold. Each of the three rooms uses a different color as a counterpoint to the gold — a pale and a darker green and, in the final room, a rich deep red. Each domed ceiling is painted in an architectural trompe l'oeil so that the pillars seem to move overhead as one passes through. The giant library tables are carved and inlaid with woods from Brazil and Goa.

The books on the upper shelves appear inaccessible until the innermost room. There on the upper gallery one of the gold and black pillars that separate the sections of shelves is pulled out to reveal ladders. The ladders tilt for climbing, and from them any book is within reach.

The fragile tapered pillars that support the galleries are black, ornamented in gold leaf scrollwork. The floor is inlaid black and white marble. The frame around João's portrait, even the "draperies" that surround it, are polychromed carved wood — carved in folds and painted so finely that it looks like brocade fabric.

There isn't much that will impress right after the senses have been so boggled. The neo-classic new cathedral, Sé Nova, in the plaza to the left above the University is pompous at best, and after the library, it is like a mediocre dessert following a great meal. But it has its charms — a plethora of smug angels hover over it saving it from its own formality.

There is a window over the main door where there once was a niche with a large statue of S. Ignatius, founder of the Jesuits. The Marquês de Pombal, who ruled as virtual dictator during the reign of José I, detested the Jesuits with even greater venom than he had for the rest of the powerful holy orders of the times. He dropped a broad hint to the Bishop of Coimbra that a window over the portal would let in more light, and S. Ignatius disappeared forever. Not long afterward, the Jesuits themselves disappeared from Portugal, and in less than a century, all the monasteries disappeared. Their vast riches and buildings became state property and their libraries fell to universities, Coimbra among them.

The old cathedral, the Sé Velha, faces on a slanting square below the University; all streets seem to lead past it. I never see it without the chords of "A Mighty Fortress Is Our God" coming to mind. It is an austere twelfth century crenelated church built over a mosque. The interior was once softened with azulejos which lined its columns (even the puritan tastes of Baedeker, who scorned the library, passing it off in a single sentence that mentioned only the books, had to admire these tiled columns). But they, as well as the tiles that covered the walls and much of the beauty of the adjoining cloister fell to the "restorers." Fortunately, the Sé retained its fine gilded and polychromed high altar retable.

S. Cruz is just below the Arco de Almedina and to the right along the main street. This busy street is so filled with cafe-bakeries that we call it the pastry street. In fact, Coimbra's most famous cafe sits elegantly in an old Chapel of S. Cruz, with a vaulted ceiling and marble tables.

The church's facade is incongruous in its present environment, a mass of carved stone figures beginning below the present street level. Instead of ascending the steps, you descend into S. Cruz. The azulejos that line the nave are set in sections, each capped, not by the usual straight line of border tiles, but by a baroque scroll, giving it a cut-out effect.

Just to the left of the altar is the Gothic tomb of Alfonso Henriques, first king of Portugal, and across from it, the tomb of his son, Sancho I. Although the spires of Alfonso's tomb are impressively carved, the real treasure of S. Cruz is the beautifully carved Renaissance pulpit with its high reliefs of several saints. In the coro alto, the stalls are richly carved, in an exuberant relief style, depicting scenes from the travels of Vasco da Gama. There are so few medieval choir stalls left, that these would be historically interesting, even without their exceptionally fine artistry.

While S. Cruz is the favorite of artists, S. Clara Velho, across (and almost in) the river, is the favorite of romantics. Partly for its history, and partly for its grace and grandeur in ruin, one cannot help but be touched by it. Once another of the elegant monasteries of the Poor Clares, it was endowed by the sainted Queen Isabel who retired there as a widow. Her tomb was there, along with that of Ines de Castro, mistress, and perhaps wife, of Isabel's grandson, Pedro I. Ines left first to be entombed at Alcobaça, and the queen was removed in a procession of nuns to the new convent up the hill when this one was abandoned.

The Mondego, a peaceful river most of the year, becomes a torrent when swollen into spring floods, and it gradually made the area around S. Clara into a marsh. The convent was flooded so frequently that a new one had to be built. Taking no chances, they chose the high hill overlooking the river.

Now S. Clara stands a forlorn shell, half below the silted-up land around her, stagnant backwater filling her undercroft. The delicate stonework of the rose window is intact as is the bell tower, but the portico rises out of the water, and the lower arches stand just barely above it, giving the church a squat, low appearance instead of the grandeur of its original setting. One is not meant to look a great church straight in the eye.

The best view of the church is not from its entrance side, but from a dirt lane that runs between it and the river. Walk around the end of the adjoining block, and follow the lane to the right. The gate on this side is left unlocked, and it is possible to go right up and look in the windows. Usually, when visitors arrive, someone will find the man with the key and he will open the door to the nave.

Inside there is an eerie glow, caused by the light reflecting from the green algae covering the water under its arches. There is some very fine stonework, but most of the floor is gone and the overall effect is one of desolation.

The church of the new convent, S. Clara-a-Nova sits high on the hill above, facing Coimbra, with a fine view of the city across the Mondego. This is a good place to become oriented with Coimbra, since the landmarks that sit in layers along the hill are easily spotted from here.

Inside, in the lower choir, is the original stone tomb, which Isabel ordered built for herself, showing her in the simple habit of a nun. But when she was canonized, a grander, more suitable silver tomb was placed in the chancel. Along the side aisles are good polychrome relief panels of events in her life. Two very good early tombs are at the back of the nave.

There is a Renaissance double cloister, considered an even finer example than the one at Tomar. Like the Tomar cloister, this one was a gift of King João V, whose fondness for nuns has been mentioned in connection with Mafra.

Also in the S. Clara district of Coimbra, and not far from the convent, is Quinta das Lagrimas, at the site of the palace where Pedro and Ines lived, and in whose garden she was murdered. The garden is open to visitors. Below, directly behind the old convent, is Portugal dos Pequeninos, which although designed for children, is delightful for adults as well. Here are miniatures of famous landmarks in Portugal and her colonies, very well done and nicely kept.

There are other attractions in Coimbra, for those who take the time. The botanic garden has exotic trees and flowers, set in graceful stairways and terraces behind the University. The museum in the former Episcopal Palace by the Sé Nova is filled with a priceless collection of art taken from local convents when the holy orders were dissolved. Below, displayed amid the supportive vaulting of the palace, are Roman and pre-Roman artifacts.

Now that there is finally a good hotel in Coimbra, it is tempting to stay there and see the surrounding countryside using Coimbra as a base. There are interesting destinations in every direction.

South of the city is Conimbriga, a major Roman settlement which has been under competent excavation for some years. The foundations of the villas are clear to see, with fine mosaic floors still intact, and pools and fountains in their atria. The foundations for the baths are fascinating, with sections for hot, cold and tepid water. A museum was added recently to display those artifacts that could not be left in place.

Running right across the site is a crudely constructed wall, roughly built of whatever the Romans had at hand — stones, broken columns, pieces of statuary. This had been thrown up quickly, in an effort to protect themselves from the Suevi, but it was ineffective. Somehow that crude wall, built over so much that was fine and artistic, illustrates far better than any history book, the panic of these civilized Romans at the advance of the barbarians. Standing on the delicate mosaic floors, looking up at the wall, it is easy to picture the Germanic hordes swarming over it and into Conimbriga.

To the west, along the north bank of the Mondego is the hilltop castle of Montemor-o-Velho, overlooking the lowlands bright green with rice paddies. This castle was rebuilt in the eleventh century, an imposing walled fortress with a church inside. The best view of the castle and its surroundings is from a road which ascends a small hill on the opposite side of the main road; photographers will find the best lighting in the afternoon.

Beyond is the wide Atlantic beach at Figueira da Foz, a popular seaside resort despite its often treacherous seas. There is an excellent museum of archaeology with artifacts found all over Portugal. Nearby is Casa do Paço, with eighteenth century Dutch tiles in astonishing numbers.

North of Coimbra lies Bucaço with its famous forest of cypresses, planted there by Carmelite brothers and once protected by a Papal Bull which promised excommunication to anyone harming a single tree. In the midst of this park stands a former royal palace, now a hotel. It was built in the late 1800s, shortly before the monarchy went into exile, and its architecture is a sort of decadent Manueline.

Designed, it is said, by a set-painter from the Lisbon opera house, it is a riot of towers and parapets and decorative details of all sorts. Its portico is supported by deeply carved columns, and the wall of its grand staircase is covered in azulejos. The antique furniture and interior decoration carries out this theme of a good thing gone wild, creating a most enjoyable hotel. Visitors are welcome to wander through it or stay for lunch, even if they are not staying there. It is set in a formal garden, completely surrounded by forest. Like Pena, no-one could possibly take it seriously; it is another of Portugal's delightful architectural romps.

Under the palace is the remainder of a convent with a chapel full of ex-votos of plastic extremities, and several cork-lined cells.

In one of these, Wellington spent the night before the decisive Battle of Bucaço, which took place along this ridge, less thickly forested then. There is a small military museum in the park, for those with a special interest in the Peninsular War.

The forest is beautiful to drive through and even better to walk in. Its well-kept paths lead past little shrines, all under a canopy of giant trees — everything from Tasmanian eucalyptus and sequoias to Himalayan cedar and magnolias. There are forests of fern, fragile wildflowers and pools fed by mountain springs. It is an especially pleasant cool retreat after the heat of Coimbra in the summer.

Adjoining the forest is the spa town of Luso. We admit to a penchant for little European spas and their grand hotels; there is such an air of ancient gentility about them, to which Portugal adds a charming provincialism. They aren't glitzy or pretentious, even Luso, which is among the best known of them. They have an enthusiasm and a holiday air.

The springs are in a sort of sunken plaza where people fill their gallon jugs at a row of flowing faucets. In the late afternoon, everyone sits in the plaza and strolls along the streets and through the brilliant flower beds that lead up the hill toward the Bucaço Forest. The hotels are pale yellow and pastel pink, and the more modern emphasis on fitness is evident in the jogging trails and sports facilities.

The main Coimbra-Porto road is so congested with traffic that it is best to plan on a byway route to these towns. Fortunately there are two good ones. The first leaves the main road just north of Coimbra with a right turn toward Souzelas. It winds through little villages and tree-filled countryside to Luso and on to Bucaço.

The other road makes a very pleasant circle route, leaving Coimbra to the east along the north bank of the river (following signs to Penacova) and up the Mondego valley to Rebordosa. The route is a beautiful one, overlooking the river cut into its deep valley. Below are women washing clothes, which they lay out to dry in the sun along the wide beach. There is considerable river traffic, most of it in narrow wooden boats with tall curved prows. Red-roofed villages cling to the steep slopes. It is like this all the way to São Comba Dão, where a road from Luso joins.

Another smaller road turns north at Rebordosa toward Lorvão and later connects with the back road between Coimbra and Luso.

Whichever route is chosen, the town of Lorvão is well worth a stop or a detour.

Set in a narrow cleft above a little river, Lorvão is so crowded that its main street is one-way as it winds between the houses; a traffic light alternates its direction and pedestrians step into doorways to let cars pass. Fortunately, there is not much traffic.

When it widens out into a square, there is a little boxwood garden with mosaic sidewalks, flowering trees and a very nice baroque arch, the gate of a long-fallen wall. Behind it stand the great white buildings of a Cistercian monastery founded in the sixth century. The church, which is entered from the side, has a particularly fine choir covered with intricate and well-designed wood carving. Under each seat, and showing only when these are folded upward, is a face carved in deep relief in the dark wood. Each is different, all caricatures, like fat-cheeked gargoyles. The choir grill is lovely as well, in iron with bronze medallions accenting the junctions.

In the cloister are box hedges and orange trees, and carved stone arches have been reset at the entrances to small altar niches. Here also are the original tombs of the two daughters of Sancho I, who entered holy orders here after it had been converted to a convent. They were later moved to the more ornate tombs at either side of the altar.

There is a charming small museum in the sacristy, to which the sacristan has the key. The painted cabinets are as fascinating as their varied contents, with false graining and naive country painting. There are illuminated manuscripts, reliquaries, vestments and a seventeenth century portable organ, set on poles like a sedan chair, covered with scrolls and swirls of eighteenth century provincial painting.

With all these things to poke about at, it is easy to forget the first rule of sacristies: look up. There is a fine painted wooden ceiling in this one. We always browse in guest books, and in this one we found no overseas visitors during the previous six months, a shame, since it is a lovely place in a very interesting town.

Lorvão is a maze of tiny streets and lanes zigzagging up the steep slopes between stair-stepped layers of little houses. Porches and balconies are lined with pots of geranium, and women carry huge loads of firewood and cornstalks along the narrow passages under them.

The chief cottage industry here is the carving of toothpicks, which the local women do with incredible speed. The women often gather to work in the shade of the monastery wall, or if a visitor expresses an interest, one of them will bring her knives and little leather strap out onto her doorstep and carve a handful of toothpicks in minutes.

They begin with a split log, which looks much like a piece of firewood. It is then further split with a sickle-bladed knife into thinner strips like kindling wood. With astonishing speed, these are split, cut, sharpened and finished into toothpicks.

Up the hill, in a tiny three-storied house with one room on each level, Sabino Torcato has a workshop the size of a closet, where he is building a scale model of the monastery below. His shop is so small that he keeps the work in sections because assembled it won't fit in his workspace.

One could spend all day in one of these little hill towns, where everyone wants to show something — the view from their garden, the little chapel or the work of a friend. Travelers are rare and everyone tries to outdo the next in hospitality.

Coimbra At A Glance

University city, 117 km south of Porto, 200 km north of Lisbon. It can be reached by train from either.

LODGING: The dearth of decent lodging in Coimbra has been a common lament for many years, and we're happy to announce that there is now a beautiful new hotel just across the river in the S. Clara district. Overlooking the city, the Hotel Dom Luis (39/ 841 510, telex DLUIS) had just barely opened when we stayed there, and it was so nice and so well-run that we decided to stay longer and tour the surrounding area from here. Large doubles with balconies and mini-bar are $60. There are other hotels: the Astoria was once quite grand, but efforts at reviving it have fallen short. The Dom Luis is the only one we can recommend in good conscience.

The top choice out of town is the Palace Hotel do Bucaço (31/ 931 01), described previously. Doubles are about $80. In nearby Luso, the Grande Hotel das Termas (31/934 50) is right by the springs, with good health and fitness facilities and even a dance floor. A double is between $40 and $50. The Hotel Eden (31/ 934 50) overlooks the spa from the other side, next to the public gardens. It's a modern hotel with less character than the Termas, but in the same price range. There are a number of pleasant pensãos and a very helpful tourist office across from the Hotel Termas to help visitors find one.

Figueira da Foz has a wide assortment of seaside lodgings, from the Grande Hotel at $35-$50 for modernized but unimaginative rooms, to the modern four star Estralagem da Piscina (33/ 224 20) with sea views, balconies and a pool, in the same price range. Figueira is not a convenient place from which to explore Coimbra.

FOOD: There are restaurants in Coimbra, but they are not always apparent to the hungry traveler in search of them. We once wandered for over an hour without ever passing one until at last we happened upon the tiny Ruas das Azeiteiras, almost an alley off Praça do Comércio, and found at least a dozen of them side by side. Most of these aren't fancy, but all serve good local dishes. Kanimambo, Ciro Churrasqueria, the tiny Viela and the Funchal are all good choices in the $5-10 range. You can read menus and look right into any of these before making a choice.

At the other end of the scale, but still not expensive, the dining room of the Dom Luis is excellent. Although in most countries we shy away from hotel restaurants, in Portugal these have maintained the old continental tradition of fine dining rooms at prices competitive with local restaurants.

The food at the Dom Luis is meticulously prepared and the service outstanding, even when they are very busy. I am not a great admirer of liver as food, but knowing it to be a Portuguese specialty, I ordered it here. The chef raised it to such gourmet heights that I vowed never to malign it again. A full course dinner with a fine wine and unparalleled view over the lights of the city was $10 apiece.

For late dinner and fado, quite different from Lisbon fado, the best place is the elegant Trovador, right across from the Sé Velha (old Cathedral). This whole square and the surrounding streets come to life at night as cafes spill out onto the streets and students fill their tables. Some of these don't open until around 10 p.m. Be sure to have your concierge call Trovador for reservations since it is quite popular.

Near the old S. Clara convent, just down from the Dom Luis there are several good restaurants including Alfredo and Pinto d'Ouro, both in the $10 range.

The Palace Hotel at Bucaço serves outstanding full course dinners at about $25. But we prefer the local specialty of the nearby town of Mealhada, whose culinary fame rests on roast suckling pig. The town is literally lined with restaurants charging about $15 apiece for platters *of this delicacy. Plan to be here at lunchtime, and toss a coin for which restaurant. We've tried several and can't find any difference in quality among them.*

If you are in Lorvão at lunchtime, we must recommend the little Cafe Lorvãoense, just south of the convent. Not only is it one of very few choices, but it serves wonderful sandwiches on thick crusty rolls. But be prepared for the price: the bifanas (grilled veal steak) is the most expensive at 90¢, and a sandwich of juicy, plump grilled sausage is 30¢.

SHOPPING: *There is an excellent artisinato at the Torre de Anto in Coimbra (go right at the foot of the steps just below the Sé Velha) with weaving, wood carving, embroidery and other local crafts. Shops on the main street have good embroidered linens.*

FESTIVALS: *On September 27 there is a Mass and parade in old uniforms at Bucaço commemorating the victory there.*

IF TIME IS SHORT: *Don't miss Conimbriga or Coimbra. Park near the bridge and walk up to the library and back down past the old cathedral to S. Cruz. Across the river, see the two convents of S. Clara, then go north to Bucaço. With a little more time, take the longer route up the river turning at Rebordosa for Lorvão, continuing on to Bucaço.*

Aveiro

People insist on calling any city with a canal "the Venice of...."
Aveiro has also been dubbed the Amsterdam of Portugal because
of the slightly Dutch looking houses along the water. Dropped
there suddenly, it would take a few minutes to figure out exactly
where one was, since in front of the pink and white step-roofed
houses, boats with long curved prows glide by, their painted designs
intricate and colorful.

Aveiro's principal artistic treasure is the chapel of the Convento de Jesus, an entire room filled with gold baroque wood
carving. Covering everything but the floor underfoot, this riot of
gold would be overwhelming, but for its size, which gives it intimacy
without claustrophobia.

Whether the adjoining tomb of S. Joana, the daughter of Alfonso V, is a masterpiece or a monstrosity has been widely argued,
but to us it is the real gem of this convent. At first glance, this large
piece seems painted with intricate designs in delicate pink, green
and white, but a closer look proves it is made entirely of inlaid
marble. Tiny flowers and vines entwine the entire tomb. Entire
borders are inlaid in unbroken sections of black and white marble
in interlocking designs. These are not formed of small shapes set
in a mosaic, but of long marble strips carved to interlock. At the
end is a medallion of flowers, even more fragile a design than the
rest. The effect of the entire work is that of painted china. It is
one of the most extraordinary and beautiful works of inlaid marble
we have ever seen.

There are other lovely things in the museum which is now set
in the convent, but the traveler's mind keeps returning to these
two, and in retrospect, when the details of the chapel have blended
into the memories of other golden chancels, the tomb remains,
unlike any other.

In Aveiro the first time with our daughter we almost missed
these, since we arrived when the museum was closed. But across
the street in the little cathedral, the priest took an interest in Julie,
who took interest in everything that she saw. Had we seen the
chapel? We couldn't leave Aveiro without that, he declared and

shepherded us across the street. He pulled the bell rope, and from somewhere deep within a bell summoned a man who let us in, with the priest as our guide.

West of the Cathedral is the Carmelite Church, known locally as Igreja S. Cruz, also covered in gold. It is larger than the convent chapel and reminiscent of S. Clara in Porto. The Misericordia is covered with azulejos.

Congested and endlessly urbanized at its outskirts, it is tempting to bypass Aveiro, but it is an interesting city. Approaching from the pleasant little beach resort town of Mira, south of Aveiro, the road crosses above the lowlying marshes filled with rice paddies and salt beds, often overlooked by mounds of salt. North and west of the city is a vast marshy area cut by rivers, a wild land which can be explored by boat (enquire of your concierge, who will know the schedules).

This is a delightful excursion, taking the bulk of a day among Aveiro's canals and marshes, where visitors see fishermen, seaweed gatherers, salt flats as well as the wild life of the rivers and islands. Bico is a little fishing port which can be reached by road. Farther north is the fishing town of Ovar, whose name is the source of the name of the Lisbon fish sellers. "Varinhas" was originally "Ovarinhas," or women from Ovar who sold fish. Just to the north of Ovar is Vila da Feira, with an eleventh century castle set among the trees.

South of Aveiro is Ilhavo where there is a little folk museum of the local maritime people. Vista Alegre, nearby, is home of the well known pottery works which can be visited. Ask to see the chapel of the quinta where the pottery is made.

Aveiro At A Glance

Maritime city 69 km south of Porto, accessible by train (through a fine station decorated with azulejos).

LODGING: The Hotel Alfonso V (34/ 25191) and the Hotel Imperial (34/ 22141) are equally good and doubles at each are priced between $35 and $45. Our choice, however, is the former senhorial manor of Paloma Blanca (34/ 26039), set in gardens with a swimming pool. Regional style furnishings and high ceilings add to its charms. Doubles are $35 to $45. There are two pousadas, one in the unusual setting of the coastal marshes. Pousada da Ria in Murtosa (34/ 48332) is about 30 km north of Aveiro on a strip of low land between the

ocean and the lagoon. Rooms are from $40 to $60. The Pousada de
S. Antonio (34/ 521230) is inland near the main Coimbra-Porto road
north of Agueda. It is in a villa, and in the same price category as the
Pousada da Ria .

FOOD: The local dish is a seafood stew called Caldeira a
Pescador, also made with eel — Caldeira de Enguias. Mexihoes de
Escabeche are local mussels in a marinade. Centenario on Praça
Mercado is a very good restaurant with meals at about $15 each.
Cozinha Velha on Rua Direita is smaller and just as good at about
two thirds of the price, but it's closed on Saturday. Marnoto on Rua
Santas Martires is a good substitute at the same price level; it closes
Sunday. A Marisqueira in Ilhavo is a good seafood restaurant and
quite inexpensive. Tigre in Vila da Feira has a reputation for good
food although its prices are higher — about $15 for dinner.

SHOPPING: The pottery factory in Vista Alegre has a shop which
is open weekdays, as is the factory itself. Fine linens are also produced
in this area.

FESTIVALS: At the end of July the La Ria Festival includes a
colorful contest for the finest painted prows of the elegant local boats.

IF TIME IS SHORT: Make a quick detour to see the canal-front
buildings and the Convento de Jesus (except on Mondays, when it is
closed).

Viseu

Because the list of "things to see" in Viseu looks so short — a cathedral, a museum and a couple of churches — it is tempting when planning an itinerary, to brush it off with a quick pass through. While certainly better than not seeing it at all, this would be a shame. For there is much to see in Viseu's little streets and gracious gardens.

It is a walking city, although it is possible, even easy, to drive right into its old town to the Cathedral. Better to park in one of the streets off of the Praça de República (the Rossio) and stroll. Overlooking this square, really three squares strung together, is the fine facade of the church of S. Francisco (confusingly referred to by the locals as Terceiros) atop its wide stairs. The interior is worth the climb, all baroque and gold.

Behind it is a large public garden, and below it is a tiny one with a pool and formal beds full of bright annuals. The Rossio is full of cafes and trees, a fine combination, and ends at a curved wall of azulejos. Above the wall is a beautiful flower garden and the smaller cafe of the Pensão Rossio Parque. To the left of the garden is the town hall with a courtyard worth peeking into. A street leads up through the Porta do Soar, past a little eighteenth century chapel, and into one of Europe's loveliest squares.

The Sé, huge and elegant, dominates one side; facing it in perfect counterpoint is the wide, graceful, Misericordia with its rounded steps spread in front like petticoats. It is creamy white and carved granite, and were it not for its twin bell towers, it would look more like a palace.

The great central doors of the Sé lead directly into the nave with its remarkable vaulted Manueline roof. This is a remarkable church for its ceilings, with unusual vaulting in the Chapter House (over the cloister) a richly painted chancel ceiling, and the best one of all in the sacristy.

We've mentioned sacristies before, but cannot emphasize how important it is to seek these out in Portugal. Even in the most modest church (of which there are few here) the sacristy is not the sparse little anteroom with sink and closet of most American churches. Care and artistry were lavished on these and, because they were not in the "public" part of the church, they usually have escaped "restoration". They are, in fact, quite often the place where lovely pieces of statuary purged from the nave have found sanctuary, where the favorite pieces of the priest or parishioners, were hidden from the scrap pile. But *always look up*, for the ceilings in these rooms are often breathtaking.

And with this introduction we submit Viseu's as the best we've seen. It is painted in scenes of animals, some real, some not — and tropical flowers in rich colors. The blue and yellow wall tiles, which ought to clash terribly with it, do not. Portuguese artists seem to be able to carry off terrible combinations with panache, and this is one. If the traveler must run through the nave and lovely Renaissance cloister to do it, they should see the sacristy.

Next to the Sé, forming another side of the square, is the former Episcopal Palace, now an outstanding art museum specializing in the Viseu school.

Down the street beside the cloister is a lovely little square which leads into the Rua Direita and other shopping streets, many with fine old baroque houses. While Viseu is not as purely baroque as Lamego, it mixes its styles well and has a lively lived-in feeling, even on a Sunday afternoon with the shops closed.

A few blocks later, a cross street to the right leads back into the Rossio. Or, following the cross street to the left will lead to a largo and the Igreja Carmo, with azulejos, a gilt pulpit and a painted dome over the apse. Any street back from that square leads to the Rossio or the public garden.

Northeast of Viseu, on the way to no place in particular, is Aguiar de Beira, a very small town with an almost perfect set of medieval buildings. The main square sits on a slant surrounded by a crenellated tower, a Romanesque fountain house and a house with an outside staircase, all of local stone. In the center is an almost delicate pillory.

The fountain house appears to also have housed the town council in its upper story, for there are stone benches around the walls, much like Bragança's, but unroofed. Above this is the castelo about which there is even more doubt and conjecture. It is constructed of dry stone — without mortar — which would seem to date it before the many Beira castles built by King Dinis. The wall surrounds the crest of the hill and some large granite blocks. Whatever its origins, both it and the town are fascinating.

To the northwest is S. Pedro do Sul, its town hall in a former baroque monastery. The church is richly decorated with statues, gold retables and a fine sacristy ceiling. The facade of the Misericordia is done in azulejos. There is a spa just outside of town, and the road beyond leads into a nature reserve covering the slopes of the Serra Arada.

To the southeast is Mangualde, with its old stone mansions and the seventeenth century Paço Anadia whose huge pink facade faces the town square. The palace is open for tours and is well worth seeing, since it is lavishly decorated and contains outstanding azulejos.

The Misericordia chapel is quite lovely, reached from the courtyard of the school, and the old town is a warren of narrow streets and stone houses. About 12 km north is Penalva do Castelo with the fine manor house of Casa da Insua with a crenellated white facade. The gardens are beautifully kept and open to the public, along with the chapel.

To the southeast via Tondela is Caramulo, on the edge of the botanical reserve high in the Serra do Caramulo. There is a spa here and museums of automobiles and Portuguese art as well as post-impressionists. There are a number of viewpoints and some short climbs into the mountains. Nearby is the pousada.

Viseu At A Glance

A provincial capital 82 km north of Coimbra.

LODGING: Although Viseu is an easy day trip from Coimbra, it is also a very pleasant town to stay in. The Hotel Avenida (32/ 234 32), just off the Rossio, is small, personal, and decorated in antiques, with rooms between $20 and $30. If motels appeal, the Grão Vaço (32/ 23511) is also centrally located and has a pool and very nice rooms starting at $40. If you like to stay in a classic Portuguese pensão with high ceilinged spotless rooms and a fine location, try the three star Pensão Rossi Parque (32/ 257 85), overlooking the flower garden just above the azulejo wall. It offers rooms with private bath in the $20 to $25 range and has a nice suite for very little more.

The Pousada S. Jerónimo (32/86291) on a mountainside in Caramulo has only 6 rooms, giving it the intimate atmosphere of a private lodge. Rooms are from $40 to $60 depending upon the season. In Mangualde, the Estralagem Cruz da Mata (32/ 62556) is very nice but expensive, and the three star Hotel Senhora do Castelo (32/ 62796) is *less expensive and also pleasant. If you love decaying grandeur and slightly blowzy old hotels that once hosted queens and prime ministers, the Hotel Urqueiriça in Canas de Senhorim (32/ 672 67) near Nelas (south of Viseu) is for you. All is dark and paneled, and even in the hottest, driest, summer in recent history, the rooms were damp, cool and musty smelling. But the tapestries are still there, as is the grand sunken dining room, and their prices reflect the era of their grandeur too. A double is $40.*

FOOD: This is the homeland of the Dão wines, the prospect of which overshadows any cuisine. Order dinner to match the wine here — roast kid, local sausage. Trave Negra, Alvorada and Cortiça are all good restaurants in the $10 range. The Pensão Rossio Parque has a good little restaurant where dinner is about $7.50. In Mangualde, Luciano at Quinta do Salqueiro on the Nelas road is good (under $10 and closed on Monday) and the Solar at the Hotel Senhora do Castelo is slightly more expensive, serving dinners only. The Pensão David at S. Pedro do Sul is a good lunch stop at under $10. Pousada guests will find the best food right there at about $16 apiece. Be sure to enjoy one of the Viseu sweets at one, or more, of the pastry shops with sidewalk cafe tables.

SHOPPING: Weaving, especially carpets and bedspreads, is a major occupation here. The local Molelos pottery is black. There is also lace-making in the area. There are two artisinatos opposite the Sé, but they carry mostly souvenirs. Look in better shops down in the commercial area near Rossio or shop at the big Tuesday market. Most of the merchandise is everyday necessities, but there are craftsmen as well.

IF TIME IS SHORT: Allow at least a two-hour stopover to see this attractive town, and remember the sacristy ceiling!

Lamego

There are many baroque buildings in northern Portugal, but no where do we see them all together in a baroque city as we do in Lamego. Mansions, palaces, churches and public buildings sit along garden filled squares and broad avenues, one of which leads to the monumental baroque stairway of N.S. de Remédios.

Lovely architecture is almost everywhere, and a short walk southward from the cathedral (which is the least interesting of Lamego's churches, although it has a nice cloister) passes several fine mansions. The Bishop's Palace, thirty-odd rooms of it, is now a museum containing an entire chapel from the S. Clara convent which fell to ruin and was torn down in the 1920s.

Their church still stands at the end of a lovely public garden and like anything associated with the Poor Clares in Portugal, is sumptuous. These nuns had good, if expensive, taste in their surroundings, and this church is richly ornamented with gold and has a painted ceiling whose trompe l'oeil architecture rises to a red cupola surrounded with flowers and people looking down into the church. There is a joy to their piety, an alleluia resounding in every church.

N.S. do Desterro has an interesting ceiling with azulejos and good carving. The key is just across the street if it is locked.

The pilgrimage church of N.S. dos Remédios stands above the town, its stairs rising in elegant stages through the trees, all white and granite with fountains, azulejos and statuary. At the top is a circular plaza surrounded by tall pillars, arches and statuary. Although not as well-known outside Portugal, it is better than the Bom Jesus at Braga.

Opposite is another hill with a twelfth century castle. Its walls are Moorish and it has a most unusual vaulted cistern.

North of Lamego, at Balsemão, is the seventh century chapel of S. Pedro, a Visigothic basilica. Although there has been interior restoration, its architecture is thought to be in more original state than the only other building this old, the chapel at S. Frutoso at Braga. Be sure to ask for directions since the way is not sign posted very well.

South of the city is the Raposeiro winery where a sparkling white wine is made. It is possible to visit the caves and see the process during normal weekday hours.

On the road southeast toward Moimenta de Beira is the twelfth century Cistercian monastery of S. João set in fields once terraced and cultivated by the friars. The convent is now only a ruined wall of windows, but the church is filled with riches. It is almost regrettable that it once contained the painting of S. Peter about which there is so much discussion by art historians, because the church is usually mentioned only in this connection, ignoring the vast array of other interesting things.

Not one, but two azulejo borders surround the walls and rows of handsome choir stalls and are decorated with amusing carved "portraits." The gold work is staggering in amount and artistry — on the high altar, all six side altars and the organ case. There is an excellent painted ceiling and the gigantic Gothic tomb of yet another of King Dinis's illegitimate sons has good relief carving.

Nearby is the town of Ucanha with one of the few fortified bridges remaining in Portugal.

Lamego At A Glance

Baroque town 153 km east of Porto, 40 km south of Vila Real.

LODGING: The Estralagem de Lamego (54/ 621 62), just south of the city, is housed in an old villa overlooking the vineyards and the city. Double rooms are about $45. The Albergaria Cerrado (54/ 631 64) is a comfortable businesslike hotel with little charm but a good downtown location, and only a little more expensive. The Hotel Parque (54/ 621 05) is next to N.S. de Remédios, a lovely location at the top of the stairs (a road goes up, too). Doubles are about $35. Vila Hostilina (54/ 623 94) is a nineteenth century house set on a hilltop with a good view. There is a pool and sauna as well.

FOOD: The local ham is excellent, especially with the melon and figs that grow here all summer. Breads in this region are varied and delicious: pao de centeio is a crusty rye. The Parque and the Estralagem both have good dining rooms and the Avenida and the S. Bernardo are both good restaurants with regional cooking. Don't forget to try the sparkling wine.

SHOPPING: Local needlework is exceptional and you are likely to find elegant crochet and net darned tablecloths and bedspreads hanging over fences along the roadsides above Lamego. These are for sale, and you will do better here than in the shops of town.

FESTIVALS: *The whole first two weeks of September are filled with the Feira at N.S. dos Remédios, with processions and dancing and a giant fair in the park adjoining the shrine. This is one of Portugal's best, but hotel rooms are booked months in advance (in a pinch try Vila Real area).*

IF TIME IS SHORT: *Don't cut Lamego, even if it means just spending an hour or so there to see its lovely exteriors. If there is time for one church, choose S. Clara.*

Vila Real

Although the capital of Tras os Montes, Vila Real is neither its largest nor its most interesting city, and lies barely within its boundaries. But it is attractive, with a number of old mansions and an overlook at Terreiro do Calvario with lovely views of the countryside and of the confluence of the rivers. It is the gateway to the mountain province with roads to Chaves, Braga and Miranda do Douro.

The Capela Nova (Clérigos) church has a most unusual baroque facade, long and narrow between two pairs of enormous columns. On top of its curved pediment stand three statues, below which is a deeply carved crest. It's hard to miss. Its interior is less interesting as though its architect had put all of his energies into the facade.

S. Pedro is the other way around, with a poor exterior and richly decorated inside. Its gilded carving is excellent and its ceiling among the finest, coffered and painted. Whenever we see a ceiling like this we offer a little prayer that the "restorers" won't find it.

Not far from town is Mateus, with its villa made famous on wine labels. This great villa is open for tours which take one and one half hours (9-1 and 2-4) and are worth the time if only to have a rare look inside one of these quintas. The ceilings are excellent and the eighteenth century Portuguese furniture and art collections extensive. The fine facade is best appreciated from the gardens, where the spires, stairways and graceful baroque lines of the house and chapel are reflected in the water and framed in boxwood trees.

Three km south of Mateus, in Panoias, is an early Roman rock temple. This is on the road to Sabosa where Magellan was born. The only routes from here to nearby (as the crow flies) Alijo and its pousada, form a long triangle north through Balsa or south through Pinhão, each over a winding mountain road.

This is the lovely land of the upper Douro, demarcated as the port wine growing region. The terrain is steep and the slopes covered with vines. The Quinta do Noval near Pinhão (east of Regua) is open on weekdays from 9:30 to 1 and 3 to 6 and visitors can see the wine making process as well as the vineyards and fine views.

On the road north to Chaves, about 26 km from Vila Real, is Vila Pouca de Aguiar, with its ruined medieval castle high on the Serrado Alvão. There is a Belle Epoque spa park at Perdas Salgadas, 6 km further on, and the entire area to the west is sprinkled with ancient dolmen. The road west toward Ribeira de Pena passes near several groups of them: ten at Cha Araca, five at Lixa de Alvão, four at Portelo da Cha and another group just beyond Ribeira de Pena.

The new road to Braga passes through Murça, which can also be reached from Alijo. Its main interest is the largest and possibly the oldest of the stone pigs, dating from the third or fourth century B.C.

Vila Real At A Glance

Provincial capital, 116 km east of Porto, 64 km south of Chaves.

LODGING: The modern hotel Mira-Corgo (59/ 25001) has 76 rooms and a wide range of facilities. There is more charm at the Albergaria Cabonelas (59/ 23153), at the same price, around $50 for a double, and the smaller Hotel Tocaio (59/ 23106) is modest but clean and hospitable in the $25 to $30 range. The Pousada do Barão de Forrester (59/ 95215) in Alijo is small, remote and comfortable with a swimming pool. Those traveling between Vila Real and Bragança can reach it best by a 16 km detour 10 km west of Murça. Rooms are $40 to $60 depending on the season. Closer than Alijo and to the west is the Pousada S. Gonçalo (see Amarante). In Regua, the residential Columbano (59/ 23704) has a good reputation and moderate prices.

FOOD: The pousada is the best choice for the people staying there. In Vila Real the Espadeiro features roast kid, trout and feijoada — a delicious bean and meat cassoulet popular in this region and similar to the famous Brazilian dish. Expect to pay around $12 each. O Mantanhas is also very good and in the same range. Lino, on the road to Murça, is good, and quite inexpensive. In Regua the Castelo Negro is popular and Gato Pieto, although smaller, is also good at under $10. For a lunch, stop in Vila Pouca and try the Nascente do Corgo.

FESTIVALS: The Feira de S. Pedro in Vila Real is the end of June.

IF TIME IS SHORT: Pass right through Vila Real, stopping only at Mateus to see the villa and gardens.

Amarante

If we were to choose Portugal's most beautiful church based on its setting, it might be Amarante's S. Gonçalo, set under a steep hillside, overlooking the river. The largo is retained by a stone wall that drops to the river on one side and is bordered by steep steps which lead up to a chapel and eventually to a street. The street is at the height of the bell tower!

But the great convent manages to occupy this narrow niche with spacious grace. The vistas toward it and the arched stone bridge are best from upstream across the Tamego, the willows trailing their long branches into the water. The round dome covered in red tile is almost Italian, but its azulejo lantern and the open crowned bell tower built into the hill behind it bring it clearly back to Portugal.

Set into the steep bank next to the bell tower, suspended so like the second tier of a stage set, is the white church of S. Domingo. It is a delightful assemblage — bridge, church, chapel, tower and largo, especially when bathed in morning sunlight.

Like so many churches, S. Gonçalo is entered from the side, quite near the chancel arch, so that the design of the church is broken up. It's best to go left from the vestibule and walk to the great barred door at the back before turning around to see the church as it was meant to be seen. There is nothing to draw the eye away from the painted arch that brings the nave into the altar and puts the improbable angels in their place. From here, this overdressed pair, all in frills and tassels with curly wigs, serve to soften the juncture of the columns with the floor of the nave. But viewed face to face without first having seen them in the context of the nave, they are hard to take seriously.

There are so many of these touches in Portuguese churches — reminders that even in churches, architecture can be fun, that they seem to have been designed for the great festival days — Easter and Christmas, and for the sacraments of marriage and baptism, not for Lent and funerals.

Perhaps, in this church dedicated to the patron saint of unmarried women, these angels and the funny little cherubs in powdered wigs at the very top of the high altar, are a reminder of the importance of maintaining a sense of humor!

The tomb of S. Gonçalo, himself, is in a tiny chapel on the left just beneath the elevated gold high altar. There are always fresh flowers and women there praying, for it is promised that a touch of bare skin to the tomb brings a man within the year. However seriously this is taken, Gonçalo's festival the first weekend in June is celebrated by the unabashed exchange between unmarried men and women of little phallus-shaped cakes. This custom is not thought to have been begun by the saint himself, but to have its origins in much earlier times.

A door to the left of this chapel leads into a passage with a richly carved ceiling and to the sacristy with its coffered ceiling, before opening into the cloister. This is a two story Renaissance work with a richly paneled ceiling and painted reliefs of the saints in each corner. The second cloister, larger, severe and boxy has become a museum of modern art.

Although the church, with its splendid altar, lovely cloister, sense of humor and perfect setting might very well be our favorite in Portugal, the real reason for coming to Amarante is because it is such a pleasant town. Across and overhanging the river are wooden balconies, many of which house restaurants and pastry shops with outdoor tables overlooking the church and the bridge. From these its deep arches reflect in the river to make full circles, and the traveler can spend a restful hour or so watching ladies below do their laundry in the river, boys fishing from the opposite shore and couples boating in the slow moving waters.

Unfortunately, the trip from Porto through Penafiel is tedious. The countryside here is filled with clutter instead of the little village clusters so characteristic everywhere else, and the road itself it filled with diesel-spewing trucks. Although it isn't far, it is slow going. Faster and much more scenic is one of the backcountry routes — the twisting one along the south side of the river to Entre os Rios, where the Tamego reaches the Douro, or an equally attractive route north through Lousada and Paços de Ferreira, passing close to Citânia de Sanfins (see Guimarães).

South of the road between Lixa and Penafiel, marked by a blue monument sign, is Travanca, where there is a twelfth century monastery church in a wooded valley. The interior is quite interesting with excellent carved arches, capitals and doorways representing a wide variety of birds, animals and mythical beings.

Celorico de Basto, 23 km northeast of Amarante along the Tamego road, has an eleventh century castle and some very nice seventeenth and eighteenth century mansions. While travelers heading on toward the Spanish border will see many castellated towns, they are not as common in this area and those who plan to go no further north or east may want to visit it.

Amarante At A Glance

A lovely river town 65 km from Porto from which there are train connections.

LODGING: The three star Hotel Navarres (55/ 424036) is well rated although we've never stayed there, with doubles at $35, and the inexpensive Pensão Nove Estrella on Rua 31 Janiero has rooms overlooking the river and the convent. Our choice, although they are few, are the rooms let out by the four star restaurant Ze da Calcada (55/ 422023). Well known as the best restaurant in the area, they do not advertise their rooms overlooking the river and the bridge.

The Hotel Amarante has a full range of facilities but is far from fancy in style, or price. In the midst of the woods in a mountain pass about 30 km from Amarante is the Pousada S. Gonçalo (55/461113). It is small and has doubles for about $60 in high season, less in low. Those headed for or arriving from Vila Real will find this convenient, but we prefer to stay in the town itself where we can eat dinner and enjoy the evening without a mountain road ahead of us.

FOOD: Roast kid, tripe with beans and a variety of pastries are the specialties of Amarante, along with trout from the Tamega served with local vinho verde. Tops for restaurants is Ze da Calcada, with entrees in the $10 range. Their impeccable dining room overlooks the river and is regarded as the area's best. At the corner of the same street, right under the bridge, is an attractive restaurant with dinner for around $5. Farther down is Lailai, a pastry shop where you can enjoy the many sweets Amarante is known for on their balcony overlooking the river.

FESTIVALS: Feast Day of S. Gonçalo is the first weekend in June.

IF TIME IS SHORT: You can say you've seen Portugal even if you haven't seen Amarante — but you'll enjoy it if you go. Possibly a lunch stop between Braga or Porto and Vila Real.

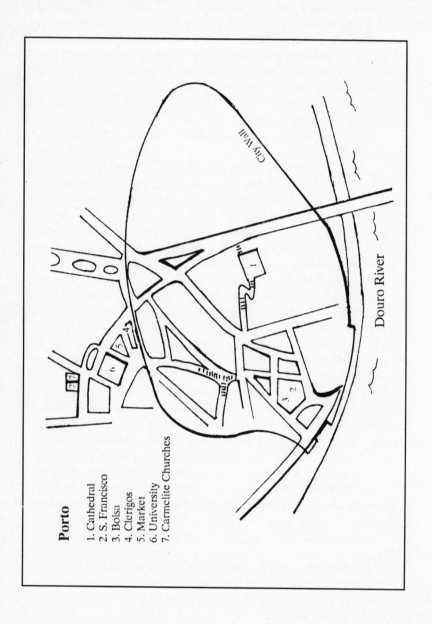

Porto

1. Cathedral
2. S. Francisco
3. Bolsa
4. Clerigos
5. Market
6. University
7. Carmelite Churches

City Wall

Douro River

Porto

Portucale to the Romans, Porto has given name to both the country itself and the wine which is its most famous product. It is a huge, sprawling city, whose outskirts seem to keep billowing forever and whose center is a tangle of tiny streets and passages only somewhat organized by squares, rotundas and broad avenues. To complicate this, it is set on hills, just as Lisbon is. It is hard to love a city when introduced to it at night trying to find one's way through a maze of streets.

It isn't until daylight that its narrow streets full of cats, kids, balconies, flowers, laundry and fountains become charming, and its rows of red rooftops patched along the hills become beautiful. Then it's very easy to love Porto, and forgive the complexities of its layout. It is wise to allow at least an hour to get through the traffic in its surroundings and locate your hotel before dark.

For all its size, most of Porto's attractions are within walking distance of each other. The Sé commands one hilltop, with the facade of the former episcopal palace beside it. It is Romanesque, but much of it has been altered by bad restoration, especially the cloister. Fortunately the baroque chancel escaped, as did the treasure of the church. This is the silver altar in the chapel to the left of the high altar. When Soule's army was approaching Porto during the Peninsular War, parishioners quickly covered the silver with a layer of whitewash to disguise its value and protect it from pillage. It is difficult to see the detailed silver work, but there is a light switch on the wall in the corner behind the column to the left of the arch.

Off the far corner of the cloister (for which is charged a few escudos to help with its upkeep) there is the interesting chapel of S. Vincent, with a huge gold altar filling one end, and polychrome bas relief panels of the life of Christ. Upstairs off the upper story of the cloister is the Chapter House, with a variety of art work and a good painted ceiling.

East of the Cathedral, across the major Avenue de Vimara Peres, and down the Rua Saraiva de Carvalho, there is a small square, across which is the Igreja S. Clara. The plain little exterior surrounds one of the finest gold interiors in Portugal, outdoing even the other churches of the Chagas nuns. The entire inside is lined in gold angels, scrolls, cherubs, leaves and embellishments. There is a splendid polychrome of S. Clara in the first chapel to the left. When all the gold seems too much, go into the choir, where the ceiling is painted and the stalls are beautifully carved.

Behind S. Clara, reached by continuing along Rua Saraiva Carvalho and turning right, is the best remaining section of the old town walls.

Descending the stairs from the Cathedral in the other direction, heading north, there is an area of steep lanes which plummet downhill (and can easily send the pedestrian plummeting, too, when they are wet). These pass little tilted largos with fountains where women do their morning laundry.

The area is bounded at the bottom by a long largo, and a left turn leads downhill to the cross street, Rua Infante Dom Henrique. A short distance to the right is the renowned Igreja S. Francisco, the epitome of gilt interior ornamentation. Inside it is a riot of unrestrained gold woodwork added to the church in the seventeenth century. The effect is currently diminished by a general cleaning underway, with scaffolds and drop-cloths covering each section in turn, but they are doing it in such a way as to leave as much as possible visible, and the cleaning will brighten it considerably.

There is no place for the eye to rest as the richly ornamented columns rise along the nave to a gold covered ceiling. The chancel arch is astonishing, with layer upon layer of angels, combings, swirls and other ornaments. It frames an equally ornate high altar, well lit by chancel windows, its spiral columns echoed in the supports of the chancel arch.

The coro alto is lit by a rose window, and only here in this section added later, is there a white wall to set off the gold between the rich ceiling and the lower wall decoration. Most of the nave columns are covered with gold embellishment, with a little of the Romanesque stonework showing. It is interesting to see this, since so many of the churches have been "purified" back to the bare Romanesque columns.

What is particularly interesting is that here, the stonework was not stripped of its painted decorations — the later gilt woodcarving was put over it. So there are still places where this painting, which has been stripped away from most churches by the restorers, is still visible. Look especially in the chapels of the right transept, inside the arches, and under the pulpit, where there are remnants of false marbling on the stone.

Behind the church is Porto's stock exchange, the Bolsa, with its neo-Moorish Salon Arabe, another room completely covered with decoration, this time all in blue and gold. It was in this neighborhood, although probably not in the house so labeled, that Queen Philippa gave birth to Prince Henry the Navigator. João I and Philippa traveled so much throughout their kingdom that no two of their children were born in the same town.

Beyond the Bolsa is a stairway leading up in a series of switchbacks, almost directly to another hilltop. At each turn in the stairs there is a little balcony with beautiful views over the rooftops of Porto. The hilltop is crested by the eighteenth century Torre dos Clérigos, below which there is a little oval church, with the traffic splitting to either side, leaving it in an island like S. Clement Danes, London. This is not only an unusual church, but it is important as the first example of genuine structural baroque in Portugal. Up to then (1732-50) baroque in Portugal had been almost entirely ornamental. Beyond the baroque portico, the interior is oval, and the nave floor is higher than the vestibule, reached by steps. Above is a paneled oval dome, everything well-proportioned and entirely in control. It reminds us of a nicely made jewel box.

Behind the tower is the busy Mercado do Anjo, which fills another square. Past the market and around to the far side of their huge university building, is another square. At the far end of it are the twin Carmelite churches, easily spotted by the blue and white azulejo-covered exterior. These two churches are an excellent example of the differences between baroque decoration of the seventeenth and eighteenth centuries, with the newer church at the right more highly ornamented.

Completely around the hospital just beyond, located on Rua Dom Manuel II, is the Museu Soares Reis. It is set in a fine eighteenth century palace and contains, along with other art treasures, a complete historical collection of Portuguese ceramics. During the Peninsular War, this was the French headquarters in Porto, and so sure was Soule that Wellington's forces couldn't attack from across the river, that he failed to believe the news of their advance. The story goes that the subsequent battle was so short that Wellington enjoyed the lunch that had been prepared for Soule, and was comfortably headquartered in the same palace that evening.

Across the river are the port wine houses in Vila Nova de Gaia. Several of these are open to the public and their films and tours are quite interesting. The Ramos-Pinto cellars are open from 10-6 on weekdays and until noon on Saturday, and others have similar hours — a pleasant occupation during the afternoon hours when the churches and museums are closed. Vila Nova is a short taxi ride or can be reached on foot via the lower level of the Dom Luis Bridge.

South of Porto on the coast are several seaside resorts, including Espinho with its casino and the smaller, nicer Granja. While these are good resorts for local residents, they are not the ones that would be likely to interest overseas visitors. The charm of Espinho is well reflected in its imaginative street names: 1, 2, 3, 4, etc.

East of Porto, along the banks of the Douro, there is beautiful scenery, although it does take a while to get past the edges of the city. The roads wind along the corniche above the river, on which there is considerable small boat traffic. The crossing at Entre os Rios is lovely, with the Douro and the Tamego converging just above the bridge and the mouth of the Tamego filled with little boats.

To the south is wine country, with towns and vineyards clinging to steep slopes, the green landscape brightened by the rich red of the vine leaves in autumn and by the red roofs and white walls of little farmhouses. Castelo Paive is a pretty town set along a hillside, with a broad, busy public square filled with flower beds.

Autumn is a good time to travel here, especially on weekends, when wine festivals seem to spring up out of nowhere. On a Sunday, it is almost impossible *not* to come upon at least one in progress. Arouca's Feira de Colheitão is a longer, bigger festival, with streets bordered in decorations and filled with people. Music from a loudspeaker fills the square and dancers in traditional costumes dance on a makeshift stage. At the other end of the square, a few older couples may join in, swirling across the pavement in a sort of polka step to the lively music. The fountain is covered with children balancing along its rim for a better view of the stage.

We had sought out Arouca to find a Cistercian convent with the extraordinary good fortune to have been endowed by a queen. Queen Malfada was the daughter of Sancho I and former wife of Henry I of Castile, and she chose Arouca's convent for her retirement. What makes Arouca's story especially interesting is that its riches were saved from the government confiscation that followed the dissolution of the religious orders in 1834. Townspeople and farmers in the area hid the treasures from authorities, and after the furor died away and the riches of the convents had been forgotten, they, and in some cases their descendants, returned the treasure to the church.

For many years these were stored away and the great square of convent buildings that line Arouca's main street were empty and forlorn. But recently a large number of these have been beautifully restored as a museum to house the collections. No dark crowded repository this, but a well-lit building with well tended examples of every sort of ecclesiastic art displayed in the former nuns' cells. Along with vestments of intricate gold embroidery, there are paintings, sculpture, furniture and reliquaries. One particularly fine multiple reliquary is displayed under special lighting and visible from both sides. The polychrome statues are especially fine. Miniature enthusiasts will like the dollhouse-sized cell of S. Ambrose, fully furnished (although a little more opulently than one would imagine a monk's cell) complete with a tiny gold songbird cage.

The choir of the church is particularly good, with life-sized statues of nuns in painted habits looking down from its upper gallery. The carved choir stalls have seats like those at Lorvão, with faces carved in relief under each one. They are of the same period, since two of Queen Malfada's sisters were abbesses of Lorvão.

On the south side, almost hidden, is a fine relief sculpture of S. Theresa. The best view of the choir is from the organ loft (in which another stone nun is hiding) and in the afternoon when the sun is streaming in the windows. Access to the loft is from the third floor of the museum.

It is clear why the people of Arouca took the risks they did to save this collection. They have since done an extraordinary job of caring for and displaying these treasures — a job any museum could use as an example.

Another very pleasant excursion from Porto, and one which does not involve driving, is the boat trip up the Douro. Excursion boats leave from the Praça da Ribeira (324 236 for reservations) in all months except January and every day but Monday. These go as far as Entre os Rios or all the way to Regua in the middle of the port region.

Porto At A Glance

Wine and industrial capital, 313 km north of Lisbon, with access by air and train.

LODGING: *Contrary to our advice to stay right in the center of Lisbon, Porto's traffic access is such that we find it better to stay in the western neighborhoods toward the airport, with easy access to the Estrada da Circunvalação which rings the city and provides easier entrance and exit.*

This plan is made all the more attractive by the fact that one of Portugal's best hotels is in this area, along the wide Avenida da Boa Vista. The Meridien (2/ 668 863, or telex 27301) is not an old grand hotel — it is a new grand hotel, modern and stylish in glass and marble. But its hospitality and service are in the finest old continental tradition. The staff remembers your name and your special requests. Any hotel that provides us with a well-lighted room with both a full-sized desk and a sitting room alcove will get high grades, but when they add washcloths (unknown in Portugal) and terry robes, we're ready to take up permanent residence!

The charm of the Meridien is in its stylishness combined with personal service; the two do not often come together. Doubles here are about $130; if you plan to be there over a weekend, there are special packages that have the effect of throwing in a free dinner in their restaurant, Porto's top dining place. The Meridien is not inexpensive, but it is worth every escudo. The Meridien is on a direct trolley line to the downtown area, or a $3 taxi ride from the Cathedral.

Closer to the sights, but harder to get to by car is the Hotel Infante Sagres (2/ 281 01, telex 22378), an elegant old world hotel built in the 1950s, but decorated and furnished in turn-of-the-century style. It is only a few blocks from the Cathedral and close to S. Bento Station, a good choice for those arriving by train. Doubles vary in size and rate from $75 - $110.

The Hotel S. João (2/ 21662) is technically a residência, the privately owned top floor of a modern building behind the Infante de Sagres. The fine furnishings in both public and guest rooms set this hotel apart, along with the personal attention. Doubles are in the $45 range.

If you arrive without a reservation, there is a tourist office near the Infante de Sagres which is open weekdays from 9 until 7, Saturday until 4, and Sunday until 1, to help you find a room.

If you want to stop just short of Porto for the night, the Hotel Praia Golfe in Espinho is right on the beach with doubles at about $45. But it is very crowded during the summer (2/ 720630).

FOOD: *Unlike Lisbon, Porto's restaurants don't seem to clump in groups, making shopping around a little harder. For a midday meal, there is a whole row of little restaurants in all price ranges in the block next to the University near Torre dos Clérigos. Unfortunately, most of these close in the evening. There are some near the riverfront in the streets around Praça da Ribeira, and several on the Campo Alegre near the Hotel Ipanema. Restaurants in the better hotels are excellent, especially Les Terrasses in the Meridien and the Navegador in the Dom Henriques.*

Aquario Marisqueiro near the city hall is an excellent seafood restaurant, serving straight through from lunchtime until 11 p.m. Dinner will cost between $10 and $15. Regaleira on Rua Bonjardim is dependable for local specialties and shellfish, in the same price range. The Standard, near S. Francisco church is a bargain at $5.

SHOPPING: *The best shops are in the area of Rua S. Catarina, where there are small shops as well as Galerias Palladium, Porto's major department store. There is a morning market at Torre dos Clérigos, and every Monday in Espinho.*

FESTIVALS: *The harvest festival in Arouca begins the third weekend in September, and Porto's big festival centers around June 23 and 24.*

IF TIME IS SHORT: *See the churches of S. Clara and S. Francisco and walk in the old streets below the Cathedral.*

Póvoa de Varzim and Vila do Conde

Póvoa de Varzim is a large seaside resort and fishing town, greatly overshadowed for the traveler by its much smaller southern neighbor, Vila do Conde. The latter town reached the peak of its prosperity in the days when Prince Henry sent his ships to push the boundaries of the unknown. His ships were built here, and today, Vila do Conde's wooden-hulled vessels carry fishermen to the codfishing waters off Newfoundland. It is a fascinating sight to watch the great hulls take shape under methods that have changed very little since Prince Henry's time.

In contrast to the heavy masculine artistry of the ship builder, the town's other art is a fine and delicate lace. Known as bone lace, it is made on a round pillow with 30-50 bobbins. The lace is fine and delicate and the speed and precision with which the artists move the bobbins is astonishing. Watch them at the Escola de Rendas on Rua Joaquim Maria de Melo.

Bright with flowers and rich with festivals, Vila do Conde is a joyful town. On the feast of S. John (June 23-24), the lace-makers form a procession that is escorted to the beach by the whole town, and during holy week, entire streets are paved in stunning mosaics of fresh flowers.

The convent of S. Clara rises above the river with almost fortress effect because of its height. The feeling is softened once one is inside its cloister, its simple delicate arches rising roofless and open to the weather as a result of "restorations" in the 1940s. In the center, its graceful fountain was once fed by an aqueduct of 999 arches that brought water the 5 km from Póvoa.

The Gothic church contains exceptionally well-carved tombs of its founder, Dom Alfonso Sanches (one of the several illegitimate sons of King Dinis) and his wife and children.

The Igreja Matriz, in the square adjacent to the market (Friday, and a fine one) has a very good doorway, rising in a series of arches finely carved in stone. There is a delicacy here, missing in some of the later, heavy, Manueline. Just above the shipbuilding yard, down the riverbank from the Praça de República, is the Moorish style Sacarro Chapel.

In contrast to the easy pace of Vila do Conde, Póvoa de Varzim is a slightly frenetic newer resort, with casino, tennis, roller-rink, and beaches. There is still a fisherman's beach and quarter, which is especially colorful when boats come in on weekdays and the fish is sold from the beach.

Since the coastal area here is in a stage of unrestrained development, and there is little of interest, the better route is inland toward Vila Nova de Famalicão, passing near Rates. This is reached from a northbound road just past Rio Mão (where there is a good twelfth century church built by the Templars). S. Pedro in Rates is regarded as one of the best Romanesque churches surviving in the country. Its capitals, the pair of twelfth century statues near the font, the extensive stone carvings in the shape of mythical beings and human forms are extraordinary and well preserved.

Those interested in agriculture will want to go about 4 km north of Póvoa de Varzim to A Ver-O-Mar where a unique kind of farming is practiced. Digging deeply into the sand dunes until they reached moisture, farmers have planted a variety of vegetable crops. The sandy walls of these gardens are shored up with grape vines, which also produce well.

Póvoa de Varzim and Vila do Conde At A Glance

Fishing, shipbuilding and resort towns 29 km north of Porto accessible by train.

LODGING: There is a four star Estralagem Do Brasão (52/624 016) which is very nice with doubles at about $35 right in Vila do Conde, and a number of hotels, residéncias and pensions in Póvoa. For modern high rise luxury in Póvoa de Varzim, the Hotel Vermar Dom Pedro (52/ 683 401) is good, at $35-$40, but our choice is the charming Estralagem de S. Felix (52/ 682 176), a four-star inn set on a hilltop above that town with the windmills, and fine views down on the resort scene below. It's not far out of town, so if you decide to sample the local high life after dinner, you can.

FOOD: Restaurants abound, of course, in Póvoa's beachfront area, where Pescada a Poveira is a popular local seafood stew. A number of good restaurants are along the beach road just north of town, including the Chelsea and the often overcrowded Casa dos Frangos. The Estralagem S. Felix has a very good restaurant as does the Estralagem do Brasão in Vila do Conde, although its fixed price *menu at $12 is a bit limited. The local pastry is, of course, Pasteis de S. Clara.*

SHOPPING: *The best bobbin lace can be purchased at the lace school itself, and at the Centro Artisinato opposite the market in Vila do Conde. The town is also known for its handknit fisherman's sweaters which are sold here and in the shops at Póvoa. The Friday market is a good place to buy hand-carved wooden ox yokes, as well as local breads and cheeses. In Póvoa de Varzim there are crafts shops on Rua dos Cafes and the Galerias Ambiente has good antiques.*

IF TIME IS SHORT: *Vila do Conde can be seen briefly on the way north or south, or skipped over entirely.*

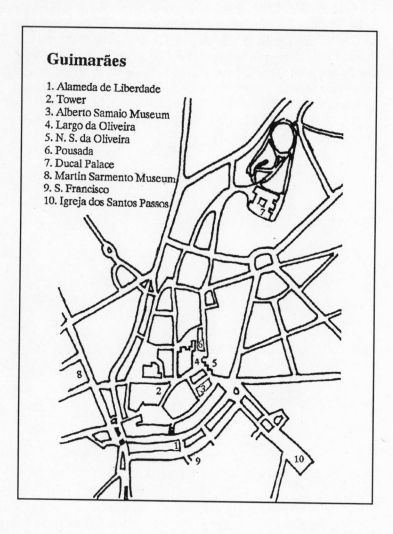

Guimarães

1. Alameda de Liberdade
2. Tower
3. Alberto Samaio Museum
4. Largo da Oliveira
5. N. S. da Oliveira
6. Pousada
7. Ducal Palace
8. Martin Sarmento Museum
9. S. Francisco
10. Igreja dos Santos Passos

Guimarães

It's a shame that so much space is given in guidebooks to the the endless controversy over whether the rebuilding of the Ducal Palace in Guimarães was a good thing or a bad thing. Good or bad it is there, and it contains some very fine furnishings and tapestries which look much better in its well-lit rooms than they would stacked in a museum. There is so much more to talk about in this delightful medieval city.

Everything in Guimarães is within walking distance, with a lovely pousada right in the middle. While there are other cities with the same narrow twisting streets closely lined with ancient buildings, few have retained, along with those stones, their character as well. In Guimarães, it would not seem out of place for a fully-armored knight to ride down Rua S. Maria.

These old streets often lead through stone archways into largos, among them the beautiful Largo de Olivera, in early Gothic and Manueline buildings, several of them arcaded. Although enclosed on all sides, with only narrow streets leading off its corners, the small square seems light and open, since there are no cars there — only a sidewalk cafe which, along with the flower boxes, gives the gray-brown stone some color.

In the opposite corner in front of N.S. de Olivera is a lovely open Gothic porch covering a cross that commemorates the legend that gave both the church and the square their names. When Wanda, the story goes, was told that he had been chosen King of the Goths in 672, he agreed to serve only if the olive-wood staff he carried sprouted leaves as a sign. He drove it into the ground and, of course, it sprouted leaves, or they wouldn't still be telling the story.

The Colégio, as the church is more often called, has a nicely carved portal, good choir stalls and an unusual tile-lined cave chapel off the sacristy. The centuries of treasures that were quite recently stripped out of this once magnificent church have, at least, been preserved in the museum in its adjoining cloister. Here are the gold side altars, polychrome figures, silver triptych and crucifix, all nicely displayed in the conventual buildings and the well-restored cloister surrounding a garden.

At the far end of the square are the arches of the old city hall, an impressive building, balconied like the houses that adjoin it. The one to the left, with its lower story deeply recessed behind stone pillars, is the Pousada de N.S. da Olivera and to its left the purely medieval Rua S. Maria.

This leads past carved granite doorways and grills, wrought iron and carved balconies to the disputed Bragança Palace Museum and the little chapel of S. Miguel, where Alphonso Henrique is thought to have been baptized. This first king of Portugal was born in the castle that crowns the town with its square towers, giving Guimarães its claim as the cradle of Portugal.

The Martins Sarmento Museum containing the artifacts from Citânia Briteiros and Sabroso, including the Pedra Formosa — a Prehistoric stone slab much discussed by historians — and the far more remarkable and significant ten-foot tall seated statue, by far the highlight of the finds there. To get there follow the Rua da Rainha from the corner of the Largo da Olivera directly opposite the pousada.

Entering Guimarães from Porto, the road skirts a lovely formal garden which ends at the extraordinary facade of Senhor dos Passos. This tall, narrow, semi-circular church, belfried and covered with azulejos is one of the most unique baroque exteriors in this country of original baroque churches. After its exterior, it's almost a relief to find that its interior isn't nearly as interesting.

Not far, just below the long curving park of the Almeda da Resisténcia, is the church of S. Francisco, badly "restored," but with an interesting Jesse Tree and azulejos. We always wonder who determines what will survive in these "restorations" to purify churches and monasteries. Azulejos survive when earlier baroque altars go — maybe altars are easier to rip out!

South of Guimarães the route from Porto passes through Santo Tirso, with a very fine Benedictine monastery in a state of excellent preservation. Its use as an agricultural college is not only appropriate (the deep arches of the convent's lower story seem quite at home with corn drying under them!) but in their use they are well maintained and have an air of liveliness and activity.

There is a lovely fourteenth century cloister, its small double arches supported by delicate columns. These, a fine wooden ceiling and a graceful fountain, make it a place where the traveler cannot resist resting on the low wall, leaning for a moment against the cool stone pillars. Only in the peaceful cloisters of Portugal, their arches designed for both inspiration and contemplation (as well as isolation) can we understand the appeal of convent life.

The church has a gold baroque high altar so well lit by three chancel windows on each side that they are lightly curtained to diffuse the flood of sunlight. The columns are twined in gold grapes and vines interspersed with little pink cherubs. These light touches are common in the altars and churches of provincial northern Portugal, giving them a human, joyous, quality which is missing in many of the more formal churches.

There is fine painted wood in the bases of the side altars, some of which look so much like panels of fine embroidery that we touched them just to be sure. The entire ceiling of the transept altar is carved and gilt. There are no side aisles, only the five ornate altars in the tall nave, each surmounted by a window.

Since there are several small works of art here, such as the exquisite polychromes in a glass case in the Chapel of the Holy Family, the good light is welcomed. With the exception of the one rococo chapel, the church is baroque throughout, a uniformity of style unusual in an active church which grows and changes over the centuries. The result perhaps of some restoration? If so, this time it was skillfully done.

Nearer to Guimarães and off the same road is the fine Romanesque church of Roriz. Follow the signs to Beneditanas, going right up the hill from the main road and right again in the town at the top of the hill. There is little left of the monastery that once adjoined the church, but there is majesty in its present use as a quinta, with great wine vats under the vaulting and arbors around what appears to have been the cloister.

The church has a good rose window and carved portal, with two unmistakable cow heads over the door. The key is at the neat white house down the lane past the fountain — follow the wall until there is a gate with a beautiful rose garden and ring the bell to the right.

North of Guimarães on a side road marked S. Torcado, slightly past Torcado, is Taide, a smaller village with the shrine of N.S. do Porta de Ave. There is a set of granite stairways set in terraces with white plaster and granite walls — all very ornate and formal with gardens, fountains and statuary. At the bottom is the church which has some nice details such as its red and gold choir lofts held by centaurs, but it is the gardens that are its main attraction. There were no pilgrims here when we were, so we could only wonder whether one backed down the stairs on his knees since the church is below, not above.

Off the road between Santo Tirso and Paços de Ferreira is the Citânia de Sanfins. Follow the turn to the town of Sanfins, then keep bearing left and uphill. Some of the forks have signs, most do not. There is a sign for the small museum, which is a little off the "main" road; to regain this road, go uphill from the museum and turn right when that road ends.

If Citânia de Sanfins were in England, it would be run by the National Trust and tour buses would include it in their regular routes. But in Portugal, where tourists have not yet scoured and catalogued every corner, it is almost unknown.

To finally come upon the Citânia after having searched, followed signs until they failed us — asked of farmers headed home in ox carts, women carrying firewood on their heads, girls filling jugs at a fountain and finally a group of neighbors gathered at a fence — had about it the air of an expedition finally reaching its mountain summit.

And like all these Iron Age hillforts of the Celts and their predecessors, it was at the top of the highest hill, commanding not only the best view, but a good defensive position as well. Having spent considerable time in our search, it was already late in the afternoon, the sun growing larger and redder as it slid into the band of autumn haze that hangs above the hilltops there.

We ran up the trail and over the remains of the outer wall like invading Romans, and then stopped short. Spread before us in the pink-orange light of the late sun, lay an entire city of stone. Its streets, now growing with grass, were lined with stone walls; the foundations of its houses, sturdy and round, covered the entire hilltop, except for its very crest.

There was no one there but us, and as we walked the ancient streets in silence, the Celts walked with us. To stand alone on this hilltop, to walk streets of a town that thrived, not just centuries, but millennia ago, somehow spans the ages. Nearby Porto, with its cobbled medieval streets and its wine houses, does not exist yet, its gold baroque altars undreamed of.

We longed to ask questions of the silent ghosts who carefully shaped and fitted these stones into double-faced walls, setting their homes along streets and avenues. The artifacts found here, and housed at the small museum in the village below, show the settlement to date from the sixth to the third century B.C. But there is much more to learn about these castros.

For example, at the crest of the hill, in an open central area without houses, there were small rectangular depressions lined in carefully cut stones. Tombs, we wondered, but at only 12 to 18 inches wide and 3 to 4 feet long, these hardly seemed large enough even for Celts buried in a crouched position. One still had part of a capstone, reminiscent of ancient tombs in England.

But I spoke no common tongue with these men who walked here over 2000 years before me. All we shared in that gathering evening was the hilltop, the setting sun and the mist — and whatever it was that urged us both to travel so far from home. For they had been strangers there as much as we.

Guimarães At A Glance

Commercial city 50 km north of Porto, from which it can be reached by train.

LODGING: The Pousada of N.S. da Olivera (53/ 412157, in US 212/ 680-9213) overlooks on one side a medieval street and on the other one of Portugal's finest Gothic squares. Set in a series of restored old homes, it is furnished in antiques and its public rooms carpeted in Arraiolos over tiled floors. Its sixteen rooms are between $60 and $90, depending on the season. But beyond its physical beauty, the hospitality of its reception staff is equaled only by that at the pousada at Miranda do Douro. Add that to its location and you have a nearly perfect place to stay. Given its proximity to Braga and the scarcity of good lodging in the old town there, we usually choose to stay here and visit the Braga area from this base.

About 3 km from the center of town the convent of S. Merinha da Costa (53/ 418453) has been converted into a pousada. It is lovely, providing a way to preserve these fine old buildings and let them live at the same time. One wonders what the nuns would think of the bar in their cloister! The surrounding gardens are beautiful with some of the rooms overlooking them. Its atmosphere is different from the in-town pousada, and it is priced in the highest range, $75 to $110. The modern four-star Hotel Fundador Dom Pedro in the newer part of town has nothing of the historic ambiance of the first two, but it is a good alternative at about $55. There are several pensions including the Mamede (53/ 413 781).

Two private residences under the TURIHAB association are near Guimarães. The beautiful Paço de Cipriano (53/ 481 337) is in Taboadelo, just south. This wide-porched manor is built around a crenellated tower, and the whole set in manicured gardens. Priced at *about $70. Casa do Ribeiro (53/ 410 881) just west in S. Cristovão is in an old estate entered through a monumental gate. Both can be reserved through TURIHAB (58/942 335).*

FOOD: *Our favorite restaurant in town is the Jurica located on a little tree-lined largo up a few steps from the Alameda da Resistência. Unlike most restaurants, their extensive menu is available in half or full servings. We each order a half, which is so much that we have never dared to ask for the larger! Their Feijão with Bolinhos would make any Bostonian feel at home here — a rich bean stew served with codfish balls. There's a hint of cumin in the beans and of fresh cilantro in the fish, just to remind one that it's Portugal.*

At lunch time, go before the shops close at one, or wait until the crowd subsides at around 1:45; it's a favorite with local residents. Dinner for two, with wine, is under $10 here. There is no topping the pousada's lovely dining room overlooking the square. Meals are $15 to $20 each. Jordão is another popular restaurant, with prices somewhere in the middle. For coffee and the local almond pastry of Rocha de Penha, go to the Pastelaria Ribela on Rua S. Antonio.

SHOPPING: *Dedicated collectors of fine handwork will love Guimarães, the linen center of Portugal. The village of Trofa, only 7 km from Guimarães on the Amarante road, specializes in lacemaking. Local linen is hand spun from flax bleached only by the sun, and it is woven either plain-weave for embroidery, or in intricate patterns. Casa dos Linhas on the Avenida de Resistência is an old and well-respected store where you should at least look at this fine work. Enxovais, near the tourist office at the end of the Alameda is also good.*

FESTIVALS: *The four days surrounding the first Sunday in August is the Feira de Gualter and the second week in August there is a craftsmen's fair in Santo Tirso. There is also a Romaria here during the first week in September.*

IF TIME IS SHORT: *Allow at least a stop to wander in the streets and drive up to the castle; miss the churches in order to see the Sarmento Museum if Citânia Briteiros is in your itinerary. For a short walk, park in the long Alameda and walk up the stone steps about midway in its upper side into the largo. Take the street to the right, out the other side, past the tower, bearing right into Largo de Oliveira. Take Rua S. Maria to the right of the pousada, continuing to the castle or going one block to the left and circling back through the arcade of the old city hall, then out the corner past the church, peeking into its cloister as you pass.*

Braga

So much is made of the pilgrimage church of Bom Jesus on a hillside a few kilometers from the city that it tends to overshadow Braga itself. It shouldn't, for Braga is a place of fine buildings and brilliant parks. And, in a country known for its fine carved and gilt church interiors. Braga stands out as the capital of these.

A city of flowers and fountains and church bells, it is a city to savor on foot, happening on its treasure by chance. Most would begin at the cathedral, although we personally would begin in the breathtaking garden of S. Barbara in front of the medieval walls of the Archbishop's Palace — or in one of the pastry shops adjoining it.

The Cathedral is a bit overwhelming and it is very easy to miss something, or to have some large piece command the attention so completely that one misses the smaller perfection nearby. It has so many little chapels, each reached from a courtyard, or cloister, or outside door, that it is as though one had come upon a whole village of chapels. It is almost better to treat them as separate churches. Like most, it has been built and rebuilt and restored and added to frequently, and its main doorway arch and south door just around the corner are the only Romanesque features left. Having once passed through either of these, one passes as well into later centuries.

Two elaborate gilded and painted baroque organs draw attention upward at once, away from the fifteenth century tomb of a royal prince and the Manueline font at either side of the entrance. The chapels, except for those flanking the main altar, are all reached by the cloister and courtyard to the left of the nave. S. Gerald's is lined in azulejos; The Gloria Chapel is set in Arabian Nights frescoes, but somberly so. The early Gothic King's Chapel contains the tombs of the parents of Portugal's first king, and S. Catherine's Chapel is usually filled with votive offerings.

Note in the cloister the especially touching Pieta — the face of Our Lady older, almost angry, in contrast to the young, serene, face of the graceful N.S. do Leite in its little stone lace canopy on the outside of the Cathedral, directly behind the high altar. The treasury takes up two floors and is, like so many, a mixed lot. But there are some very fine pieces here including solid gold ecclesiastical pieces. Its main attraction, however, is access to the impressive organ loft and choir.

Of Braga's other landmarks, most are churches. The Misericordia is right behind the Cathedral on a street spanned by a very fine Renaissance arch. Inside, the entire chancel wall is covered in baroque gold work. While the exterior of the church of S. Cruz may be a little extreme, its interior is beautifully proportioned, its swirls and arabesques and gilded organ and pulpits flooded with light from large windows. In contrast, S. Vitor's plain exterior gives its rich interior an impact of surprise, crowned by its radiant chancel arch.

The tiny chapel of Penha de Franca is filled with baroque altars, set off by azulejo panels reaching high along the walls. When all of this sumptuous gold fru-fru seems too much, it is time to visit the Biscainhas Museum, set in one of Braga's fine townhouses and a good chance to see the interior of one of them. The real reason, however, is to see the elegant formal garden set in tiled walls.

There are some pieces here that have been discovered in excavation, closeby, of Roman Bracara Augusta upon which in later centuries modern Braga has arisen. The excavations are not, at present, open to view, but those with a particular interest should ask at the tourist office for the name of the person to contact for access. Just off the Avenida da Liberdade is the Roman (some claim earlier) fountain, Fonte do Idolo.

The pilgrimage church of Bom Jesus is 5 km from Braga and may be reached by a funicular, by a winding road, or on foot or knee (as pilgrims must) up the stairs. Since the stairs themselves, the gardens that border them and the views they give upward toward the church are what accounts for much of the charm of Bom Jesus, it would be a shame to miss them. One solution is to walk at least halfway down the stairs and reclimb them — also easier than the entire series which is enough of a penance on foot, let alone on one's knees! It is a good place to visit on the way to or from the Iron Age city of Citânia de Briteiros.

There is a story which local men are fond of telling, of the lady devoutly climbing on her knees when she caught her heel in the hem of her dress. Her foot fast, she was unable to move without ripping her skirt. She noticed a man a few steps behind her and pointing to her caught heel asked if he would mind lifting her skirt. Never looking up, he replied, "That, Senhora, is what I am doing penance for!"

The landings are set with chapels and fountains, all quite original in mythological motifs, representing the five senses and the three virtues. Inside the chapels, in terra-cotta figures, are scenes from the passion. The steps and the church itself are bordered by beautifully terraced gardens. Below the facade is a formal area whose beds echo the baroque scrolls of the church itself in flowers and herbs chosen for their color. This is a popular place for weddings, often several in one day.

The road to Bom Jesus leads on to Citânia de Briteiros, passing close to Monte Sameiro, a devotional shrine which, although of awkward architecture, sits in very nice gardens with a fine view of the countryside below.

Of the many tourists who visit Guimarães and Braga, few know and still fewer stop to see, the remarkable Iron Age sites that crown nearby hills. The best preserved is Citânia de Briteiros, its ancient paved streets and walls shaded by thick dark cork trees, the only sound the bells rising clear and melodic from the valley below. Briteiros is fenced and open only during regular hours, so one can not simply wander in and watch the sunset as at Sanfins, but it is larger and shows the development of the castro from its early Celtic origins into Roman times.

The stone foundations rising in terraces now grown with heather and ferns show this development clearly. They progress from the round earlier houses, some with small vestibules similar to those at Sanfins, to round buildings whose foundation stones are great neat slabs of stone set on end at an angle, like bricks set on their corners that border garden walkways. (The same pattern here is echoed in local buildings, where crenellation is often in the same saw-toothed shapes.) Finally there are the rectangular foundations of Roman buildings, for unlike the others, this city was occupied well into Roman times.

There are three rings of wall, only a short stretch of the outer one still intact, which crosses and then runs along the hill beside the road to Braga, about 150 yards north of the parking belvedere. The middle wall runs alongside the same road for a distance and continues about half way around the Citânia. The original inner wall is intact around the south side and has been restored along the north side.

There is a definite plan to the streets here, with wider ones forming a square and houses set along the streets. Stone gutters carried water (a good one remains intact); there is a well near the top of the hill and a primitive fountain near the entrance gate.

It would be nice to see this castro with all of the structural artifacts in situ — the elegant carved doorway, and lesser decorated lintels, which are all in the Museum Martins Sarmento in Guimarães. We do see two reconstructed houses near the unspeakably ugly chapel erected there in 1853. Downhill, beside a monument alongside the road leading toward Guimarães, is a chambered tomb with a curious house-shaped lintel and some carving, about the only ornamented stones remaining except for a few spiral inscriptions on stones near the restored buildings. Here, too, are more of the same small rectangular stone depressions as at Sanfins.

It is easy to stand here in the afternoon silence looking down into the valley and picture the well-armed Roman legions approaching the steep hillside, storming the walls of this last-held bastion of Celtic power.

Much easier to find than Sanfins, Citânia de Briteiros is signposted from the road between Taipas and Póvoa de Lanhosa and from the road leading south from Braga via Bom Jesus. Closely by, just north of Taipas is Sabrosa, another smaller hill-fort which has a larger wall, but only about thirty houses. It is assumed to have been abandoned earlier than Briteiros.

Just outside of Braga, about 2 km along the route to Ponte de Lima, are two places usually bypassed, which is a shame. Just past a block of arrestingly bright tiled buildings in an old village is a sign to the right for S. Frutuoso. Only a short way on, this small white chapel is connected to a Franciscan convent church built eleven centuries later.

The small, very plain building is all that is left of seventh century Byzantine architecture in Portugal. Surviving the Moorish domination, it is thought to have been rebuilt in the eleventh century. It is in the form of a cross, its arms surmounted by a central dome, its marble pillars topped with very fine carving. There is considerable controversy about this little chapel, with some scholars classifying it as Visigothic. It's an enigma whose history may never be clear.

Outside there are recessed arches and bands of very finely carved marble. The lines are so simple and clean that, combined with the stark whiteness, the effect is quite unlike the churches we had come to expect in Portugal — especially having just left Braga's surfeit of gold baroque. Although it's a jolt after this Byzantine gem, the attached church is quite nice with an excellent sacristy and choir.

From a sense of awe at S. Frutuoso, comes a sense first of wonder and then of frustration at Tibaes. This monastery is reached by returning to the main road and taking a road just off it in the other direction. Tibaes, of eleventh century origin and rebuilt in the nineteenth, was the first Benedictine monastery in Portugal. Long a victim of its joint control by the Ancient Monuments Commission and its private owner, it lies crumbling with restoration of one section just now beginning.

Only the church itself, which is clearly the responsibility of the ecclesiastical authorities is cared for, and very well. The church rivals any in its baroque goldwork. The organ and choir stall are particularly interesting, the former supported by a pair of satyrs and topped by statues. There are very fine polychrome statues at the high altar. But the four cloisters and remaining building, with fine azulejos, painted ceiling and lovely details, are in deteriorating desolation.

The gardens, long overgrown and deserted, are set around a large pond with aqueduct and fountains. Its miniature stairways are thought to have inspired Bom Jesus. Any good Garden Club member visiting here would itch to make their restoration a civic project.

Póvoa de Lanhosa, 16 km east of Braga, has a twelfth century castle perched high on a rock above it. There are Iron Age foundations at Citânia de Lanhosa, on the way up to the castle, but not as complete as those at Sanfins and Briteiros.

Braga At A Glance

Agricultural and commercial center, 53 km north of Porto, from which it may be reached by train,

LODGING: The Hotel do Elvador (53/ 25011) at Bom Jesus is very nice, although it may be handier to be in town. All rooms are spacious, have good views and cost $35 to $40. The usual choice in town is the modern Turismo, although it is a fifteen minute walk from the old part of town where the treasures are. If you are using Braga as the center for touring the area it is well located on a main route. Also *new and less expensive is the Caranda on Avenida de Liberdade (53/77016). There are several pensãos in town.*

The Quinta de Bela Vista (53/82518) is a private estate in Bom Jesus or Quinta de S. Vincente (2/687472) is in Portas near Póvoa de Lanhoso, or call TURIHAB (53/82519).

FOOD: The Caranda has a very good dining room. Conde Dom Henrique on Rua Forno and Cruz Sobral on Rua Campos das Hortas both specialize in regional foods at prices under $10. The Lusitania, on the corner of the S. Barbara gardens, serves splendid little sweet pastries for an afternoon or evening pick-me-up.

SHOPPING: Braga is not a major center for handwork, but there is a very nice artisinato in the old municipal library building, and several antique shops in the old city. José Luis Soares, on Rua S. Marcos carries local baskets.

FESTIVALS: S. João Baptiste (June 23-4) is a major celebration here, with parades, fairs, costumes and general celebration. People come from all over, so be sure to reserve a room early.

IF TIME IS SHORT: Depending on your own personal interests, Bom Jesus, Citânia de Briteiros or the old streets and Cathedral of Braga are the highlights of the region.

Barcelos

Because we spend so many of our days wandering about the countryside, climbing in ruined castles, exploring the stones of Celtic cities and searching for lost monasteries, we often arrive in cities in the late afternoon or early evening. We've had our first view of so many Portuguese towns and cities in the golden light of sunset or the afterglow of evening, when they are at their loveliest, that we want everyone to have the same first impressions we did.

Barcelos is a charmer at any time of day, but late afternoon arrival, especially if you are just passing through, allows time to see the few "must do's" and an entire evening to do what Barcelos is best for — strolling and enjoying. Like so many small cities there is no one site the traveler can't leave without having inspected.

Its treasures are small gems well set. To stroll its streets, peek through its doors and gateways into vestibules and gardens, explore its small churches and enjoy its pastries is a lovely way to spend the early evening. On Thursdays, however, it is better to arrive earlier, when the entire enormous Campo de Feira is full of market stalls — one of the best of the weekly markets, especially good because it is in this region so rich in handcrafts.

At one corner of the Campo, sort of mid-street in front of the row of old balconied houses that line one end, is the small octagonal church of S. Cruz. It appears round from a distance, white and domed in the center, like a wedding cake. At the south side of the Campo is a baroque garden, its beds set in swirls and arabesques that seem to match the buildings of Barcelos.

The church of S. Benedict (known as the Terço) has a splendid gilt altar and azulejo panels of the life of the saint, which reach halfway up the tall nave to the barrel ceiling. The Igreja Matriz, by the ruins of the Ducal Palace, is very early Gothic with a fine baroque side altar on the right. The Palace overlooks the river, its ruins now home to an excellent architectural collection — armorial crests, a stone lavabo, azulejo panels in the park-like setting of the castle's remaining walls. There is even a fourteenth century monument to the cock that has become the symbol of Barcelos.

It's impossible to leave Barcelos without hearing the story of the cock. A pilgrim on his way to N.S. de Compostela was accused of a theft in Barcelos and sentenced to hang. He called upon S. James to prove his innocence by causing the roast cock upon the judge's plate to rise and crow. It did, and its crow earned it a place in local history (as well as the freedom of the prisoner!). This accounts for the little ceramic painted roosters everywhere in town.

On the coast just to the west is Esposende, a resort and fishing village with some nice old houses, and Ofir, mostly given over to a seaside resort. A Roman city is being unearthed at Esposende. A little south is Fão with nice houses and, when the tides are right, its seaweed gatherers with long rakes and nets.

To the east off the road to Braga about 7 km is the village of Villar de Frades with the church of a Benedictine monastery, baroque, but with one Romanesque portal from an earlier church and one Manueline portal.

Barcelos At A Glance

Market town, original home of the Dukes of Bragança (the Avis dynasty) 55 km north of Porto.

LODGING: The four star Condes de Barcelos (53/ 82061) is near the center of town, nicely decorated in handcrafted furniture, a very attractive hotel with doubles from $30-35. We have a particular fondness for the less fancy but beautifully located Pensão Arantes (53/ 82326), what may be the most elegant two-star pensão in Portugal. It is in a lovely old home and second floor rooms open out into a marble parlor overlooking the Campo de Feira. Rooms on the front, although a bit noisier, open onto wrought iron balconies overlooking the octagonal church and Campo. With high ceilings and modern marble baths, this former grand mansion is now a well-run pension with rooms in the $25-30 range. There are two TURIHAB country homes, Casa dos Assentos (1/ 2184773) a fine, ivy covered manor in Quintães and the equally lovely Casa do Monte (53/ 82519) in its gardens at Abade do Neiva, just barely north of town. (Book both by calling 58/ 942335 in Ponte de Lima). If you prefer the sea, there are several hotels in Esposende.

FOOD: The Arantes, across from S. Cruz church, specializes in regional dishes, as does the second floor restaurant of the Pensão Bagoeira by the municipal market building, both very inexpensive.

Fancier, and more expensive are the Casa dos Arcos and Dom Antonio.

SHOPPING: *For those who like handcrafts, Barcelos is a good stop, especially on Thursdays when a quarter square mile of market stalls sell goods from the entire area. There is also an excellent Centro Artisinato in a tower in the square below the town hall. They have a good selection of the work of Julia Ramalho, carrying on the tradition of the late Rosa Ramalho whose inspiration was drawn heavily from Portuguese history and folklore — her Queen Isabel with the apron full of roses is in the Museum de Arte Populare in Belém. Their work is easy to spot with its almost caricature quality, and ochre high glaze. Below the municipal market building (do look into this spotless public building with the marble meat counters) are some craftsmen's shops including a coppersmith with very reasonable prices. Back up on the Rua Antonio Barroso, a walking street, are more shops, including some with crafts.*

IF TIME IS SHORT: *You can combine Barcelos with Braga and even Guimarães, but it would be a shame to miss this lovely small provincial town. If you see these other cities during the day, plan to at least overnight in Barcelos, skipping the churches if they are closed and simply enjoying its streets and gardens.*

Ponte de Lima

There must be more to Ponte de Lima than we found there — some magical quality, some vantage point to hide the garbage strewn on its river bank, some church that wasn't stripped of its treasures. Writers have made much of it over the years, but even visiting Ponte de Lima during its famous harvest festival, when it should have been at its gayest and brightest, didn't bring it to life. It is an attractive place, certainly, but it didn't come close to living up to its much vaunted reputation.

An important Roman settlement, a portion of its long bridge is Roman; the nearer end had to be added when the river changed course. Except in the spring, the riverbed is a wide sandy beach where, unfortunately, it has become the custom to toss a wide variety of debris. Along the bank an avenue of giant sycamores creates a cool, shady walk to the two Renaissance churches they almost hide. These have been secularized, and S. Francisco is a fine museum of ecclesiastical art with some very rare wood pieces. Admission is by guided tour which takes an hour.

There are lovely old houses interspersed and crowded by box-like modern buildings. The broad square at the head of the bridge is lined with cafes from which one can enjoy the passing world as well as the nicely proportioned buildings that line the other three sides of the square.

Across the bridge is the onion-domed spire of S. Antonio de Torre Velha. Small, light and curiously un-churchlike, it could almost be the parlor in a palace. From here there is a nice view of Ponte de Lima, mountains rising behind it and the bridge in the foreground. Although there are only a few of the narrow closed-in streets characteristic of many towns of its age, Ponte de Lima is pleasant to stroll in, especially for its abundance of little street-side shrines which the locals call "little souls."

The Monday market is Portugal's oldest, and a lively, busy, place. If one is bent on seeing the town, this is a bad time since it is very crowded, but for those of us who love market days, it's the time to be there.

The road along the banks of the Lima is a succession of lovely views, as the river grows narrower and its banks steeper. Shortly before Ponte da Barca is Bravães, the portals of whose Roman church are a delight even to those who are not as fond as we are of Roman stonework. Chunky little figures of people, animals and other designs form a series of columns with griffons and birds surrounding both the west and south doors. There are also nice rose windows and some interesting murals inside for those who can find the sacristan who lives in a house on the north side of the church.

Ponte da Barca, less known but equally lovely, sits on a hillside above a Gothic arched bridge with a little park overlooking both bridge and river. Its parish church has two giant angels guarding the high altar.

Next to the church is a lovely eighteenth century manor house, its ochre yellow walls rising from its attractive garden. Ponte da Barca is well worth exploring, and is the gateway to one of the roads into the Peneda-Gerês National Park.

Although the park is all one piece, roads into it do not connect, partly because of the mountains and partly to preserve its wild areas. The road from Ponte da Barca to Lindoso is not for the timid as it climbs above the Lima River along the Serra de Soajo. It clings to the corniche with spectacular views all the way to Lindoso, passing Mosteiro, where the granaries are like the tall oriole's nests made of twisted willow reed, and Citadelhe, a little village of almost perfectly preserved mountain architecture.

The castle at Lindoso is much restored, but its attraction, in addition to the view, is the cluster of stone granaries just at its walls. Surmounted by stone crosses, these group around a community threshing floor. Although some date from the early eighteenth century, the espigueriros are not just relics of an earlier way of life. Some are fairly new, and this way of threshing and storing grain is still a part of the harvest here. The cluster of granite houses give the traveler in this remote place the feeling of having stumbled upon an ancient castro still in use.

The return can be made through Arcos de Valdevez via a road to the north not far west of Citadelhe, marked Soajo. It runs along the park border, leaving it at the Mezio entrance. To the right of the entrance, past the trees, is a very good pre-historic dolmen — one of several in this area and the easiest to get to.

Arcos de Valdevez is a busy market town just north of Ponte da Barca, with some very nice baroque churches. One of these is on the main route through town, an oval church set on a hill, which accents its facade with a two-storied entrance and a curved, pointed cornice. It is a most unusual facade.

The road between Arcos and Ponte de Lima along the north bank of the Lima passes the small Castro de Cendufe and the magnificent Paço de Gloria with fine gardens and an arcaded stone mansion. Beyond is the imposing Paço de Calheiros; a right turn to it is shortly past Refóios. Neither of the palaces is open to the public for tours, but are worth a stop to see the outside. Between the two paços, in Refóios do Lima, is a Benedictine convent and church. Much of the convent is in ruins, but it has a nice cloister. The church, although heavily restored, is filled with fine baroque woodwork, a riot of gold ornamentation.

The entire area around Ponte de Lima is dotted with lovely country homes and palaces, many of which can be seen from the road and some of which take in guests. Whenever a solid wall borders the road, watch for a gate and stop to look through it, for a good chance of seeing one of these homes.

Ponte De Lima At A Glance

A market town 20 km east of Viana do Castelo, 30 km north of Braga.

LODGING: One of the best reasons for spending time in Ponte de Lima is its central location for exploring the entire northern corner of the Minho. Braga and Barcelos, the western part of the national park, west to the coast and north to the border are all within easy reach of the day driver, with roads diverging so conveniently that each area can be covered with very little backtracking. Not only is it well located for this, it is well prepared with an enormous number of the local palaces, manorial estates and quintas welcoming guests as part of the TURIHAB association. Calheiros and Gloria, mentioned above are the most elegant, but each of these has its special charm and the standards are very high. Remember, however, that you are in a private home, not a hotel; this requires a different attitude on the part of guests, who are expected to be prompt for meals and reasonable in their arrival and departure times.

Paço de Calheiros (58/941364) has been in the same family since 1336 and is kept in perfect condition. Rooms are furnished in family antiques, but the bathrooms are all modern — a fine combination. They serve breakfast only, but since Ponte de Lima is only 7 km away, dinner is not a problem. Expect to pay a little less than the pousada rate, about $80 for a double.

Paço da Gloria (58/914477), between Ponte de Lima and Arcos de Valdevez, is a small seventeenth century manor with an arcade set between two square towers. It is beautifully restored and furnished with antiques. There are 10 guest rooms, equally divided between the main house and the converted stables, with the most luxurious ones in the manor house at about $80.

There are several more nearby: the wine quinta of Casa de Covas, the lovely Casa das Torres with its elegant facade and sculptured hedge, the Manor of Casa de Barreiro with its antiques and lovely architecture, Casa de Agrela near Ponte da Barca with its iron balconies and bright gardens and the equally fine Paço Verdo nearby. These and more can be arranged through TURIHAB in Ponte de Lima (58/942335 telex 32618PTPL). The Pensão S. João in Ponte de Lima is clean and inexpensive.

FOOD: Local specialties include Sarrabulho, a pork dish with many variations. Restaurants in Ponte de Lima include Clara Penha, the oldest in the Alto Minho, Encanada overlooking the river, Padeiro across from the market and Gaio, specializing in regional cooking. All are quite inexpensive.

SHOPPING: Craftsmen in the Ponte de Lima area include embroiderers, basketmakers, tinsmiths, woodcarvers, lacemakers and weavers. Their work can be seen in Ponte de Lima shops and in a very nice artisinato on the main street of Ponte da Barca just uphill from the bridge. Ponte de Lima's market is on Monday, Arcos de Valdevez is on Wednesday and the third week in September there is an artisans fair in Ponte de Lima.

IF TIME IS SHORT: This area can be passed in favor of the border towns or it can be seen quickly on a day trip from Braga or Barcelos.

Viana do Castelo

Viana do Castelo is a good-sized city, but its river mouth location has always allowed it to spread, so its size is forgotten in the grace of its wide avenues, plazas, and low white buildings. It is a lady, well-dressed, well kept and always smiling.

Viana is a city for strolling and browsing, with good parking along the riverfront. Sacadura Cabral leads away from the river at the opposite end of the garden from the bridge, past Rua S. Pedro with its fine old homes. The Igreja Matriz on the right is not especially notable except for its trompe l'oeil ceiling, most impressive, and the fine Gothic stonework of its west door. Beyond is the Praça de República.

Enhanced, not diminished, by the combination of styles present there, the Praça de República is one of Portugal's loveliest squares. The square crenellated and granite town hall is flanked by the Renaissance facade of the Misericordia, probably the best known building in town. Rising in three tiers, the upper two are supported by granite caryatids. Most of the year its imposing gray face is brightened with boxes of red geraniums. In the center of the square is a fine Renaissance fountain and beside the caryatid facade is the entrance to the Misericordia chapel, with a provincial painted ceiling and azulejos.

A short stroll up and back along the street to the left of the Misericordia gives a view of some fine housefronts. Viana do Castelo became a very prosperous city from the maritime trade, and its wealth shows in its private and public buildings. Back in the square, where it is hard to resist stopping in one of the open air cafes, there is a narrow street bearing to the left off its lower end. One side of this street is lined with butcher shops, their wares hanging outside, as is common here.

In contrast, the other side is lined with embroidery shops. These are well worth exploring for anyone interested in needle-arts. This street leads to a broad avenue, which, on turning left, leads back to the riverfront.

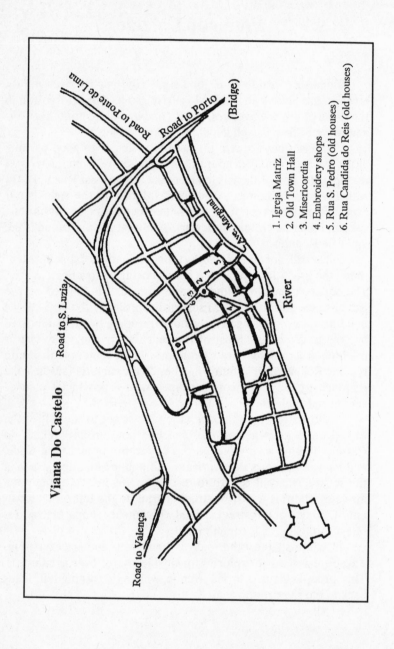

Viana Do Castelo

Road to Ponte de Lima

Road to Porto

(Bridge)

Road to S. Luzia

Road to Valença

Ave. Marginal

River

1. Igreja Matriz
2. Old Town Hall
3. Misericordia
4. Embroidery shops
5. Rua S. Pedro (old houses)
6. Rua Candida do Reis (old houses)

Instead of retracking on the Rua de Candide dos Reis, one can continue to its end near the train station, behind which is the funicular car to the Basilica of S. Luzia. Or, there is a winding road to this church and further on, the lovely hotel and Celtic Citânia.

The basilica on its belvedere is square, topped by a central dome with a lantern turret which, along with its large rose windows, lights the interior. Above is the Hotel de S. Luzia, and a small but very well preserved Celtic Citânia which, unfortunately, has been closed to the public recently. No one seems to know why, or when it will reopen; there is a hole in the fence along the approach road to the hotel. No more said.

North of Viana, the road passes a number of seaside resorts, including Vila Praia da Ancora, where there is an exceptional, well preserved dolmen. It is off the road toward Ponte de Lima about 100 yards down the road marked "VP Ancora". There is a plaque in the wall enclosing the courtyard in which the dolmen stands, but it is not visible. For directions ask for the Dolmen da Bairrosa.

Further north, at the mouth of the Minho, is the old town of Caminha, fortified and almost surrounded by water, retaining both its medieval air and buildings. The Gothic Pitas Palace is on the main square, its clocktower part of the original fourteenth century fortifications. At the far end of its Rua Direita (the name almost universal here for the main street inside of fortifications) stands the Igreja Matriz, whose sixteenth century carved wooden ceiling is exceptionally fine, at least as good as the celebrated one in Funchal. The Renaissance carving on the doorway is also very good.

Viana Do Castelo At A Glance

Seaport on the north coast, 71 km north of Porto; train connections from Porto.

LODGING: Top choice, in more ways than one is the Hotel de S. Luzia (58/ 22192 or in US 212/ 686-9213), on the crest above the city. A grand hotel of the turn of the century, it is now government run, although not technically a pousada. Art deco and modern touches highlight its structural elegance; it is a top-rate hotel in the middle price range — $50 to $70 for a double. Literally in its backyard is the Celtic Citânia de S. Luzia, which abuts the swimming pool.

The Hotel Alfonso III (58/ 24123) is right near the garden by the river, a shiny modern hotel with good service and a price range close *to the S. Luzia. In a lower range, but clean, comfortable and hospitable is the Hotel Aliança (58/23001). It is family run, a bit tattered at the edges and offers doubles in the $35 to $40 range.*

Over these downtown hotels we would choose to stay in a country home through TURIHAB, such as Casa de Cortegaça (58/971639) in Subportela on the road toward Ponte de Lima. Paço d'Anha (58/28459) is a stately, porticoed manor house set in vineyards just south of town and Casa de Ameal (58/22043) nearby in Meadela sits among lovely gardens. Those interested in old costumes will want to stay here just to see the collection. In Caminha is the beautiful Casa de Esteiro (58/921356), in a wooded garden setting. All of these may be booked through TURIHAB in Ponte de Lima (58/942334).

FOOD: Local specialties here include seafood, as might be expected, cabrito (goat) and lamprey. Restaurants are abundant in Viana do Castelo, in the downtown area and along the coast north of town. Of course, the S. Luzia's dining room is among the best, with dinner in the $15-$20 range. Os 3 Potes specializes in regional dishes at around $10, but you'll need a reservation during the summer. The Alambique and the Espigueiro also serve specialties of regional cuisine at slightly lower prices. At one of the cafes in the Praça, try one of the local pastries; we like Torta de Viana best. In Vila Praia de Ancora the Vordes Lirios has a panoramic view and shell fish specialties, at $10-$15 each. Restaurante João Ratão (also a pensão) in Caminha is a good choice.

SHOPPING: One of the major handcraft centers of Portugal, Viana offers beautiful embroideries, both in the colorful peasant embroidery and in finer examples of white on white. Shops line the streets off the Praça de República. Don't judge it all by the bright skirts and blouses displayed outdoors; the best work is inside the shops. The local folk embroidery style is one of light, flowing designs with lots of space, worked in primary colors on white for clothing. A slightly more stylized, but also open, flowing style is done on white with shades of blue embroidery, or ecru with red, white and blue or on black with bright primaries. These styles are used on clothing and household linens, especially tablecloths, which are quite lovely and moderately priced. Do look for quality pieces since good and poor examples may be side by side.

Collectors of miniatures should seek out the shop of S. Raphael, across from the tourist office in Vila Praia de Ancora. It is filled with miniature wooden furniture. The street behind the church in Caminha is lined with antique shops, as well as brass and copper ware, a specialty here. Friday is market day in Viana, a good place to find good handwork from the region.

FESTIVALS: The weekend nearest the 20th of August is the major festival, centering around the pilgrimage church of N.S. da Agonia in Viana. The fair includes market, dancing, music and general celebration, much of it in traditional costumes which are rarely worn otherwise.

IF TIME IS SHORT: Viana do Castelo can be included in a day trip from Barcelos or Braga, or in a circular tour of the border area and Ponte de Lima.

Valença and the Minho Valley

The best time to arrive in Valença, if one is staying at the Pousada S. Teotónio, is after dark. Not that we generally recommend night driving, but the entrance to Valença's walled citadel is so beautifully lighted and so dramatic, that the traveler should first see it, like a footlit stage set, appearing suddenly at the top of the hill. It should be accompanied by a blast of trumpets, heraldic flags flying.

Another reason for night, or at least Sunday arrival, is that the shops spill their merchandise onto the streets and cover the facades of the buildings. There is a daily stream of Spaniards who come to shop here for mundane household goods, far cheaper than in Spain. While all this commerce is not objectionable, nor ugly, it does cover up many fine housefronts and changes the appearance and atmosphere of the town. At night it is a medieval town; it is easier to accept its Common Market era if first seen uncluttered and lit by street lights and the warm glow of its restaurants and cafes.

There is nothing one "has to see" in Valença. Wandering in its streets in the evening or in the early morning is enough. In warm weather restaurant tables spread onto the streets, and pots of geraniums on iron balconies and tiny door stoop gardens set the scene alive with color.

Not for its artistic significance, but for its charm as a much-loved Portuguese village church, stop and look into Bom Jesus chapel, behind the statue of S. Teotónio in the square. The tiny chapel of S. Sebastian just inside the gate is a classic of folk art with small primitive polychrome statuary, including a S. Stephen whose face bears an expression of abject boredom.

Walk the perfectly preserved walls for beautiful views, as well as for a fascinating look at how defensive walls worked. There is one area just beyond the corner battlements near the pousada, where an army, if they scaled the outer wall, would be forced to drop down into a walled-in field in which they would be trapped, a perfect target from the battlements above.

Outside the walls is a more modern town with a busy Wednesday market covering the wooded hillside below the castle walls.

These markets, even if one is not shopping, offer a fascinating slice of local life. Farm women with baskets of herbs, ripe fruits and vegetables and furry baby rabbits catch up on news with customers. Bakery stalls are piled high with broa, the traditional bread of the region, and enormous displays of ceramics, cooking wares, rugs, clothing and goods of all types fill row upon row of canopied stalls.

To the south of Valença, Vila Nova de Cerveira is a fortified town with a pousada created out of several old homes inside the castle walls, a rocky barren slope rising straight behind it.

The route along the Minho River from Valença to Melgaço, or São Gregório only 50 km away, is through farm country, passing carts pulled by the local lyre-horned oxen with their carved yokes, and shepherds accompanied by big shaggy dogs. At Ganfei, just off the river road about 5 km from Valença is a Romanesque monastery and about 5 km further is a right turn to the sixth century church of Sanfins, one of the outstanding Romanesque churches of northern Portugal. The road at Friestas passes the enormous gate of the Quinta do Crasto, set in the middle of nowhere, stranded, somewhat below the new road. Comical as its placement is, the gate is none-the-less impressive with a deeply carved crown at the top of the arch.

Lapella, clustered right on the river bank, is worth a stop not so much for its fine twelfth century tower, but for the warren of streets at its foot. Vineyards overhang the road, barely held back by the stone walls peculiar to this area: cut granite slabs set side by side on end in a solid row. In the town, grapevines hang from the balconies over the narrow streets, and cars have to stop while housewives shoo chickens from the path.

Every doorstep and balcony seems covered with flowers and a huge sundial is set overhead in a facade. Leaving the car parked under some trees on the riverbank, we walked up a little lane toward the tower. Its base sits in the dooryards of a cluster of houses, next to the finest collection of Minho granaries we had seen. These long, narrow wooden corncribs are set on stone posts, each capped by a flat stone as a barrier to vermin. Painted dark red, these granaries are a fine contrast to the gray tower wall and the golden haystacks nearby.

It was lunch time and everyone, it seemed, was grilling sardines in their dooryards. A rosemary bush our own height filled the air with its delicious scent as we brushed past and the combination was almost irresistible. It was a detour well worth the 15 minutes it took and put lunch as the first priority in Monção.

Seated at the next table was a much-worn couple who took great interest in us. They listened in delight as the waitress explained the menu — a process which usually involves pointing out which of the items on the printed list they really have that day. They watched fascinated as we changed film with a buzzing of auto-winders. As they left, the man stopped at our table, pointed at the platter of fish, and said "bom peixe" (good fish). Then he pointed to the plate of kid liver stew (sometimes our Portuguese fails us and our sense of adventure takes over), shook his head and said in Portuguese "not so good." We grinned and agreed and wondered where he was when we needed him.

In the main square at the end opposite the tourist office (one of the most helpful in Portugal!) is a little Misericordia church with primitive statuary, a nice Madonna and S. Augustine at either side of the altar and a fine painted ceiling.

Igreja Matriz, a block behind the tourist office, near the river, has a fine Roman portal. The chapel in the right transept has a splendid rococo altar surrounded by azulejos, and richly carved doors. The church is a mixed bag — with a strange S. Christopher in a glass case and old vaulting with stairs superimposed — but it is one of the best examples of how churches grew and evolved.

About 3 km south of Monção a long wall to the right of the road ends suddenly with the gate of Brejoeira Palace, designed after the Ajuda Palace in Lisbon, and the last of the great houses built in Portugal. Although it isn't open to view, the entire facade can be seen through the wrought iron gate.

East of Monçao, on the road along the Minho (which becomes more tightly contained within its wooded slopes), is Ponte de Mouro with a deeply arched Roman bridge over a chasm. Just before the bridge on the main road there is a lane to the right which leads to a largo and a church. Below the steps of the church the old bridge is almost beside the newer one. Although there are many Roman bridges remaining in Portugal, none of them seemed quite as perfect as this one, with its single arch too narrow for modern traffic, and a plaque marking it as the meeting place of John of Gaunt and King João I in 1386 to arrange the marriage of the King to John's daughter Philippa. The houses between the church and river are built on Roman foundations.

There is another Roman bridge at Barbeita as well as little-explored pre-Roman ruins. We haven't explored them ourselves, so can only report their presence from the advice of local residents.

Melgaço has a square castle keep with pointed crenellations and a good thirteenth century church, N.S. da Orada, about 1 km east of town. São Gregório, at the Spanish border, is a fortified town, but unless one is crossing the border here, a more interesting and beautiful drive goes south from Melgaço, about 25 km into the Peneda-Gerês National Park to Castro Laboreiro.

Here granite espigueiros, granaries for the storing of corn, have replaced the wooden ones of the Minho valley, but they are built much the same way with broad flat stones set upon stone pillars for foundations. On the way up to the ruins of the eleventh century castle in Castro Laboreiro there is a large rock which has been so eroded as to look like a giant turtle climbing the hill. There is a megalithic tomb in Castro Laboreiro and several others along the plateau. Since the road ends just south of the Spanish border beyond, the route must be back-tracked as far as Monção.

Valença And The Minho Valley At A Glance

A walled border town 53 km northeast of Viana do Castelo, across the Minho River from Tuy, Spain.

LODGING: Lodging is fairly plentiful in the area with pousadas and private estates as well as hotels. The Pousada de S. Teotónio (51/ 22252, US 212/ 686-9213) is a lovely modern hotel, built inside the walls of the fortress. Balconies overlook the garden, especially beautiful in the morning sunlight when the river mists still lie below. Beyond and below, where there were the twinkling lights of Spain the previous evening, there is nothing but mist.

Lingering over breakfast (it's impossible not to, since it takes 10-15 minutes to get a cup of coffee here!) we watched the mists rise and the mountains and fields appear. Rooms are furnished with carved beds, handwoven rugs and very nice details. The view from any window here is splendid. In the middle of the pousada price range, a double is $80 in high season and $50 in low season.

Also in castle ramparts, the Pousada do Dom Dinis (51/ 95601) at Vila Nova da Cerveira is in a group of historic buildings complete with its own eighteenth century chapel. In the highest pousada range, a double costs from $70 in low season to over $100 in the summer.

In Valença, the Lara Hotel (51/ 22348) offers doubles at about $56 in high season and $40 in low, or if you travel light and don't mind a three-flight climb, a room here is $20-25. In Monção the Albergaria Atlantico (51/ 52355), located on the main square costs about $50 to

$70 and is quite nice. *Requiring advance reservations, but well worth it for the experience of staying in a lovely private home is Casa de Rodas in Monção (51/52105) or call the central reservation office for these "casas antigas" in Ponte de Lima at 58/942335.*

FOOD: *Fresh ingredients here include fine garden produce and fish from both the river and the ocean. Lamprey is so popular here that people travel from all over Portugal to enjoy it in its season from March to April. Salmon, trout, and ocean fish are fresh and well prepared. The local honey is divine, and the broa, the hearty corn-based bread, is a particular favorite of ours. Perna de Vitela a Costa Verde is roast leg of veal, Rojoes a Minhota is roast pork. The local wines are vinho verde, of which Alvarinho from Monção is the best known.*

There are a number of good restaurants in Valença within the town walls, but our favorite for a warm evening is the Fortaleza, where outdoor tables face the lighted inner gate and its grass-topped walls and bridge — fine setting for their Pescada a Romana (a firm white fish cut thin, then lightly breaded and fried) or the braised cabrito. Prices range from $7.50 to $15 for 2 with wine. The Restaurant Bom Jesus, beside the church, has an upstairs dining room overlooking the square and is more elegant and more expensive. Restaurante Balvarte also has a pleasant upstairs dining room. The town is small enough to walk through, reading menus as you go, before choosing.

In Monção the Chave de Ouro is famous for its lamprey and Mane is also good and a little less expensive. Casa Matraquilhos is a tiny local restaurant off the flower-filled public garden just uphill from the main square. Family run, it's far from fancy, but the fish is excellent and the price for two, with a bottle of Alvarinho, was $12.

SHOPPING: *Local crafts have remained strong in the Minho, where embroidery, woolen blankets, wood carving and pottery are still made by individual craftsmen at home. You will see some of these in the Wednesday market, especially beautiful copper ware, and in the shops along the streets of the walled town. You may have to look hard between all of the everyday things put out for the Spanish trade, but you'll find some nice little shops in Valença.*

If you plan to travel into the Peneda-Gerês National Park, where there are a number of spectacular picnic sites, consider buying bread, cheese, local cured sausage or ham, and the incomparable local olives at the market before you leave. Food is sold every morning in the municipal market building at the intersection of the main roads below the old town.

FESTIVALS: *When traveling through this area on Sundays in the summer, look for wood and reed arches covered with paper which announce local festivals. You are welcome to stop and join in, and you should, since its a good way for you to see and take part in the local folk life, which always includes dancing and singing as well as food and wine. This is the poorest province, but the richest in color and customs.*

IF TIME IS SHORT: *Valença and the Minho valley are at the very northern edge of Portugal, and while they are a must for those who love unspoiled countryside and have lots of time, they aren't practical for a very short trip. If you are just passing through quickly from Viana do Castelo, make Valença a stop over then go to Monção and south to Braga. You can do a lot of wandering between Valença and Braga in one day, especially if you leave out the trip to the park.*

Caldas do Gerês and
Peneda-Gerês National Park

Gerês, strung along a narrow crevice overhanging a rushing river, is a busy little spa and resort town without the feel of either. Completely devoid of glitz, it is a Portuguese mountain resort with very few foreign visitors. It is located inside the park.

In the center of town, along the main street like everything else, is an arcaded semi-circular building — the spa, with the mineral spring in the center. At the other spas, such as at Luso, people come to the mineral spring to fill their plastic jugs, but at Gerês the flow is slow and an almost reverential air prevails, as though it were a holy pilgrimage shrine, not water from a geological fault. From early in the morning people are lined up carrying special little glass containers inside tiny oval baskets or white crocheted reticules. Patiently they wait while two old women fill the jars from the spring's flow and hand them back.

There is a relaxed holiday air, with cafes and shops, but entirely different from the beach resort towns not far away. There is no formal parking, one simply drives on up the street until there is a space. The Turismo office is in the spa building and there is a park office in a stone building a little farther uphill where maps of the park are available.

The road climbs out of Gerês above rock-strewn forested glades, through rich green forests which thin to reveal sheer cliffs on the opposite wall of a deep ravine. It's first and second gear all the way; in places one can look straight down on three layers of the road just climbed. The plateau opens out to magnificent mountain scenery — rocky peaks framed in dark pines above green meadows. Wildflowers spring through the grass — tiny pink crocus-like flowers without leaves, heather, columbine, laurel, soft ferns and a variety of iris peculiar to this region.

Farther north, the road splits and the left turn loops back to the south following the Homen River. This is an old Roman military road, part of the Via Nova linking Braga to Astorga in Spain. There are milestones still standing, columns like weary groups of legionnaires resting beside the road. Further south the road goes along the valley, forming a full circle at the bridge at Rio Caldo below Gerês.

Not far west of the Rio Caldo bridge, on the north side of the reservoir, is the town of Bouro with the ruined Cistercian monastery of S. Maria. Although by this time the traveler cannot avoid having seen a lot of monasteries, many in ruin, the huge gray hulk of S. Maria's facade commands attention as it dominates the center of the town.

On the facade, which was once plastered in white, are unusual stone carvings of the kings of Portugal. Inside (just push on the door to enter) is desolation. The roof is entirely gone, having been sold for its lead and iron in the 1940s by a man from Porto who bought the whole place for a few hundred dollars.

The kitchen with its great chimney, the refectory and cloister are all open to the weather, their fine frescoes all but gone, the once fine azulejos stripped off. There is an air of desolation here, as compared to other monasteries in just as bad condition which seem almost ethereal and splendid in their abandonment.

The church, at the top of the stairs, is still in use by the parish and has fine choir stalls, good paintings and an exceptional painted sacristy ceiling. There is usually someone in or around the church, or ask at one of the buildings across the street for the whereabouts of the key if it is locked.

There are two routes between Rio Caldo and the eastern end of the park. One follows the north shore of the reservoirs, along a steep slope inside the park. The other road leaves the park and rides along the high south shore overlooking the reservoirs below and the rocky slopes of the park. Not only is the road better but the views are breathtaking from the belvederes cut alongside.

To the right are strange bare hilltops covered with rounded boulders that look as though they could roll down at a breath of wind. There are farms and vineyards set in terraced fields. The air is fresh and, even in autumn, smells of green and growing things. Camomile and gorse share the roadsides and the rock walls are hanging with heather or covered by ripening brambleberries, sweet and juicy. We kept stopping, we claimed, to admire the views, but always climbed back into the car with our hands full of berries.

Pastoral scenes are all around these red-roofed farming towns, herdsmen with cattle or sheep, ox carts laden with hay creaking along the road, carts of grapes headed for the cooperatives, hay in giant house-shaped mows and corn drying in town squares.

Montalegre is a hilltop town crowned by a well-restored late medieval castle. The walls of its keep are about eight feet thick with huge inside window arches narrowing to four-inch slits. Few other places illustrate so clearly just how a bowman could stand with plenty of room inside to shoot through this tiny slit. There are fine views from here across the green and amber farms to the mountains. The Misericordia church just below the castle has a good altar flanked by salomonic columns that continue twisted right into the arch. For all Montalegre's bustle, no one is surprised that a flock of sheep, two goats and an ox cart piled with hay stop traffic, each in turn, along the main street.

The road into the far eastern end of the park goes west from Montalegre through a valley of farms. A right turn in Covelães leads north along a beautiful open moor whose stone walls, hedgerows, heather and gorse make it look quite English. At the far end is Tourém, with its painted house decorations and carved stone house columns (some with gaunt stone faces as capitals). A turn west off the Tourém road leads into Pitões das Junias.

Pitões das Junias really is at the end of the road — although it seems to be at the end of the earth. More often, when the map shows a road ending, it simply means that the towns beyond are too small to mention or that the road dwindles to the class not shown on the map.

Not so of Pitões das Junias. Its steep cobbled streets don't allow a car to go very far along them. Narrower and narrower, steeper and twisting more sharply, they become impassable shortly beyond the fountain where the old men gather in the afternoon. From there on foot, with the first bend in the steep street, the parked car is out of sight and one is suddenly aware that this is a medieval village. The traveler may well be the only thing from the twentieth century in sight.

Like so many hill towns, the streets are often steps carved into the bedrock, and the rest covered in rounded paving stones worn by centuries of water and feet. No carts ever wore stones at such a pitch. The stones are covered with a layer of straw and the droppings of farm animals which share the area. Chickens and goats make way for pedestrians who make way in turn for donkey and ox carts and the only twentieth century vehicle, an occasional tractor.

The homes, barns and farm sheds that line the streets (actually the streets are simply alleys winding between the buildings, more of an afterthought than planned) are all of stone with red tile or thatched roofs.

There was almost no-one in the town in the late September afternoon when we first saw it. We could see them below in the fields, harvesting potatoes.

The street led us upward past wooden wheeled carts, onions spread to dry, piles of green broom, laundry, firewood, brush, farm tools and chickens until at last it reached another fountain. Then we realized why the road ended at Pitões.

Before us over the low flat roofs of the final buildings lay nothing at all. The foreground had dropped suddenly away. And beyond that, grayed slightly by haze, was the meanest, steepest, sharpest face of mountains that we'd ever encountered. We were face to face with the great Serra de Jures of Spain, its sharp peaks of Fuentefria like the lower jaw of a wolf rising sheer and menacing. We love mountains, but would find it hard to love these. Our road too ended at the fountain at the top of the hill in Pitões.

We had not traveled into the heights just to see if the road really did end there. The moor-covered mountains over which we traveled were the Serra Gerês, Portugal's northern range. We had come in search of the ruins of a twelfth century Cistercian monastery which we had heard were hidden deep in a glen below Pitões.

It was clearly not on the side of the town toward Spain, so we followed another set of streets back downhill to the car. "Don't you have the feeling that if we don't get out of here by sunset we'll disappear into the mists for a hundred years like Brigadoon?" Tim asked as we drove out.

We asked some men building a house at the edge of the village about the monastery, and they pointed to a road — really a track — off to the left just as the road dropped into the lower edge of the village. It led off across a barren rock-strewn moor, which dropped off before us on all sides, led us to the left and obviously nowhere.

When it finally became too rocky to risk (or a few hundred yards past the point where we were sure we couldn't get out again!) we left the car and walked down the stony track, which soon turned into a path leading into a glen whose bottom we still could not see.

The path clung along the edge, through broom and rock and suddenly below us, its bell tower catching the last few rays of the evening sun to reach so deep, was the monastery. Lying along a little river in the deep green of its narrow glen, the church, cloister and walls of S. Maria das Junias seemed like a toy. We climbed down and found that even inside its walls it was like a monastery in miniature, entirely hidden by the steep slopes at either end.

The remaining few arches of the cloister were small and low, the now ruined kitchen, refectory and dormitories tiny and over-grown with brambleberries, and the church itself, the only part still intact was like a little parish church. Its single nave was without side chapels or transept, with two small side altars of carved stone in perfect proportion as the only accent to the plain stone walls lit from tiny windows high above. We wished only to have seen this small gem of a Romanesque cloister intact.

Visitors are almost certain to be alone there, few have ever heard of Pitões or of the little monastery hidden below it, let alone ventured on foot to see it. But it is these hidden corners with their tiny treasures that fill Portugal with daily delight.

All over Portugal are towns like Pitões at the end of the road and nearly forgotten, carrying on life much as their ancestors have for centuries.

Gerês At A Glance

Spa town 34 km in the mountains of the Peneda-Gerês National Park.

LODGING: The Pousada S. Bento (53/ 57190), like the one at Valença, has a dramatic approach — depending upon which direction one arrives from, it's either straight up or straight down. The road snakes up the almost sheer face of the mountain above the Caniçada Reservoir, with outside turns that bring you face to face with the sky and nothing else before reversing direction in another hairpin turn. The passenger can (if he dares) look straight down into the evening mist and water far below. Never has a pousada entrance looked so welcoming. It is also one of the loveliest of them, an elegant, rustic country lodge with spectacular views, well-kept gardens and a light, open architecture. Rooms are set off a mezzanine which provides small, almost private, sitting rooms for the guests. It is in the mid-range for pousadas at $80 in high season and about $55 in low.

There are several pleasant places to stay in Gerês, the Parque (53/ 65112), Das Termas (53/ 65143), and the Universal (53/ 65141), venerable old resort hotels right in the heart of town, all moderately priced. The Pensão S. Antonio and Casa de Ponte are newer and just

*outside the center, but the town is quite small and everything is within
an easy walk. In Vieira do Minho, near the pousada, is a country
home with a splendid granite granary in the yard, with rooms available
under the TURIHAB program (53/57452).*

FOOD: *Guests at the pousada will want to eat dinner there for
two reasons: it has, by far, the best food in the area and few would
want to drive that road after dark. Their chef brings the classic peasant
soup, Caldo Verde, to new heights, with fine strips of shredded kale
suspended in a semi-thick potato soup, delicately seasoned. The trout
with ham is excellent, as is the kid. Meals are fixed price, about $20
for a full meal with both fish and meat courses, and $16 for one or the
other complete with appetizer, soup, main course and dessert. There
are several restaurants in Gerês and Croisanteria, on the way into
town opposite the wood craftsman's shop, has a very pleasant outside
cafe and modern restrooms. There are restaurants in Montalegre and
few between. It's a good area in which to consider a picnic lunch.*

SHOPPING: *Gerês, although not the shoppers' capital of Europe,
has some very nice little shops and stalls where local knit woolens are
inexpensive and well made. The pottery shop on the main street has
a very good selection of the work of Julia Ramalho (see Barcelos) at
prices you won't find elsewhere. There is a woodworking shop (opposite the Croisanteria) where you can watch a family team do the local
fretwork in the backyard. Roadside tables sell mountain herb tea,
honey, and beautiful mineral specimens from the mountains.*

FESTIVALS: *The most colorful local festival of this region takes
place between August 10 and 15 at São Bento de Porta Alberta near
Rio Caldo.*

IF TIME IS SHORT: *This area is for the traveler who is not in a
hurry, with its steep winding roads and cul-de-sac villages. It should
be skipped by those who don't like mountain roads, or be viewed from
the top along the main road from Braga to Chaves, which is quite
good.*

Chaves

The public gardens of Portugal are among the loveliest in the world, so to say that one stands out above the rest is a compliment indeed. But the garden that surrounds the castle tower in Chaves has the perfection of a classic baroque church — lovely, exuberant, but restrained and tasteful. Beds of only two varieties — brilliant red salvia and rich blue ageratum are arranged in semi-circular bands accented with round beds on perfect lawns inside the belvedere of the castle walls. Interspersed among them are ancient stones — carved slabs, a graceful small arch and columns, a segment of pillar — providing a balance to the almost electric colors.

Above it rises the straight battlemented keep, built and maintained to discourage Spanish incursion from over the border fewer than 10 miles away. Since Roman times, Chaves has been the key to this region, with its wide, flat, fertile valley — its very name means key. The Palace of the Dukes of Bragança which backs onto the tower faces a lovely small square enclosed by fine balconied homes and two churches.

The Igreja Matriz at the end of this square shows little of its Romanesque origins, but has, in one of the walls of the apse, a statue of Mary considered to be among the oldest ecclesiastic statues in Portugal.

The early baroque facade of the Misericordia commands attention at once, with its double stories supported by salomonic columns. Inside, the walls are covered to the ceiling with azulejos of scenes from the New Testament.

Inside the Bragança Palace next door is an excellent collection of ancient artifacts, part of which is displayed in the garden. With the few escudos admission fee comes a complete listing of these which are all numbered to correspond to the list. In an adjoining room, the collection of pieces and pictures from the several sites of prehistoric rock carvings nearby are a must for anyone interested in prehistory.

The Tamega River is crossed in town by a bridge built by the Romans. On the near end are legible Roman inscriptions. Just over the bridge, to the left, is an octagonal church, with a fine baroque facade. It faces a street so narrow that it is impossible to see it, but we discovered by walking up the next street, that above the tile roof tops we could see the pair of granite angels set in a scroll above a richly carved crest. The scene, with the rough walls and balconies of old homes in the foreground and the elegant facade above, is pure Portugal.

Out the Estrada de Outeiro Seco, past the stadium and fort of S. Neutel, the road leads past the remarkable church of S. de Azinheira. It contains the best sixteenth century frescoes remaining in Portugal and though badly faded with age they are still visible. The sacristan lives some distance away, so it is best to ask a passerby.

Or, more likely, one will ask you. We were just entering its gate as a man was driving by on a donkey cart. "Do you want to see inside?" he asked. There followed a long description of the way to the house of the lady who had the key. We couldn't understand it, of course, so he motioned us to follow him. Off we set, Citroen following a donkey cart in which was a bleating baby goat. With the goat bouncing, the donkey puffing, the driver urging him faster, and the Citroen in first gear following, we turned left at the fork. About 250 yards down the road on the right side sat an old house, one side fallen in but the other side freshly roofed and whitewashed.

"Maria, Maria" he called but there was no answer from Maria. The man apologized and we thanked him for his troubles (although not for the morning's entertainment) and returned to the church. We admired its fine exterior, and peeking through the keyhole, a large part of the interior. We've seen many a church through the keyhole, or through cracks in the door and not a few by boosting one another up so as to be able to see in a window.

Even if Maria isn't home, this beautifully carved portal with a rabbit and two dogs, and the corbels make it worth the short diversion. Each of the corbels is different — wolf, bear and others. The last one on the west side before the chancel is especially endearing. There is also an excellent tomb in the portico and an interesting early monument in the west yard.

Behind, overlooking the fields, farmhouses and olive groves is the parish churchyard, with modern marble tombs (often including a framed photo of the deceased) mixed with a few old granite stones, all in a profusion of roses, zinnias and other flowers in full bloom.

On the north of the road at the national park, marked by a blue monument sign, is Castro de Coralha, a Celtic settlement. (The obvious path to the right leads to a rock scramble — go uphill instead, through the small trees at the left end of the little parking area.) They are doing some work to restore the massive outer wall encircling this small hill fort, but, like most, it is deserted, especcially at sunset, which seems to be our Celtic calling hour.

Finding the prehistoric rock carvings at Outeiro Machado looks very easy on the little map from the tourist office. Simply take the street to the right at the foot of the beautiful garden in front of the Turismo and follow signs toward Soutelo until you come to the monument sign. That far it works, but from there it is simply toss a coin at each fork in the maze of dirt tracks that wind among fields and past vineyards heavy with grapes.

Briefly, leave the main road turning right onto a dirt track, go left at the first fork past some new houses, then right in the trees, then left quickly (a small sign encourages you here). The carved stones are a short way on the right, off a small place where you can park.

The stones are badly covered with lichens, but a search will turn up a variety of carved symbols on the large ledge and on the adjacent ones to its right.

In Mairos, north of Chaves on the Spanish border, there are more of these carvings, but even harder to find. At the spa town of Carvalhelos, near Boticas, is another Celtic settlement and a fourteenth century castle tower is at Monforte, along the road to Bragança. There is a popular spa and a lovely park at Vidago, on the road south toward Vila Real.

But of all the attractions in the region, we read about what must be the most curious, if one is to believe the brochure from the Valpaços tourist office, only long after we had left the mountains. At the Sanctuary of N.S. de Saude (and here I must quote from the English version of the brochure — unfortunately we don't have a copy of the Portuguese one to make our own translation) "The visitor's attention is always attracted by the so-called Pedra Furada, a real local curiosity, with its monumental aspect caused by a circumference of 26 meters of diametre and more than 6 meters of profundity." The Portuguese "furada" is from the verb furar, to pierce, drill or puncture, so we can only picture an 80 foot stone with a 20 foot hole through it, like a monumental donut!

Next time, without fail, we shall track down this six-meter profundity!

On the way to Valpaços there is another curiosity, the huge Pedra Bolideira, a balancing stone that moves with a gentle push. Much of the countryside in the mountains is strewn with giant rounded, freestanding, boulders, some of which are poised disconcertingly above the road or overhang villages and farms.

The road toward Bragança climbs above the low farmlands to a high and lovely plateau, with the Serra do Coroa rising to the north.

Short of Rebordelho, we stopped at a little bar just off the main road in the town of Lebucão to buy wine for a picnic. Tim came out empty-handed and said "There's a nice little restaurant inside, let's eat here." We asked for a menu and the lady apologized. "We have only one thing today, only the leitão." The name rang a bell from the previous night's menu where we had skipped it because of its very high price. We were brought a big platter of roast suckling pig. We had stumbled into their Friday "Blue Plate Special," more expensive than their usual at almost $10 for the two of us, including a bottle of good local wine!

Chaves At A Glance

Farming center and spa since Roman times, 64 km north of Vila Real, 100 km west of Bragança.

LODGING: What Chaves needs is a pousada, and the perfect place for one would be the abandoned convent of S. Francisco. By converting and restoring it, as they have done with the one in Guimarães, this could fix a missing link in the pousada chain and save travelers from the fairly grim assortment of lodgings now offered. Actually, the Hotel Trajano (76/ 22415) is fairly nice with doubles in the $35 range. It is located in the center of town on a side street near the Tribunal of Justice. Beside the court is the Estralagem Santiago (76/ 22545) which no longer merits its four-star rating, but still charges for it. It is clean and comfortable, however, and both of these hotels are perfectly acceptable although far from luxurious. This is not a place to try the pensions, as even the three-star Jaime is dismal, noisy, and has primitive plumbing. But double rooms are only $20.

During the spa season, from June 1 through October 15, consider the fading grandeur of the pink Palace at Vidago (76/ 97356). It is in the $50 range, but that includes dinner, a pool and sport facilities. As *these old spa towns regain their popularity, the hotels are being modernized — in the sense of improvement — without losing their charm. It has a neighboring annex, new and more expensive, which is open in the winter.*

FOOD: Chaves is famous for its ham — presunto, and the local wine is called Mortos de Boticas because it is bottled, then buried in the ground. The Trajano Hotel has a pleasant dining room with dinner for two at about $20. The Dionisyos, opposite the castle, is more lively and less expensive, and the Flavia, a little family-run place across from the Trajano offers good meals at about $5 each. There are several restaurants in Vidago, including the Palace's dining room which, although expensive for the region (about $15 each) is excellent.

FESTIVALS: All Saint's Day, November 1, brings a big local fair in Chaves.

IF TIME IS SHORT: You can go straight from Vila Real to Bragança, but you'd miss some of Portugal's loveliest scenery. There is nothing in Chaves you "must see." It is just a pleasant city with a beautiful garden and hospitable people, surrounded by spectacular countryside.

Bragança

"The traveler..." we had read, "who expects much of Bragança will be disappointed." Yet, in spite of this sour warning we expected a lot and were *not* disappointed. Nor have we been since.

The castle, with its enormous and well-preserved towers and walls, stands out over a base of uneven red tile roofs which cling to the hill all around it. Behind is the great stretch of the Parque Natural de Montezinhos ending in mountains at the far horizon. In the morning the castle walls are dark against the sunlit roofs, and in the afternoon, the whole face is bathed in sunlight.

On the way up or down the streets, narrow and faced with homes on the uphill side, traffic may be slowed by a herd of sheep from the town below being shooed up to the green hilltop pastures for the day. Bragança, for all its size and stature is still a country village at its edges. Whether from planning or the availability of land, its growth and new building has been at the lowland edges where new neighborhoods neither threaten old ones nor ruin the view.

The castle is everyone's first goal and it should be, since it is one of the best remaining medieval military castles in Portugal. Unlike most, it was kept up instead of having been allowed to fall apart prior to restoration. If you are traveling with children you may never be able to extract them from this exciting place, where there are ramparts to walk, towers to climb, crenellations to peer between, narrow windows through which to vanquish assailants. Each round tower of the walls forms a little belvedere with views out to the fields, or down into the town that has grown at the foot of the castle.

These castle towns inside the walls with their tiny houses and backyard gardens and front yard laundry and chicken and flower-pots on the doorsteps are a charming feature of several Portuguese fortresses. House walls are often built into the castle itself. There is talk of "restoring" these later-built warrens out of existence, which would be a shame for they give it life and color.

In the case of Bragança, these also provide someone to keep the keys to the church and twelfth century Romanesque town hall.

A visitor doesn't usually get to the door of either before one of the women crocheting in front of her door will ask if they would like to go in. She sends someone for the key, or sends for whoever has it. There is no admission charge, although a small tip, 50 escudos or so, is always appreciated.

The five-sided town hall is about the only original Romanesque civic building remaining in Iberia. It sits alone above a cistern and its council chamber is open, with stone benches around its walls. Stone-carved supports under the ceiling are of human and animal faces and flowers.

Next door is the baroque facade of S. Maria. Word will have reached the key-keeper that there are visitors (can you imagine a system like this working in England) and she will already be there to unlock it.

The overwhelming memory of churches in Bragança — and there are nine of them — is of their painted ceilings. S. Maria has one of the best, a trompe l'oeil of the Assumption. The main altar doesn't quite seem to fit its arch and there are pieces missing in some of the side altars, but here is good gold work and some exceptionally fine polychrome statues. The painting has not been stripped from the chancel arch — although it is faint, and there are splendid little cherubs throughout.

Near the castle gate, where until recently there was a lovely garden (which has been unaccountably torn out), is the famous pig. Carved in stone, it has a stone stake through its middle and a bowl-like depression in its brow. These pigs are of ancient but uncertain origin, and are found in a number of towns in this area. Because these were Celtic settlements, they are thought to connect to the Scottish use of the boar as a symbol of kingship. It is interesting that their name in Portuguese is always in the feminine form: sow.

Igreja S. Bento stands below the castle walls to the right outside the gate, its facade on the side. In a refreshing change, it is often open even when there is no one there — just push on the very center of the door and a panel swings in. The light switch is just inside the door. The ceiling here is quite different, in a colorful combination of classical columns and figures — very Italian — painted on the barrel-arched wood. An earlier and very well-preserved ceiling is in the choir loft (stairs in the rear) which is also a good viewpoint for the church as a whole. There is an exceptionally fine high altar as well, and the new freestanding altar is well made and in a compatible style!

The cherubs, which are plentiful throughout Bragança, wear little black capes here. There are so many fine works and details in S. Bento, and they are all so nicely taken care of, that it is obvious that its parishioners know what treasures they have. There is a little coffer near the entrance for the restoration of the church and we hope that S. Bento visitors remember it as they leave so that S. Bento's upkeep can continue. Don't forget to switch the lights off.

Down the hill is a largo with the Igreja S. Vincente in it, and yet a different splendid ceiling — this one with carved figures of the Evangelists at the corners. The azulejo plaque on the outside wall records that it was from this church that General Sepulveda urged the citizenry to rebel against French domination. Legend holds this to be the church where the future King Pedro and Inez de Castro were secretly married — an event that would certainly not have been recorded, since his father had forbidden it. Cantahede near Coimbra makes the same claim.

Beyond, on Rua Abilio Beca, past a very good local museum, is the Misericordia, one of the earliest. Its Renaissance high altar is particularly fine as are its polychromes. A right turn here leads to Igreja S. Clara. As we entered, two women were in animated conversation — when they saw us, they knelt quickly and began their rosaries. Amid this devotion, we hesitated to poke about in the chancel for light switches, so we didn't see the richly painted ceiling as clearly as we would have liked.

The Sé, which has only "recently" held that honor, the bishopric having been moved here from Miranda do Douro in 1770, was obviously not built as a cathedral. It is a relatively plain little church, less grand and more like a neighborhood parish in its decoration. The fan tracery in its Gothic roof is excellent. The prize of this church is its sacristy, reached through a graceful little cloister almost lost in overgrown apple trees.

Two ladies of the altar guild were in the small sacristy fixing vases of flowers from huge bunches of fresh blooms in buckets. More flowers kept arriving in armfuls until the room smelled like a florist shop. After each had been accepted with great appreciation, the ladies returned to showing us the treasures: two very fine polychrome statues — S. Francis Xavier on the right and S. Ignacious on the left, and a paneled ceiling painted with scenes from the life of S. Ignacious. What the ceiling lacks in artistry it gains in enthusiasm, and the sacristy, with or without the flowers, is lovely.

The street directly off the Sé leads back to S. Vincente and on up the street through the castle gate, making a long circular route. Lining both these streets are fine houses.

Although Bragança rises from a wide and fertile plain, it is surrounded by distant mountains, so its approach from any direction is through magnificent scenery. To the west the landscapes are alternately wild rock-strewn mountains or terraced landscapes of walled sheep pastures, gardens and grape vines set into hillsides. Chestnut trees with their huge twisted trunks line the road, and smaller ones are lined up in orchards.

In the spring, when they are in bloom, and the entire landscape is covered with wildflowers, it is spectacular, but at any season it has been rightly described as one of the great drives of the world. No jagged Alpine peaks, simply row on row of mountains blue to the horizon, set in a foreground of fields, meadows and forests.

The Montezinhos Natural Park lies between the road and the Spanish border to the north, with roads extending into it from Bragança and Vinhais. This long narrow corniche town has two churches, set together on the downhill side of the road so that their towers are at street level. Once a great and wealthy convent, the lower church is now a school, its cloister ringing with shouts and hung with swings and climbing ropes — a happy use, far preferable to crumbling decay.

One or two of the boys will gladly open the church, which has an outstanding gold and polychrome altar and a most unique reliquary display case full of little windows. Ask the boys to turn on the lights from the switch in the sacristy — and be sure to see this room with its carved vestment chests whose arched backs meet the rounded ceiling. Two excellent polychromes which once were in the church are now in the sacristy.

The upper church is not such a happy story. What was once considered the finest painted ceiling in Portugal — one of delicate line and coloring and perfect execution — has now been painted over in white.

South of the road between Vinhais and Bragança is Castro de Avelas, with a twelfth century monastery, mostly in ruin. Its round brick walls are quite unusual in Portugal, set in rows of closed arcades, like great boarded-up windows, giving it a "Little Orphan Annie" look. It could quite easily be set in Spain.

Drives north from Bragança into the national park offer spectacular scenery from tortuous roads. Just east of Gimonde on the road to Miranda do Douro is a good Roman bridge, then the road ascends dramatically along the edge of a beautiful green valley. As it climbs there are lovely views back at the roof tops of Bragança, framed in chestnut trees.

Bragança At A Glance

Medieval city, until recently much isolated from the rest of Portugal, 100 km west of Chaves, 137 km north of Vila Real. It can be reached by train from Porto.

LODGING: The most lackluster of the pousadas, S. Bartolomeu (73/ 224 93) is in a prize setting overlooking the old city and the castle. This is not a criticism of its service; it is just one of the early pousadas and showing its age a bit. But it is up to standards in other ways and it is still the best hotel in town. It's in the lowest price range at $60 for a double with a balcony. The Albergaria S. Isabela (73/ 22427) in the old city has a four-star rating with doubles at around $25 and the Hotel Bragança is on a broad avenue in a newer part of town with rooms at about $40. There are pensãos, including S. Roque (three stars) under $20 and the Tulipa (three stars) at about $25. Remember that these far northern towns more used to European tourists and lodgings don't tend to be fancy. But what Bragança lacks in luxury it adds on in hospitality. You'll be treated like Queen Catherine herself.

FOOD: Bola de Carnes is a meat pie, and Coelho Bruxa is "Rabbit Witch Style," both Bragança specialties. The local chourico sausage is excellent and Nogado is a popular nut cake. The pousada serves the most elegant meals, but the Solar Bragança and the Restaurante Cruzeiro, both overlooking the cathedral, are very good, as is La Em Casa, a block away from the Misericordia. Right below the pousada is the very pleasant Restaurant Fervença where dinner for two with wine will be under $15.

SHOPPING: Terra-cotta and copper ware are found here, as well as handwoven fabrics, blankets and rugs. There is an artisinato across the street from the museum on Rua Abilio Beca.

IF TIME IS SHORT: There is no way around the fact that this is Portugal's most remote corner, and a long trip. The countryside around it is as attractive as the city itself. There is no reason to spend days here; an overnight stop with some time the next morning would be sufficient. See the castle and the buildings within the walls, then S. Bento and S. Vincente which are very close to the castle. Avoid Thursdays when the castle is closed.

Miranda do Douro

It is difficult to say exactly why the traveler should go to Miranda do Douro. Hydroelectric dams are not our favorite scenic wonder, but this one filled the bottom of an enormous chasm, out of which rises the sheer rock wall of Spain, creating a gorge of wild beauty. From the balconies of the Pousada S. Clara the view is of the sun rising over this in a big red ball — or at the right phase, of the moon in a big white ball.

We decided that we would not want to be slung across its span in a basket as Wellington is reputed to have been, but it gave us new respect for the English hero of the Peninsular War. I wouldn't even want to cross it on a bridge. Fortunately, the Spanish border crossing is at the dam level far below.

Of the castle, little remains, it having been blown to bits along with 400 inhabitants in 1762 when a cannon shell hit a powder magazine. Far better castles fill the region. Of the old town within its walls, and its once fine houses, little remains, but wandering through its narrow streets one notes, on glancing upward, some fine gargoyles and other remnants of the stonework of ancestral homes. Grimacing little faces, and one that can only be a human bottom, jut from occasional housefronts.

It is not over-tidied and painted like some pousada towns, which, although lovely, appear almost as stage sets. It is an active rural town where on Sunday mornings the strolling visitor may easily see a lady selling her cow and calf in the street beside the cathedral.

The former cathedral, still called the Sé, even though the actual seat of authority passed to Bragança over two centuries ago, was built in 1553 by the confessor to Queen Catherine, designed by the architect who did Tomar. Along with its fine baroque altars and organ it is noted for the peculiar little statue, "Christ in a Top Hat," much loved and revered by local residents.

Behind the Sé a roofless cloister has been made into a lovely garden with a cafe and public conveniences. Score one for Miranda do Douro! There is a nice little Misericordia church and nearby is a square with a fine loggia.

There are other attractions to this area as well. The road from
the north, along the ridges and through the mountains is magnificent; the road to the south is lower, through farmland, looking up
at the fascinating stegosaurus-shaped hills with rocky outcroppings
along their backs.

To the north is Vimioso, a brightly white town on a hillside,
every balcony trailing flowers. The great church here runs uphill
— its floor sloping up from the door to the baroque altar. A pair
of very fine polychrome angels top the altar columns. It has
excellent painting on the stone chancel vaulting and a fine ceiling
with carved boisseries. It is so hard to find good examples of
unrestored (read "unstripped") churches in Portugal, that Vimioso
is worth the stop for this alone.

Vimioso is also the only place between Braga and Miranda do
Douro with a restaurant — and there is quite a nice one. South
from Vimioso a road leads to Campo de Vibora and about 7 km
further to Algoso, where there is a castle well worth the detour.
(Note that one of the early books about Portugal sets this castle in
Campo de Vibora and some later books have merely repeated it,
much to the confusion of travelers who arrive there looking for a
castle.)

Algoso is an attractive little farming town where tourists are
rare and are treated like honored guests. The dour civil servants,
those misbegotten Cicerones who guard the royal palaces, could
take a few lessons from the charming women who fix the altar
flowers throughout Portugal. These ladies may not know the exact
measurement of the sacristy ceiling, but you won't miss a cranny
with them as guides.

It is their land, their town, their parish church, their castle from
under whose shadow they have never traveled. They marvel when
told that we come from a land without castles, and a look through
a zoom lens will provide stories for their grandchildren.

It was just such a lady who took us to the castle in the town of
Algoso. We stopped to peek into the church, for you never know
what treasures may be hiding in a little parish church. It rewarded
our curiosity with polychrome angels and cherubs. Those on the
side altars in the chancel are excellent examples of decoration
remaining in few churches — ecclesiastical folk art.

But its crowning achievement is the side altar on the south wall
with a large polychrome bas relief of Christ saving souls from the

fires of hell. The demons are black and wicked, leering amid tongues of bright red flame. A monk in a black robe is busy pulling little naked people from their grasp, using his cincture. Their faces show appropriate terror or gratitude depending upon their position in the scene. And above it all, a placid Christ receives them. When we write a book about the great classics of folk art, this will be on the cover.

We asked about the castle: could we drive there and which way was it. The key to the castle, said one of the altar guild ladies, a slight thing all dressed in black and old beyond her years, was up the street, and the key to the chapel was with someone else. Just the castle, we said, would be fine.

"But you must see the chapel! It has a painting of the miracle of the baby saved from the jaws of the crocodile! That is where it happened, on that very mountain — and there is the skin — this long — to prove it! The chapel is right by the castle."

There was no resisting the enthusiasm that lit her face. "I will take you" she said and we pushed aside our traveling library to make room for her in the back seat. We stopped by a Roman column in a little square where the houses had carved door and window frames and she went to a lady using a yarn winder, who took a key from her pocket.

In front of nearly every house was a woman knitting or crocheting and I remembered the beautiful needlework of all the altar cloths in the little church. Our guide waved out of the window to each of them as we passed, "Adeus, Adeus" they all called as she was born off grandly in her chauffeured Citroen.

As we drove up the hill she took out her own needlework — a nine-inch square with an intricate design, which she was knitting on crochet hooks. It takes her a year, she told us, to make a really fine bedspread. That's what the ladies were working on.

The castle sits on a pinnacle, at its foot only an olive tree, a couple of small almond trees and the chapel. She swung its door open and there indeed was the unlikely S. George, ax in hand, the fierce crocodile, the little pink baby in its mouth, the horrified mother and above, Our Lady bringing the miracle. "And there," she pointed, "is the skin of the crocodile to prove it!" Above the painting (a primitive gem dated 1917), was the skin.

The castle above was not an anticlimax. From its round walls we could see range upon range. But even more beautiful than the mountains were the cultivated fields and hilltops below, with their almond orchards and olive groves. And to the south a sheer drop to the river which had cut a path deep into the stones, but was barely a trickle in the fall. Over it, almost blending into the stones of the riverbed in the late afternoon shade was a beautiful Roman bridge, a little track winding down and across it and up the other side. It was a glimpse into history, "You should see it," she told us, "In the spring when the wildflowers cover everything; everywhere there are flowers."

Beyond Algoso, on a new road that doesn't show on most maps, is Azinhoso, just beyond the small city of Mogadouro. Azinhoso also has an excellent castle, around which a town clusters, with little farm sheds backed right up to its walls. If it is clear you can see the castle at Algoso and the one at Mogadouro.

The border here is lined with the remains of these, in now remote towns at the crests of hills. When the castles were in use, they could see signals from one to the other and alert the entire frontier of any Spanish aggression. Looking at the rocky chasm the Douro has cut between the two countries along here, it is hard to imagine an army even considering an attack across it but they frequently did.

Mogadouro is an attractive little city with a Templars castle keep built on solid rock. Right under it are the remains of a once-fine stone building with houses built into its stone walls. The old convent of S. Francisco has a fine facade and is so packed on Sunday morning that there is no room to get in the door.

The area here is filled with wild birds: swallows swoop around the castles and larks, cuckoos, nightingales and warblers sing. A list of 63 different varieties of birds spotted along the 25 km road between Miranda do Douro and Picote alone has been compiled by a gentleman who comes often to the Pousada S. Clara. Sr. Leite has a copy (with Portuguese, English, and Latin names) and guests with an interest in birds should ask to see it.

Miranda do Douro At A Glance

Border town 83 km south of Bragança, Spanish border crossing.
LODGING: The Pousada S. Catarina (73/42255) stands out for its view, hanging as it does above the chasm, but even more for its exceptionally hospitable staff. It's worth traveling to Miranda for. Under the management of Sr. Pedro Soares Leite, this pousada is the

essence of what these hosteleries were meant to be. The girl at the front desk does not have to consult a list as you stand hoping that the telex with your reservation was correctly received. She knows who the night's guests are just as the hostess in a private country home would know. This inn glows with the genuine hospitality of its director, who makes a point of meeting each of his guests personally. It is beautifully furnished, its cafe is on a balcony overlooking the river and it is well located two blocks from the castle and cathedral. Doubles are from $40 to $60.

There is also a pensão, the Planalto (73/ 42362), which is clean and well located. In Mogadouro the Lareira (79/ 32363), a very good restaurant, has a few rooms as well.

FOOD: *There is no question that the best meals are served at the pousada, with local specialties such as trout, pumpkin cream soup, Ensopado de Cabrito (kid stew) and Favas a Trasmontana (beans with sausage). These hearty country dishes take on a lighter, more sophisticated, touch here without losing their distinctive character. There are restaurants in town, some of them quite good. The Buteca across from the Misericordia serves local fare at about $5 apiece with wine, in its upstairs dining room. In Mogadouro there is a very good French restaurant, Alareira, with meals in the $15 range. In Sendim, between Mogadouro and Miranda do Douro, the Gabriela serves hearty lunches and dinner at under $10.*

In Vimioso, the Restaurant Crazeiro is in a square below and to the right of the church. The dining room is upstairs over the cafe and their vegetable soup is rich, thick and delicious — don't miss it. From soup to fresh melon, lunch runs about $7.50 with wine.

SHOPPING: *Border towns tend to have a lot of goods displayed for the Spanish shoppers, but there are some good antique shops in Miranda as well as copper, woodcarving and embroidery. Traditional embroidered capes are produced in the area — you'll not find them elsewhere. For magnificent handmade bedspreads enquire at the pousada, or go to Algoso and ask any of the ladies crocheting. You'll soon have several to choose from at prices far below the (still reasonable) pousada price. There is a market in Vimioso 9 to 12 and 2 to 7 each weekday, and shops in Miranda do Douro stay open into the early evening.*

FESTIVALS: *The major event is the Festa de S. Barbara on the first Sunday following the 15th of August. Here you will see the traditional stick dance, quite unlike the regional dances elsewhere.*

There are festivals in several of the towns in the area during that same week in August, so be sure to reserve lodging early.

IF TIME IS SHORT: *This whole corner is bypassed by many tourists who travel straight from Bragança to Mogadouro through Izeda. It is still possible to see the castles of Azinhoso and Algoso by taking a side trip north from Mogadouro. There are no "must see" sights in Miranda do Douro, except for an autumn moonrise.*

Fortified Towns of the Beira Alta

One of Portugal's most interesting regions is also one of its least visited — perhaps because so little is written about it. All along the Spanish frontier are these towns crowned with castles, most of which are in some state of ruin. Some of these are close to other attractions or large cities, such as Marvão and Castelo Vide, but most lie in a line beginning north of Pinhel and ending a little north of Castelo Branco. A few are farther inland at the foothills of the Serra da Estrela and are mentioned in that section, while border castles of the north and the south are described in the sections with their neighboring towns.

Castelo Rodrigo, an ancient town that towers over its younger brother Figueira de Castelo Rodrigo is a dramatic beginning to this route of fortifications. The road up to the castle is marked just south of the new town and leads up past the fountain through a gate in the defensive walls. Inside is a stone village and the very early church of N.S. de Reclamador. At the top of the castle, its walls and tower still standing, a bell tower is built into its walls. One of the best views of the gate and the castle is from the top of this tower, which has iron stairs clinging to the back of it. From there, too, one can look down into the streets of the village and on the pattern of tile roofs below.

There are two interesting places that can be seen in a very short side trip from Castelo Rodrigo. The road straight ahead upon leaving the gate leads to a larger road across the valley floor toward Redondo and Almofala. Only a short distance after turning right onto this road is a large church set in a lovely green farm. This is the thirteenth century convent of S. Maria de Aguiar, pillaged by Massena's troops, left empty for a century upon the dissolution of the holy orders, then stripped by the Ancient Monuments Commission. Its cloister now houses a farm, where the owners are happy to open the great nave for visitors.

The church stands nearly empty, great stone tombs along its edges, its carved and gilded altar stripped away, the remains of its magnificent choir stalls stacked in the little sacristy. Through its

Manueline door are the remaining treasures — two fine poly-chrome statues of S. Bernard and S. Benedict, and S. Catherine in marble, and some stone details including a lion rescued from the church.

The vaulting in the nave is excellent, and the Chapter House, opening off the cloister by a door in the convent wall, has a finely vaulted ceiling. The adjoining house has a lovely Renaissance loggia on the far end.

About 3 km past S. Maria is a left turn to Almofala and 3½ km further is a dirt track leading to a very curious Roman structure which can be seen from the main road. Although overgrown toward the end, the track is passable right to this "Casarão da Torre." Its foundations are definitely those of a Roman temple — and a rather imposing one. Built upon that base is what appears to be a later structure, the total effect of which is most peculiar, it being set in the middle of farmlands, standing out above the grass and trees.

Pinhel lies 20 km southwest of Castelo Rodrigo over the wild and stony Serra de Marofa past the rocky gorge cut by the Coa River. It is an attractive town, its houses graced with wrought iron balconies and coats of arms. Two towers of its castle are still standing and there is a pillory in the main square. Just south is the large dolmen of Anta de Pera do Moco, a huge slab of granite supported by five standing stones.

There is a secondary road leading to Almeida from Pinhel, across a desolate rock-strewn plateau. A crossroad leads left to Almeida. Alternately, Pinhel can be bypassed via a good road directly from Castelo Rodrigo to Almeida.

The eighteenth century fortification of Almeida are of the classic style, a six-pointed star with separate salients. They are exceedingly well preserved, and for fortification buffs, they are a must. The old town sits within the inner set of walls. The entire town is surrounded by a ditch 40 feet deep (these were always waterless ditches, not moats) crossed by two bridges leading to gates high in the walls and one road entering through a lower gate at ditch level.

During the Peninsular War the fort changed hands back and forth between Wellington and Massena, the scene of fierce battles, but today it is a peaceful, lovely, well-kept village. The new pousada sits with its balconies overlooking a fountain, doorsteps, the donkey carts and the general life of the village. These pousada towns are very well lit at night and this one is delightful to stroll in, since it has some fine homes and pleasant parks. Its white buildings should be seen at sunrise when they are starkly contrasted to the still dark streets.

Since the town was laid out within the fortress rather than having grown around it, the streets are wide and fairly straight. So much of village life takes place out of doors that it is almost like being in someone's house to sit on the balcony and overlook a series of scenes of domestic life.

South of Almeida at Vila Formoso, there is a new limited access road to Guarda which does not yet show up on most maps. It bypasses the next castles completely, so unless you plan to go directly to Guarda, drive past the Guarda signs and go west at a little unmarked triangle just past it.

Castelo Bom is only a short way, the village clustered at the top of a rocky mound. Never have we seen so many swallows or dooryard gardens. The narrow streets around the castle ruins are lined with tiny neat houses, each one with a tiny garden overflowing with flowers. The counterpoint of the bright flowers and gray stones is beautiful, and there is a stretch of remaining wall to walk. It traverses a gate before disappearing.

There isn't much left of the castle — a bit of tower and the stretch of wall with an arched gate — but the houses are built into its walls and out of its stones. This is a castle for someone who loves stone ruins and an excuse to poke about in someone's back-yard.

Across a rocky landscape strewn with boulders, cut by a deep ravine and spanned by the enormous bridge of the new highway, is Castelo Mendo. It is entered through a gate flanked by a pair of truncated towers and a pair of stone pigs. (This is supposed to be beyond stone pig country, but these certainly looked like stone pigs to us!) The gate is shared by cars, ox carts, cattle and people, all coming and going. Entrance to many of the homes here is from the second story reached by stone steps and graceful pillared porches. Both steps and porches are covered with pots of bright flowers.

The castle here is different from the rest. Although the town itself sits high above the olive groves below, the top is flat, surrounded by walls, with only low foundations remaining of the castle. The wide steps are cut into bedrock and ascend to a ruined chapel, its roof gone, its nave grown to brambleberries. The altar, pulpit stairs, font, and all the stonework remain, and where there is plaster, some of the frescoes remain.

A road south just beyond Castelo Mendo leads to Sabugal, an attractive town built on a pinnacle directly above the Coa River, which is crossed by a medieval bridge. The riverbank is planted with an attractive and very well-manicured formal garden which the castle overlooks. Entrance is through a tall arched gate and inside is a busy country village with freshly harvested corn spread out to dry on sheets in the square below the castle. Cars drive carefully around the corn and ladies sit in the late morning on their doorsteps shredding kale for their Caldo Verde.

The castle is beautifully preserved with good battlement towers and ramparts intact all around. There is a pentagonal keep with fine fan groined vaulting on two levels; the hearty can climb all the way to the top. Over the entrance gate is an overhanging battlement with a hole in its stone for pouring dreadful things onto attackers. This is a four-star castle, in fine original condition, it is about as good as you will see anywhere.

Further on and less well known, although Sabugal is hardly overrun with tourists, is Sortelha. The town is smaller and is clustered inside its castle walls, its architecture more aristocratic. Stone houses have lovely porches and stairs lined with potted flowers. At the top is a fine small castle, with its outer walls much intact, set into one edge of the stone walls.

Perhaps it's the size of this castle, or its setting, but it has a more fairy-tale castle quality than Sabugal. The wall into which it is set continues to rise, as do the stone streets cut into solid rock, and from the top of these walls one can look down on the top of the castle perched on the edge of its precipice over the valley of the Zezere. It's no wonder that Hans Christian Anderson loved Portugal.

The last four castles have stood along a rocky plateau, cut by olive groves and some agriculture, but often just rock-strewn slopes. From Sortelha the road drops into a rich green valley with farms and trees, donkey carts full of hay and people working their fields. From this fertile valley rises Penamacor. The cobbled street up to the castle is one of the more exciting vertical approaches, as it goes past a lovely church facade and becomes steeper yet. At the top, the keep rises out of fig trees and overlooks a valley full of olive trees. The sound of cow bells comes drifting up the slope. This castle is not as well preserved as the others, but the town is pure medieval. There are some good Manueline windows and doors and the women here sit on their doorsteps crocheting.

Monsanto, by some mistake, was once voted the "most Portuguese town." Perhaps it is, in the sense that the country is full of surprises and the minute you think that you know what to expect you find something different. Monsanto is certainly different from any other town. It is built not on top of, but into the side of a gigantic outcropping of rock. Most of its streets are steep steps carved from base rocks. It is the only town I know where the streets have switchbacks.

Houses are built into, under and on top of, huge boulders. Streets are so narrow that instead of sitting on their doorsteps, ladies do their mending sitting on the stone steps of the street itself. Climbing to the top we found round pig pens made of stone with beehive-like stone igloos in them. They reminded us of the walls of the Celtic houses in the Citânias of the north.

A road to the south leads to Idanha-a-Velha with its huge walled enclosure with a Roman portal and a tower built on the base of a Roman temple. The Roman settlement there has been partially excavated and visitors can see this by inquiring of anyone living nearby.

These hill towns are not far apart. With determination, and an early start, one could leave Almeida and see all the hill towns south of this in one day, with daylight to spare. Seeing means not just driving by, but climbing around in, and climbing up to the top of, and wandering the streets of, each of them.

Fortified Towns At A Glance

Strung along the Spanish frontier they run from Castelo Rodrigo, 57 km northeast of Guarda, to Monsanto, 51 km northeast of Castelo Branco.

LODGING: The new Senhora de Neves Pousada (71/54283) at Almeida is lovely, roomy, airy and bright, built around a patio, it has balconies all around the outer walls. The smell of bread baking wafts in the window in the morning from the town below. There are private lounges for guests on the upper floors. Doubles are from $50 to $80 depending on the season. Beyond the pousada, lodging in the region is widely scattered. Sabugal has the four-star Albergaria S. Isabel

(71/ 92412) which is very pleasant. In nearby Sortelha there are a number of manor houses, stately houses and old houses which are open for bed and breakfast. Casa de Patio (71/ 68113) is a characteristic country cottage in a rural setting while Casa Árabe (71/68129) and Casa do Vento Que Soa (71/ 68182) are a bit fancier. All are comfortable and give a rare chance to be inside a Portuguese home.

At Monfortinho, a spa near Monsanto, the Astoria (77/ 44205) is a classic spa hotel and 30 of its rooms have private baths. Da Fonte Santa(77/ 44104) is in the same moderate price range, but these are open only during the summer spa season. Guarda, only 40 km of good road from Castelo Bom and Castelo Mendo, has several choices.

FOOD: *In addition to the pousada there is a nice little local restaurant just outside the gate at Almeida: the Portas de Almeida serves a typical variety of dishes for about $6 a person. In Castelo Rodrigo, the Pensão Santos has a nice little restaurant. There are a few in Sabugal and two good ones in Sortelha. One, the Alboroque, is uphill from the castle inside the walled town and serves regional specialties (closed Mondays). Every bit as good is O Celta, the little restaurant shortly to the left of the town gate. It is in a new little building with cafe in front and dining room in the rear. Their Caldeiro of Cabrito is delicious and plentiful (they'll serve you seconds) and the service is exceptionally friendly. All of this, a bottle of wine and coffee at about $11 for two.*

FESTIVALS: *Monsanto's colorful procession of Marofonas on May 3.*

IF TIME IS SHORT: *Choose Sabugal and Sortelha, close together and with contrasting castles, and Monsanto, not because it is "typical," but because it is so unusual.*

Serra da Estrela and Guarda

The mountains of the Serra da Estrela which cut through the center of the Beira Baixa, were once a barrier to travel, but are now an attraction of their own. There are several roads across and among these mountains, each with scenery more breathtaking than the last. Instead of describing each route (How many ways are there to say spectacular?) we shall mention several places in and around the park and simply state that any route through here is steep, the landscape wild and the vistas grand. In the winter, check to see if the roads are open (advice not usually needed in Portugal).

At the northern tip of the park is Celorica da Beira, the large square keep of its castle rising above it. The Igreja Matriz there has a good painted ceiling. To the north is Trancoso, a walled city with lovely old arcaded streets. The wall itself has square bastions and decorated arch gates, with a castle in one corner under its keep. Photographers note that the best view of the town and battlements is from the north road where it stands against the Serra da Estrela. Once an important town, it was the scene of the wedding of King Dinis and Isabel of Aragon — and the beginning of her charitable work.

A secondary road leads into the Parque Natural da Serra da Estrela from Celorica, connecting to a crossroad between Guarda and the western boundary, passing Linhares. Another, better, road skirts the edge of the park, and Linhares may also be reached from this. It is a tiny village with a fine walled castle and many fifteenth century houses with fine stonework. Its streets are best toured on foot unless the car is very small and has very good springs. Near the castle is a fine early council chamber and two town houses, but all through the village there are fine doors and windows. Both churches have very good primitive paintings. The riches of Linhares, and other nearby ruins, make it clear that this meager road across the Serra was once the main one!

From Gouveia a tortuous road crosses a rock-strewn plateau before dropping terrifyingly into Manteigas in its beautiful mountain setting at the head of a long valley. A road to the south leads past a belvedere to the Pouco do Inferno, a gorge with a waterfall.

The trip to Belmonte is smooth, through farmland, a pleasant drive after the descent. Another of the castles built by King Dinis, Belmonte retains only its keep and battlements (and a badly restored cement front), but the walls make a fine walk. Followers of the Portuguese explorers in the New World will note the statue of Cabral, discoverer of Brazil, and his tomb in the Igreja de S. Tiago. The church is very early with an unusual pulpit and a polychrome stone pieta.

About 4 km north of Belmonte is the Roman Centum Cellas, off a road signposted to Comeal de Torre. This tall Roman or pre-Roman tower is built of granite blocks, but there is no definitive answer as to its intended use.

To the south lies Covilha, a ski resort known for its woolen blankets. This combination tells us something of its winter weather. Covilha is a mixture of new and old with modern facilities and some of the steepest, narrowest, streets west of Monsanto. From Covilha there are two routes across the Serra, the northern one passing through the ski area of Penhas de Saude and a glacial valley to the north. A short road leads south to the summit of Torre, with yet more panoramic views, then the road follows a plateau before dropping into Seia.

The southern road follows the national park boundaries along a less precipitous route through little villages clinging to the slopes. A turn north brings it to Seia, or a short secondary road shortly after Chamusea leads to the main road and to Oliveira do Hospital. Its setting is lovely and the Igreja Matriz there has a superb trompe l'oeil ceiling and good early stone-carved tombs. Three km west at Bobadela there is a Roman arch.

Guarda is Portugal's highest city at over 3,000 feet. It is not its prettiest, but it has a stern air of grandeur. It is known to the Portuguese of other regions as "forte, feia, friae, farta": strong, ugly, cold and rich. There is some truth in that: only a New Englander could love a winter there, with the raw winds and wet snow. But in the summer, its public garden on the belvedere is bright with flowers and overlooks a fertile green valley.

The old houses around its square bear armorial crests and its arcaded streets are filled with fine buildings. The baroque facade of the Misericordia stands out in fine contrast to the face of the Sé. It is said to have been influenced by Batalha, and the similarities are evident in its buttresses and pinnacles. But instead of the warm, creamy-colored stone of Batalha, it is of cold, gray granite which makes it look more like a holy fortress, more appropriate for its hilltop city and its setting beneath the gate of a medieval tower. It was once the outpost of the Roman legions and still has about it the staunch flavor of a capital of a frontier province.

Inside, the cathedral has some fine features taken from the various periods of its construction. Twisted Manueline pillars flank the chancel arch framing an altar covered with finely carved figures. The choir stalls have strange carved under-seats with grimacing faces, much like those at Lorvão and Arouca. In the south transept a stair ascends around a column to the roof, where, as at Milan, the world can be viewed from between the pinnacles.

Guarda is a good base for touring both the Serra da Estrela and the castle towns to the east. The Castelos Bom and Mendo and Almeida are easily reached by taking the new highway to Vilar Formoso.

The Serra da Estrela And Guarda At A Glance

Provincial capital 364 km from Lisbon and 218 km from Porto, near the national park and spectacular mountain scenery.

LODGING: There are two pousadas in the Serra da Estrela. At Manteigas, or about 13 km straight up from it, is the Pousada S. Lourenço (75/ 47150), a rustic mountain lodge with splendid views, in the lowest price group from $40 to $60. The other is the Pousada S. Barbara (38/ 52252) in Oliveira do Hospital on the west rim of the national park. The views are lovely and rates are between $50 and $80 for a double. In Guarda, the best hotel is the Turismo (71/ 22205), centrally located and long established, with doubles in the $50 range. The Residência Filipe (71/ 22659) is a little less expensive and the Quinta de S. José (71/ 96210) is a lovely farm villa on the outskirts. In Covilha there is the Estralagem da Varanda dos Carqueijais (75/ 24071) as well as numerous pensions. Manteigas has the Hotel Manteigas (32/ 47114) at the spa just out of town, with doubles in the same range of $45 to $50. The Casa de S. Roque (75/ 47125) is a very nice guest house, with lower rates and more personal surroundings.

Gouveia and Seia, within the park, have stately homes that accept guests, the Casa Grande (38/ 42204) and the Casa do Oitão (38/ 42688), both are in Paços da Serra just outside of Gouveia. Casa da Ponte (38/ 93351) and Vila Eduarda (38/ 92174) near Seia are two other good choices. In the park above Guarda the Quinta da Ponte (71/ 685597) is a lovely villa in the village of Faia.

FOOD: *The Serra is famous for its cheeses made from ewes' and goats' milk. The food here is hearty with excellent stews and braised meat dishes, and fish from local rivers. Along with the pousadas and hotels mentioned, there are several restaurants in Guarda. The Belo Horizonte is modest in price and long on hospitality, on the Largo S. Vincente. On the main road are the Mexicana (not Mexican, but very Portuguese) and the Telheiro, the former in the under $10 range and the latter at a little more. The Camelo in Seia and the Lareira in nearby Sabuqueiro are both good and under $10.*

SHOPPING: *Wool blankets and sheepskin crafts are made here and are sometimes for sale by the roadside, especially between Seia and Gouveia. The Fair in Covilha the last week of June is a good place to find country crafts.*

FESTIVALS: *Trancoso has the Feira de S. Bartolomeu in August, and the second Sunday in August is the pilgrimage of N.S. da Boa Estrela at the shrine near the summit of Torre. The Feira de S. Tiago is June 22-30 in Covilha.*

IF TIME IS SHORT: *There is nothing here the traveler must see, but many things worth seeing. Pass through the park en route from Porto to the Alentejo or make side trips into the area from Viseu or the eastern border route.*

Castelo Branco

We always think of Castelo Branco as much smaller than it is; it leaves the impression of a small town, with its broad plazas, cafes, little shops, restaurants and gardens. These center around the city's main attraction, the beautiful Gardens of the Bishops Palace. Set in terraces, the garden is laid out in formal beds bounded by sculpted hedges and punctuated by statuary. In the center of the main section is a fountain and pool in an elaborate arabesque shape. Winter is probably the best time to admire the beautiful design of these gardens, when the hedge design shows up clearly without tall flowers. It's all green then, in boxwood and orange trees.

Summer fills the beds with annual flowers placed in the hedge bordered beds, and sets the garden alive with color. Stairways are lined with statues of the twelve apostles and of the kings of Portugal. Always ready for a snipe at the Spanish, the kings of the period of the Spanish domination are shown smaller than the Portuguese kings. Stairs to the street level are bordered in azulejos, as are the walls of this lower garden. It is a remarkable and lovely garden, even for Portugal which is filled with fine gardens.

Next door is the Episcopal Palace, now a museum with fine Arras tapestries and examples of colchas, the bedspreads embroidered by local girls. These were traditionally part of a trousseau, but at the embroidery school attached to the museum, they can be made to order.

The Misericordia church to the left of the garden gate is not worth crossing the square to see (although you are certain to do it anyway, just in case we missed something). To the right is a bustling square with cafes, shops and restaurants — a thoroughly pleasant place to stop for lunch or coffee. Although there are castle ruins up the hill, they are not outstanding. But there is the Miradouro, a park-like belvedere near them with views out over the red roof tops of Castelo Branco and the countryside.

Northeast of the city at Idanha-a-Nova, there are ruins of a Templar castle and an eighteenth century manor with some fine houses surrounding it. Nearby is the shrine of N.S. de Almortão, where there is an enormous pilgrimage on the first weekend of April.

Further along at the old border town of Segura, there is a large gate, all that is left of the defensive walls that once encircled the town. Segura has the dubious distinction of being the first entry point of French troops during the Peninsular War, and its Roman bridge indicates that the French weren't the first army to march through town. For all of its battering, it is still an attractive old town and has a Manueline Misericordia.

Castelo Branco At A Glance

Provincial capital, 155 km southeast of Coimbra.

LODGING: Scarce in Castelo Branco, whose position halfway between the resort areas of the Serra da Estrela and the tourist meccas of Evora and Estremoz has made it a pass-through and lunch stop between Manteigas and Marvão. There are two perfectly adequate pensãos, however, the Caravela (72/ 23939) and the Arraiana (72/ 21634) are both clean and comfortable, if plain. The first charges about $15 for a double, the latter about $25.

FOOD: Restaurants are more plentiful and, while not fancy, serve good food at very reasonable prices. There are several around the square to the right of the garden. The Arcadia is further into the center of the city on the main square and the Terminal is on the Montalvão road. Meals at either of these will be under $10.

SHOPPING: The major local art here is the colcha and, although expensive, these bedspreads are quite lovely, done in muted colors usually on linen. Visit the embroidery school to see these made and to enquire about custom work.

FESTIVALS: The Romaria de N.S. de Almortão includes a market with local crafts and goods in addition to spontaneous song and dance. It's the first weekend of April. If you go, reserve a room early.

IF TIME IS SHORT: Stop long enough to see the garden, which is right on the main road from Coimbra. The road passes the garden just as a little footbridge crosses over it.

Portalegre, Marvão and
Castelo de Vide

Portalegre is well named; it is a light hearted city. In spite of its location near the Spanish border and its long history since the days when it was a major Roman center, nothing major ever happened here. But it is not without a history, however quiet it may have been. Ruins of the castle that once crowned it and the lovely seventeenth and eighteenth century mansions that line the streets leading up from the Cathedral (especially Rua 19 de Junho) are relics of its long past. Two local museums are filled with folk (José Regio Museum) and sacred (Municipal Museum) collections.

The Sé stands out for it unusual facade and has a good sacristy with azulejo walls and impressive vestment chests. Its eighteenth century cloister has oval windows over its arches. It is not uncommon to see a donkey cart in the street, and much of everyday life goes on in its streets as it does in many small villages.

To its north is Nisa, with the ruins and gate of one of the area's oldest castles, built by King Dinis in the thirteenth century. It is a market town, pleasant and busy, but quite small.

West of Nisa, at a turn to the north in Gavião, is Belver, with a castle well worth the detour. It is near the main road from this part of the Alentejo to Lisbon through Abrantes. Belver is approached by a road that winds down the steep banks of the Tagus (Tejo) to a single lane bridge. The very well preserved castle rises above the river and the town, in a setting very reminiscent of the Rhine valley.

It is a beautifully stationed castle, still retaining the elegance it knew when it was built by the Order of Hospitalers, with its rectangular walls and round towers. It is reached by a path whose stairs are cut out of bedrock. It is on the hot climb to this castle that one learns how little shade there is from an olive tree.

Ask at one of the houses near the square below for the key, but don't expect to find it between 12 and 2, and don't plan to eat at the only restaurant in town. If you have an extra minute, look into the church in the largo below — it is badly restored, but has a fine stone pulpit standing stairless on a single delicate pillar.

Both Nisa and Portalegre are overshadowed, figuratively, by the nearby fortified towns of Marvão and Castelo de Vide. Far from undiscovered, these towns are probably the most visited of all of Portugal's border hill towns, yet manage to maintain their own way of life as though there weren't people taking pictures.

Marvão is spruced up a bit more now that the pousada has opened up in three of its fine old houses, but a fresh coat of whitewash hasn't robbed it of its charm or its power. The traveler will be well fed and well housed in Marvão, and if, in the process, the local residents have been able to improve their standard of living and restore some of the beautiful buildings on their hilltop, so much the better.

It is difficult for us to be objective about Marvão. We first saw it on a foggy morning in March with nine-year-old Julie. It was her first castle, and we had chosen well. We had it all to ourselves, the mists rising about its stones, drifting past, sometimes isolating it not only from the Spanish plain below, but from its own town as well.

We explored its ramparts, then sat on the damp stones and watched as she manned each battle station, darted between crenellations, curtsied to each passing knight, rode forth in full armor into battle and returned triumphant with the victors. She was alternately the king, the queen, several knights, and a princess. She has walked the ramparts of many castles since, but Marvão will always be "Castle" to her and to us.

It's a different place in the sunlight, under the blue Alentejo sky. Its stones melt from gray to a warm honey color and the world spreads off below into mountains, plains and infinity.

Unlike other towns where tourists come, Marvão's streets aren't lined with shops. They are in fact curiously empty, as though no one lived there. But there are curtains at the windows (many of which have fine Manueline frames) and flower pots on the doorsteps, and the local baker is busy making bread for someone. We are told that most of Marvão's men work in the fields and vineyards below.

These Alentejo towns are a blinding white in the sun, their thick-walled houses rising like steps along the cobbled streets, each layer looking down on the red tiled roofs of the layer below. There is nothing here that must be seen except the castle itself. At its approach is a lovely sunken garden, with hedges of rosemary and tall, rich, red dahlias.

Just west of Marvão is Castelo de Vide, also on an outcropping of rock, but spilling down the hillside, too big for the small, walled enclosure at the top. It is possible to drive right to the gates of this enceinte, which open onto one of Portugal's many perfect street scenes. But this one is even better. Out of the tiny spaces between the stone pavement and the buildings grow shrubs and vines, and where there is no room for a foothold, clay pots of all sizes are set beside the doorsteps. Thus greenery and flowers cover the white walls, with an occasional bird cage hanging among the leaves. This Rua Direita is short, but well lived in, with people, laundry, cats and activity joining the plants in the narrow space between its walls.

The castle above is mostly in ruins, but a stairway leads up from a little outcrop of rock in one corner to a section of wall. From there one can walk along a roof to a keep. This overlooks the mosaic of roof tops of the Judaira below. The Judaira, although exceedingly steep, is well worth exploring since it contains the finest assemblage of ogival doors in Portugal. It is the best preserved and largest of the country's old Jewish quarters, and one of the few authentic ones remaining in all of Europe.

Below this steep area, the town levels out a bit into pleasant squares filled with cafes. This is a town to relax in, a busy place humming with people, in contrast to Marvão's almost ghost town atmosphere. Perhaps all of the residents of Marvão work here!

Southeast of Portalegre, almost to the Spanish border is the little town of Alegrete, certainly off of the normal tourist route. It is a tiny town completely enclosed by the outer wall of its castle. It has some fine doorways and windows and is, like Castelo Vide, covered with flowers. It is well worth the 22 km round trip.

Directly west of Portalegre is Crato with remains of a castle, and a parish church with secular azulejos. The streets that radiate from the Praça de República are filled with seventeenth and eighteenth century houses. Just outside of Crato is Flor da Rosa which has a fourteenth century fortified monastery of the Knights Templar. Although there has been a lot of restoration, this is a fine group of monastic buildings within a crenellated wall. There is a small cloister with Gothic vaulting and a simple church with a very high nave. The key is at the farm just beyond the monastery.

South of Crato is Alter do Chão, whose fourteenth century castle overlooks a square paved in black and white mosaic of a tessellated design. A road to the west leads on to Seda, which has one of Portugal's finest Roman bridges, with six arches. It is still in use after two millennia — the Romans built for posterity.

The road south from Seda to Avis passes through beautiful countryside along a river widened by a dam. The Alentejo landscape is more rolling than the regions to the north, with dark cork forests and the pale silver-green of olive trees. Avis itself retains three of the original medieval towers in its ramparts. Of particular interest is the church of the convent of S. Bento with a sixteenth century sacristy.

East from Avis through Fronteiro with its seventeenth century houses, is Monforte. Its ruined castle dates from the early fourteenth century, and 4 km northwest at Torre de Palma are the extensive remains of a Roman settlement with a villa, Paleo-Christian basilica and burial site. Most interesting here, in this site overgrown with grass, are the remains of the baths, arches intact.

The town is an attractive one, its whitewashed houses topped with fat chimneys. There is a fine Roman bridge and, for those with a flair for the macabre, there is the Capela dos Ossos adjoining the Igreja Matriz. The walls are completely "faced" in human skulls. This is the sort of place that must be seen to be believed. It defies mere words.

Portalegre At A Glance

Small provincial city 240 km east of Lisbon.

LODGING: The Hotel Dom João III (45/ 21193) is a modern hotel overlooking a park right in the center of town. Double rooms are about $30 and it has a swimming pool and elevators. Most travelers prefer to stay in Marvão or in Castelo de Vide, each of which offers excellent lodging and the chance to explore the town in the evening. The Pousada S. Maria (45/ 93201) in Marvão is small, but beautifully located inside the walls of the castle in a series of three old houses rebuilt as a single facility. There are lovely arches and decorative details here, and the dining room overlooks the red tiled roofs below. Doubles are $50 to $80 depending on the season. Facing the castle is the three-star Estralagem Dom Dinis. Although not as elegant as the pousada, its rooms are spotless and comfortable with doubles from $42 to $48. In Castelo de Vide, the Hotel Sol e Serra faces onto a wide square in the lower part of town (no narrow streets to navigate!). Many rooms have balconies and doubles are about $45. The Albergaria Jardim, in the same price range, faces the same square, with overflow rooms at the slightly plainer Estralagem S. Paulo around the corner.

FOOD: Hands down, the best dinner in the area, a notch even above the pousada, is in the small dining room of the Estralagem Dom Dinis in Marvão. This is open to the public as well as to guests. The atmosphere, while attractive, is not as plush as the pousada's since, as is customary in many inns, there is a television set in the dining room. It is, however, unobtrusive and once the first morsel of food arrives you won't care. The menu is extensive with a full range of regional specialties. Do not fail to order the Açorda Alenteja, whose English translation "soup with egg and bread" should not deter you. For just under $1 you will be served an enormous bowl of rich delicious soup into which egg whites have been poached. This is poured over thick chunks of crusty, bread creating a dish both hearty and delicate at once. The febras, thin sliced scallops of pork, are outstanding as well, and the traditional pork with clams is superb. A complete meal with appetizer, entree, dessert, coffee, and excellent wine and mineral water was $20 for two. In Portalegre the hotel is a reliable and inexpensive choice with meals under $10, but we prefer Alpendre in the same price range or the equally good and even less expensive Assentos, where you may need a reservation at peak hours! Castelo de Vide has several restaurants along the main squares, and we suggest an evening stroll to "shop" by reading menus. The Dom Pedro V is always good, in the $10 to $15 range.

SHOPPING: Portalegre is justly famed for its tapestries, and visitors are welcome weekdays at the workshop in the old monastery. Nisa is known for its pottery which has tiny pieces of white stone embedded in the surface, as well as for its distinctive style of applique. Bold scroll and arabesque designs are cut from heavy felted woolen fabric — almost a melton cloth thickness — and appliqued onto a similar fabric of a contrasting color. The technique is used for dramatic table coverings as well as handbags, placemats and other small items. Marvão is known for willow baskets and there is an embroidery school in a tiny house on Rua Direita inside the walls at Castelo de Vide. Flor da Rosa is known for earthen ware, Monforte for woodcarving, and Portalegre for painted furniture. Castelo de Vide has a Friday market.

FESTIVALS: *Monforte's Feira da N.S. do Parto is August 15-17, Castelo de Vide has fairs January 15 and August 10 and Marvão has a Romaria on September 8.*

IF TIME IS SHORT: *Don't miss Marvão, if just to walk the walls of its castle. You won't find a better one with a better view.*

Elvas

The approach to Elvas is dominated dramatically by the gigantic aqueduct, its tiered round buttresses like giant wedding cakes holding up the arches of the aqueduct. Still in use as a water conduit, the aqueduct was built on Roman foundations and took over a century to complete.

Those who love to "walk the walls" of fortified towns will love Elvas, for there are 5 km of them, some dating from the thirteenth century. The history of Elvas's defenses echo that of nearly every other of these border fortresses: wrested away from the Moors, frequently besieged by the Spanish, and taken by Junot during the Peninsular War.

The street through its entrance gate leads uphill to the Praça de República, easy to recognize by the stern face of the former cathedral and by its inlaid pavement. Usually described as a checkerboard, the inlay is not a series of alternating squares as that suggests. It is a far more interesting series of parallelograms in three colors of stone, forming, depending on the angle of view, the three dimensional impression of a series of stairs or cubes all set on end. It brings energy to the square and softens the almost grim face of the church. Although no longer the episcopal seat, it is still often referred to as the cathedral and retains some of its grandeur, with marble columns, a fine organ and a painted ceiling in the sacristy.

Behind it is the unusual octagonal church of N.S. da Consolacão, entirely lined in polychrome azulejos, its lantern supported by marble pillars. It faces onto a Manueline pillory with iron dragonheads at the top.

The way uphill (everything in Elvas seems to be uphill or downhill) divides here, the street to the right ascends through a towered arch, the one to the left leads to the parade ground in front of the castle. Just before the parade ground is a street to the right, one of Elvas's loveliest. Ochre and cream-colored houses, covered with flowers, line its narrow cobbled street. Here, as on other streets, the doorways are unusually low as though built for a town of pygmies. This street ends in another little square adjoining the castle.

From the walls there is a view out over the valley but as we walked along the street below one morning, a man saw Julie with her little half frame camera. Would the little girl like a picture of the prettiest view in all of Elvas? Of course she would.

He led us inside a building through a series of rooms to a balcony overlooking the whole city, its red roof tops and white walls set against the green valley below. It was a soldiers home, and the old men were glad to have a little girl visit them. It left us with a warm feeling for Elvas, where a stranger would invite the traveler in to share a view, and where the town would set aside its loveliest location for its aging veterans.

Along the border north of Elvas is Campo Maior, an important headquarters during the Peninsular War despite the fact that its castle and fortifications were severely damaged when lightning struck its powder magazine in 1732. Shored up, it continued to withstand attack.

A road continues northeast through a wild countryside to end at the medieval town of Ouguela. Unlike most of these walled towns that are a warren of narrow streets full of houses all crowded inside the wall. Ouguela is spacious, its houses set around a campo with the ruins of a noble house. In good weather, life goes on in this common area which is living room, kitchen and front porch to the surrounding families. The castle overlooking this open air domesticity is from 1310.

South of Campo Maior is Castra Segovia, an important Iron Age settlement. Like all of these, it commands a hill; excavations proceed sporadically.

South of Elvas is Juromenha, another walled border town overlooking the Guardiana and Spain, and farther on, toward Redondo, the restored towers of Alandroal rise above its walls. Enclosed within them and overflowing below is a very attractive town.

Elvas At A Glance

Walled city 41 km east of Estremoz, may be reached by train and a moderate taxi ride.

LODGING: The Pousada de S. Luzia (68/ 62194) is quite small and is located outside the walls. It is also one of the older of this chain of inns, and a remodeling and enlarging has been planned for some time now. Rates are $40 to $60 for a double. More character, however, is offered at the Estralagem Dom Sancho II (68/ 62684) right on the main square. Although larger than the pousada, it is still fairly small, and reservations are a good idea. Small but well furnished doubles are $25 to $35. The largest hotel is the Dom Luis (68/ 62756), on the way to the Spanish border. Although well-equipped, its location is not within an evening stroll around town. Doubles are $35 to $40.

FOOD: Elvas plums are the definitive sugarplum, sticky, sweet and sinful. You can buy them in little sealed packets that will travel well if they last that long. The pousada in Elvas is better known for good food than it is for lodging and if you are not a guest, be sure to have a reservation, especially on Saturday and Sunday nights. Dinners are about $15 each. The Estralagem Dom Sancho II has a good dining room in the $10 range and the Cidade Nove, Aqueduto and Sagres are about the same price. Elvas is small enough that we suggest that you browse among the posted menus as you explore the town and make notes for evening reference.

SHOPPING: Besides plums, Elvas is noted for its striped woolen blankets, easily available in shops.

FESTIVALS: September 20-25 is the pilgrimage and fair of Senhor Jesus la Piedade, the major event of the area with markets, processions, and the works. You will need reservations even at nearby Estremoz during this event, since it is well attended.

IF TIME IS SHORT: Stay in Estremoz and see Elvas in a short side trip, allowing an hour or so to go from the main square to the castle and back, with short stops at the churches and castle and detours through streets that attract you.

Estremoz

The situation of the royal castle of King Dinis and Queen Isabel is unequaled: high on the rim of the protective ramparts, entered through a tangle of narrow cobbled streets inside the thick walls of the fortress. These castle-palaces were built atop hills for reasons of defensive strategy, but they offer the bonus of the finest views.

The pousada, unlike many others, is an attraction in its own right, and we strongly urge staying there even if you don't choose pousadas normally. It can be compared to living in a museum, and unless you stay you can't just wander about poking at things, especially on the second floor.

A grand marble staircase leads up from the vestibule to an encircling corridor; at the landing is a painting of the sainted queen, her skirts full of roses. At each turn in the corridor is a large arched doorway topped by an ornate gold cornice. Small sitting rooms are arranged at the corners, furnished like the public rooms, with Arraiolos carpets, Chinese porcelain — paintings, sculpture and antiques.

The doorway to each room is framed in false marble, a hand painted luxury in this land of marble quarries where the doorstep to the humblest home is marble.

Below, Estremoz is still a country town gathered around its Rossio. Its town hall is in an old convent. Not knowing its history, but recognizing it as an old and once great building, we stepped through its portal arch one morning to find city trucks being repaired in its roofless nave, and beautiful azulejos ascending the staircases along the side.

Another convent, S. Francisco, has a staircase frieze of azulejos of pink, green and yellow ribboned garlands and slender vases. The juxtaposition of these exquisitely delicate tiles with the present use of the building is quite a contrast: it is now a military barracks! But both of these convents are well cared for by their present occupants, however incongruous their uses, a far better fate than the many others which lie empty and desolate in advancing decay.

The adjoining Gothic church has a fine tomb and an interesting Jesse Tree. The hospital is in the former convent of the Knights of Malta, with two cloisters and fine tiles in the church.

The uphill town clusters about the keep, built entirely of marble. If the door is locked and the day is clear, ask at the desk at the pousada next door for the key. The view from the top seems to cover the entire Alentejo.

The sainted Queen Isabel, whose castle this was, died here and the room was later made into a chapel dedicated to her. Its walls are covered with azulejo scenes of events in the queen's life, including the one that has become her symbol, the skirt full of roses.

The good queen was generous to a fault, or so thought her husband, King Dinis, who paid the bills for her royal largess. Daughter of the King of Aragon, Isabel began her deeds during her wedding ceremonies when she invited the neighboring poor and fed them. The couple was followed by beggars even on their honeymoon, but she produced an heir before retiring entirely to her philanthropies.

Fearing bankruptcy, the king finally forbade her charities, which she continued in secret. The rose legend, also told of her aunt, the sainted Queen Elizabeth of Hungary, is that he caught her one morning as she left the palace with loaves of bread for the poor concealed in her skirt. He demanded to see them and when she opened her apron it was full of roses. Deceiving one's husband is a peculiar path to sainthood, but she was indeed a kind-hearted soul, for she welcomed all nine of the king's illegitimate children into the royal household.

While one wonders at the reaction of Queen Isabel to the present opulence of her palace, it is easier to see Dinis, "The Farmer King", standing atop the marble tower surveying the fields of the Alentejo. He was a wise and far-sighted king who encouraged agriculture by offering bonuses and establishing experimental farms: he would be pleased with the patchwork of fields and pasture below.

The king's audience chamber contains a beautiful Gothic colonnade, and the white church of S. Maria, which replaced an earlier Gothic structure, is also in the largo at the foot of the keep. There is a new municipal museum in the square with architectural and ethnographic collections, including local crafts, ancient relics, historic furniture and implements.

Near Estremoz is Vila Viscosa, a town of startling whiteness and the only Portuguese castle that you don't have to go uphill to see! The castle — Roman, Medieval and Moorish in turn — is set in a lovely garden, with a moat and white peacocks, but it is not the main reason for visiting Vila Viscosa.

Probably no royal palace has engendered such violent differences of opinion among writers on Portugal as the one at Vila Viscosa. It has been called tedious, boring, beautiful, classic, charming, sad, monotonous and magnificent. Along with the usual royal trappings and treasures with which palaces are routinely furnished, Vila Viscosa contains the everyday Bragança family personal belongings in a way that makes it feel curiously inhabited. The queen's hairbrush is on her dressing table with her perfume bottles, clothes are laid out and personal mementos and photographs are set about as if waiting to be used.

King Carlos's paintings, most of everyday scenes and subjects, also add to this personal quality of Vila Viscosa. The bad is there with the good: some curiously un-royal bits of Victoriana, in fashion at the close of the monarchy, are alongside priceless tapestries and relics of S. Thomas a Becket.

The kitchen is splendid, with its huge fireplaces, gigantic copper vessels, cooking pots and a giant spit for roasting game. All these are set against white walls and a marble floor, ready for the cook to don his toque and take over.

The palace forms one side of a large square, faced with creamy local marble, and behind it is a lovely garden. Like the palace, there is a sense of the garden being strolled in and enjoyed. The coach museum is in the stables and contains a fine collection including the one in which Carlos was riding when he was assassinated.

Perhaps because it was used into this century and because one knows from its history that the king and crown prince left from Vila Viscosa the day they died, it seems sealed in time like Sleeping Beauty's castle.

The scent of orange blossoms fills the air in Vila Viscosa, and its narrow streets are draped with flowers. The Chargas Convent sits beside the palace and across from it is the church with the pre-royalty Bragança tombs, all identical in black and white marble.

Borba lies just north of Vila Viscosa, a city known mostly for its wine and white marble. Here, as in Vila Viscosa and Estremoz, the doorsteps and window lintels are marble. There is a lovely fountain, white marble, of course, and the Igreja of S. Antonio done by the same craftsman.

There is an extraordinary little private museum of crucifixes at Vilalobos, close to Borba on the road to Estremoz. This is the sort of little travel surprise discovered as the result of following or stopping for signs, which happens constantly in Portugal.

Alandroal, south of Vila Viscosa, has a well-restored castle and very attractive walled town, and further on, Redondo is also a hilltop castle town. It has a very nice Misericordia with a Manueline choir and good baroque retables. There are some fine homes here with iron work balconies and windows.

About 20 km north of Redondo, as the Estremoz road climbs into the Serra de Ossa, near the village of N.S. Freixa, there are several good dolmen. There are other neolithic remains scattered about the countryside here but this is the most accessible of them.

Before the road passes the summit of Alto S. Gens, the convent of S. Paulo lies to the east. The widowed Catherine of Bragança lived in it and it was here that Pombal exiled the "Meninos de Palhava," illegitimate half brothers of King João V. The lovely convent, now privately owned, is a guest house. The church is the scene of a Romaria on Ascension Thursday, the only day the convent is open to the public.

Evora Monte sits just off the main road between Estremoz and Evora and can be seen in the distance through the olive groves that surround it. The town has spilled down the hill to the road and an uphill turn passes white houses, pots of geraniums and women sitting on door stoops mending and crocheting. Straw hats, sometimes several per head, protect them even from the spring sun. It is easy to see why there are no windows here, that shadeless hilltop of the Alentejo is scorching in the summer sun and the thick walls hold the evening cool well into the day. The narrow road skirts the castle wall and finally enters the thick wall in a hairpin turn. The restored keep of the castle looms ahead where ended the civil war between João VI's two sons, Pedro and Miguel. The smallest Misericordia in Portugal is next to the castle and the whole place has the atmosphere of a toy town.

North of Estremoz is Vieros, set around its castle. Only 4 km south of town is a Roman settlement reached by a road to the east, then a track to the south at the quinta gate. There are extensive remains of a villa, a Paleo-Christian church, and other fourth century buildings.

Estremoz At A Glance

Market town in the Alentejo, 175 km from Lisbon, 45 km from Evora.

LODGING: *Top choice is the Pousada Rainha S. Isabel (68/22618). The rooms are large, lovely and luxurious. Ornate tester beds, antiques or fine reproduction furniture, Arraiolos carpets, antique china and artworks. Rooms open out onto the Praça below with a view of the city and valley. In the top pousada price range, $75-110 but worth it to live in this museum. The Hotel Alentejano (68/22717) on the Rossio is well located and inexpensive. In Vila Viscosa, the Casa dos Arcos (68/98518) is a sixteenth century palace with a courtyard, a short walk from the Royal Palace. A double here is in the $50 range. South of Estremoz, on a hillside in the Serra de Ossa, is the Convento de S. Paulo (68/22618), mentioned above. This is a rare chance to see this lovely and fully restored convent. Although rooms there are not inexpensive, they are not at the pousada price range either. Call the central reservation office for guest houses in Lisbon (1/681713). It is possible to stay at Evora and see the Estremoz area in day trips.*

FOOD: *The dining room of the pousada is excellent, with a menu that varies, but usually includes Porco Alentejo, the regional dish of pork with clams. Aguias d'Oro on the Rossio has an attractive second floor dining room where a good dinner with wine will cost about $10. Ouro Branco in Vila Viscosa serves fresh shell-fish daily as well as other specialties in the under $10 range. There are other small restaurants in Estremoz, but it is not over supplied.*

SHOPPING: *The street from the pousada down to the Rossio has several pottery shops selling the traditional cream-colored Estremoz ware. There is a Saturday market where crafts are sold along with produce and household items. The street leading out of the Rossio to the left of the town hall has a number of shops selling painted wooden ware and other crafts, including pottery figures for creche sets. Borba has a number of antique shops, including one at the crucifix museum.*

IF TIME IS SHORT: *See Vila Viscosa and make a short stop in Estremoz to see the castle. Don't plan to be in Vila Viscosa on Monday, when the palace is closed.*

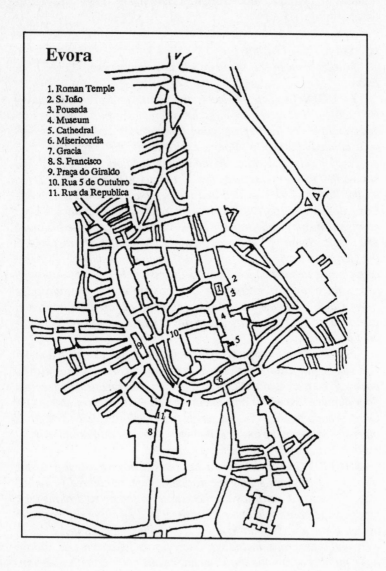

Evora

1. Roman Temple
2. S. João
3. Pousada
4. Museum
5. Cathedral
6. Misericordia
7. Gracia
8. S. Francisco
9. Praça do Giraldo
10. Rua 5 de Outubro
11. Rua da Republica

Evora

Perhaps the most remarkable quality of Evora's old city is that the area within its encircling walls remains much as it was during Evora's golden age, but without a sense of having been "preserved." It is a busy, thriving city, whose everyday life goes on around, through and in its architectural and historic treasures. It is not a self-conscious museum and therein lies its particular charm. The visitor feels that after he has seen all the sights (there are 50 odd important ones, if you listen to locals) he could stick around for a few days and just enjoy being there.

But first the sights. We begin at the Roman temple, not just because it is the earliest historically, but also because it is in the square where several other attractions are clustered. The small, graceful temple is possibly the best preserved Roman building in Iberia, with fourteen of its columns, all of its base, and a good stretch of its entablature standing. Its Corinthian columns are of granite, thin and almost delicate in proportion, the capitals and bases of local marble. All but two of the carved capitals are intact; the remarkable condition of the building is probably due to its having been walled up and fortified during the Middle Ages, then later used as a slaughterhouse. The bricks that obscured the columns for so many centuries probably also saved it. Thus encased it survived the 1755 quake.

The notion that it was a temple to the goddess Diana has become so widespread that it is even locally referred to as the Temple of Diana, but there is no evidence to support the name. All we know is that it dates from the second or third century, when it must have been a beautiful sight crowning the hilltop of the Roman city of Liberalitas Julia.

In the shadow of the temple is the Church of S. João the Evangelist, a little-known gem in a city filled with fine churches. It is a graceful blend of Moorish and Gothic styles, with eighteenth century azulejos and good Gothic and Renaissance tombs; its cloister is now the pousada. From this square you can see the unusual conical lantern of the Sé, an imposing building of more than sufficient decorative styles. These are combined in a relatively small

199

space, with major features of the architecture dating from the fourteenth (cloister) and eighteenth (chancel and high altar) centuries. Between lie a sixteenth century choir and pulpit and seventeenth century sacristy and side chapels.

The building itself is Romanesque-Gothic, built in the twelfth century. It is one of the few Romanesque buildings remaining in Portugal although it has been embellished considerably since. The chancel and main altar are especially fine, in mixed colored marble, and there is gilded wood-carving throughout. The varied styles don't clash with each other, but none is at home with the mud color of the granite pillars of the nave. To make it worse, the pointing between each stone is raised slightly and painted white, giving the effect of enormous freshly laid bricks. We assumed this strange, almost garish effect, to be the work of a recent overzealous painter, but writers of the 1950s and 1960s, whom we have since read, complain of the same thing, each also assuming that it was a recent aberration.

The cloister, down a few steps from the right (south) transept, is small and graceful, containing some fine tombs. The newest of these is in white marble, with the bishop's vestments executed almost as finely as real lace.

The Renaissance facade of the Igreja Graça is grand baroque with a sense of humor. Its stone giants, their feet dangling off the capitals of the square columns on which they sit almost carelessly, gaze out at the square. A pair of huge stone rosettes flank a central window in the upper story. One can only wonder what kind of church lies behind this magnificent, if slightly bombastic facade. But it stands in roofless ruin and has been closed for many years.

S. Francisco's claim to immortality is its chapel lined with human bones, its entrance flanked, to make matters worse, with long braids of hair left as ex votos. It's simply too many human body pieces for most, but that shouldn't put one off from what is otherwise a very fine church, one which can be seen without the Ostiary Chapel. It is Portuguese Gothic with a plain wide nave to set off the beauty of its side chapels, one paneled in white and gold, another richly carved with an exquisite Christ. Here, as in the Cathedral, is the curiously accented mortaring.

But all these are buildings and, although rich in artistic treasure and diverse and impressive in style, we needed people to occupy them. So we sought the Calvario church and convent, founded in the sixteenth century by the Poor Clares. When the Marquês de Pombal decided to marry his son off to the fourteen-year-old daughter of a wealthy and powerful family, the plucky girl refused. People did not refuse Pombal and she was forced to marry, but declined even to speak to her "husband." After three years of stony silence she was finally allowed to retire to the Evora convent, where she stayed until the death of the king and Pombal's subsequent fall from power.

After seeking an annulment, she was at last free to marry her childhood sweetheart who had waited patiently for her release. Their son became the first Duke of Palmela. It's easy to picture the young girl here in the simplicity of this small cloister, waiting patiently in the company of the Poor Clares.

Widowed queens habitually retired to convents, but when Catherine of Bragança returned from England following the death of Charles II, she retired instead to the delicate traceries and frescoes of the Conde de Basto's Palace in the Patio de S. Miguel.

Evora's heyday as the intellectual and artistic capital of Portugal lasted from the fourteenth century to the closing of the Jesuit University following Pombal's expulsion of that order. Fortunately, Evora kept, along with her other treasures, the college building. The vast cloister, with a double row of arches and pediment surrounded by statues is the centerpiece, and the azulejos are stunning even in this city that abounds in them. Many rooms have entire azulejo scenes as well as some good painted ceilings, especially the sacristy.

Each street rings with history, in the facades of fine homes, the balconies and arches, even the names of the streets, many of which reflect the city's royal patronage: Her Highness's Kitchen, The Countess's Seamstress. It would be a shame to be so preoccupied with the city's art treasures (we haven't even mentioned the rich museums here) that one misses the spirit of the place.

A walk in the warm Alentejo evening, when everyone is out for a breath of air, is a good time to enjoy its side streets, belvederes, largos and gardens. Wander in the area around Largo dos Portas Moura, with its towers, fountains, hanging flower pots, narrow streets and arches. Ghosts of the past are everywhere — in the empty windows of the ruined palace walls in the public garden, in the aristocratic faces of the people who nod as they pass, in the Roman stones with the children playing amid the pillars, in the conversations overheard in the cafes.

The Surrounding Alentejo

As though there were not enough to see within the city's walls, the area around Evora is also rich in attractions. Just outside the wall is one of Portugal's rare charter houses, with a black and white marble facade. About 3 km further along is the monastery of S. Bento de Castris with its sixteenth century double-storied cloister, and the scene of an Ascension Day Romaria. About 5 km northwest is the fortified convent of Espinheiro with its fine small cloister and lovely church.

The main road to the southeast leads through pastoral countryside to Mourão, a border defensive town with a good fourteenth century castle and typical narrow streets. A road leads due north just before the crossing of the Guardiana River to Monsaraz, 7 km away. Near the road is the Menhir of Xarez, set on a square stone base.

Monsaraz is an unrestored hill town set under its castle, whose tall keep offers a view that stretches for miles. It is difficult to drive or park inside the town walls, so it is best to travel the Rua Direita on foot, leaving the car outside the arch. The town hall has a fine verandah with coats of arms and the Misericordia has excellent baroque gilded woodwork. Enquire for the key. There are also lovely old homes, some decorated with coats of arms and others with frescoes, wrought iron gates and balconies.

There are two megalithic monuments near the base of the hill, one engraved with symbols, and the other over 15 feet tall. Ask for Bulhoa and Outeiro, since these are easier to find when someone points you in the right direction.

Arraiolos is more interesting in reputation than in fact, but for the traveler with a special interest in needlework, a visit to the workshop is worth the side trip. It is open 8-12 and 1-6 on weekdays and you can watch the making of the carpets, a process that involves an interlocking long-legged cross-stitch executed on canvas.

The castle at Arraiolos is much ruined, but just to the north of town is the Quinta dos Loios, a fifteenth century church and fortified convent with a lovely two-storied cloister. The church is completely lined with azulejos, but be warned that it is privately owned and once there you may not be able to get in.

South of Arraiolos on the Evora road is a fine example of Moorish-Manueline at Sempre Noiva. The manor house has seen both better days and clumsy repairs but it preserves some fine features. Its name, which translates to "ever virgin," refers to the girl who refused to consummate her forced marriage to Pombal's son.

Heading southwest toward Alcáçovas, a right turn at about 10 km goes to Quinta de Valverde (or Mitra), formerly a Capuchin monastery and the country home of the Archbishop of Evora. There is a lovely round church, whose cupola is supported by marble columns. A quartet of semi-circular chapels surround the central one, the entire of which is only about 20 feet at its widest point. More than just a miniature curiosity, it is an architectural work of some importance and, although its design is of uncertain origin, it has been ascribed to de Torralva, the architect of Graçia in Evora and the cloister at Tomar.

Beyond Valverde is the Chapel of S. Brissos, which is built against a megalithic tomb. This is not infrequent in Portugal, there being similar chapels over ancient tombs in Pavia and Alcobertas west of Caldas da Rainha.

Alcáçovas, a 12 km detour from Viana is worth seeing for its fine palaces. The Berahonas palace has a columned arcade and that of the Condes dos Alcáçovas retains much of its original Gothic structure and a funny little chapel decorated with sea shells. About 3 km west out of town is the former Dominican convent of N.S. de Esperanza with unusual azulejo work.

Viana do Alentejo, south of Evora is crowned, like most of these Alentejo towns, with castle walls, against which is built a much pinnacled and crenellated Igreja Matriz from the 1700s. It has an excellent Manueline doorway and a nice interior. It is quite a sight with its flying buttresses, little turrets and balustrade. Standing before it I am reminded of the old gem of grandmotherly advice to stop at the hall mirror before going out and take off something — the hat, the earrings, the scarf — so as to avoid being overdone. The architect didn't, and here we have a church with one of everything, not unpleasant, just a little bit over-abundant.

Just to the outside of the town to the east is a pilgrimage church, N.S. de Aires with a very popular Romaria. It is usually chock full of ex votos, some of them quite amusing to the less than reverent tourist.

South of Viana on the Alvito road is the palace of the Dukes of Cadaval. Alvito's castle is a fortified fifteenth century country house, with Moorish arches and round corner towers. The style is the pleasant combination of Moorish and Manueline often found in these Alentejo towns. The castle is in excellent condition with some very fine ceilings. Just south, about 6 km to the southeast at Vila Ruiva there is a Roman bridge.

Near Portel, which is southeast of Evora and has a thirteenth century castle of the Dukes of Bragança, is Ameira, 14 km to the east on a back road. Ameira's castle, built in the mid-fourteenth century, is quite well preserved, but unless one is taking that route from Evora to Beja, or has some time to spare, it is probably not worth the detour.

Evora At A Glance

Former royal and ecclesiastical center in the Alentejo, 143 km from Lisbon. It is accessible by train from Lisbon's south bank of the Tagus.

LODGING: The Pousada dos Loios (66/ 24051) is built in the former monastery, centrally located within the city walls. It encompasses the cloister and the chapter room with its Moorish doorways and a private chapel, now a parlor. It is the showpiece of the pousada system, lovely, luxurious and in their highest price range of $75-110. It is also usually booked full of American tourists, even out of season. In these heavily visited areas the pousadas tend to be more of an American preserve than in the north, where guests are often European.

The Hotel Planicie (66/ 24026), at about half the price, is in a well-restored old building retaining some fine features while offering modern rooms. When you reserve, make your preference clear between overlooking the largo or the quieter rear rooms.

A bit simpler, but very comfortable, is the Hotel S. Clara (66/ 24141), still within the walls and an easy walk from major attractions. Doubles here are about $40. In the same price range, two blocks from the Cathedral, in an old villa with nice decorative details, is the Residéntial Riviera (66/ 23304).

For doubles in the $30 range, still in a gracious old building with antique features, try O Eborense (66/ 22031). Some rooms do not have private baths, but all are clean and comfortable, with an accent on personalized hospitality. The Estralagem Monsaraz (66/ 55112) is in that medieval town. A delightful country inn at less than pousada prices, it is an excellent stop for those arriving from Spain.

FOOD: In a city so well supplied with restaurants, many serving fine regional foods, we recommend not dining at the pousada. Less expensive, but excellent, is Cozinha de S. Humberto. Its "country kitchen" decor may be a bit overdone, but the food and atmosphere are good and dinner is in the $10 range. In the same price range are Alkazar, A Torralva and the Evora, all nicely decorated and serving regional specialties. Or join the locals at the more crowded, but charming and very personal Guião. It is less expensive and has the busy, friendly atmosphere of a restaurant where people come back often. In Monsaraz, the Estralagem serves excellent meals, good to know if you are going there on a side trip from Evora.

Wherever you eat, you should try the Alentejo specialty of Porco com Ameijoas, pork with small clams. Sopa Alentejana is a delicious soup with garlic and coriander, and Gueijadas de Evora are cheese tartlets. The Borba wines resemble Bordeaux. The breads here are light and crusty and irresistible.

SHOPPING: The pousada has an excellent shop featuring local handcrafts and more can be found along the Rua 5 de Outubro. The carpet factory has a branch in Evora if you are not going to Arraiolos. Local crafts include the wood-carving often known as shepherds' art, Evora embroidery and items made of sheepskin or wool. There are several nice local ceramic styles.

FESTIVALS: There is a Romaria at S. Bento de Castris on Ascension Day, and at N.S. de Aires on the fourth Sunday of November.

IF TIME IS SHORT: Consider Evora a "must" on your itinerary and do a walking tour of the city beginning at the Roman temple, the Chapter House door inside the convent (now the pousada), the Sé (see especially the cloister, treasury and choir stalls), down Rua de S. Marcos to Rua Don Augustus Nunes to Largo dos Portas de Moura past the Manueline facade of the Soure mansion, along the Traversa de Caraca to Largo da Graça, where the church facade will be easy to spot. Take Rua de la República to S. Francisco (where you can see the Ostiary Chapel or pass it by), back up República to Praça do Giraldo and Rua 5 de Outubro back to the Cathedral. Above all, don't try to "run over to Evora for the day" from Lisbon. If you don't stay in Evora, stay somewhere in the Alentejo at least one night. Do avoid visiting Evora on Monday, when many public buildings and churches are closed.

Beja

Distances in the lower Alentejo become longer and the towns farther apart. Beja sits in the middle of a large area with relatively few surrounding towns. Its fame is literary, since it was here in the convent of N.S. Conceicão that a young nun, Mariane Alcoforado is thought to have written "Letters of a Portuguese Nun." Although there has been considerable squabble among literary historians over who really wrote them, the most recent opinion is that she did.

Whatever their origin, they have attracted considerable attention in the three centuries since their publication, and the convent is now a museum, whose chief interest is fine azulejos, some of which are Mudejar, and a rich gilt chapel; it is always a good idea to seek out chapels of the Poor Clares since they are usually richly decorated.

The castle in Beja was built by Dom Dinis and the gallery around the top gives a fine view of the plains below. Near the castle is the church of S. Amaro, of pre-Romanesque origins.

Seven kilometers southwest of Beja are the ruins of the Roman settlement of Pisões, with remains of a villa, pool, bath and mosaic floor. Excavations are intermittent, so it is wise to check at the tourist office in Beja to see when they are open.

To the east is Serpa, with medieval gateways and castle. A road here leads north to Moura, with another of King Dinis's castles (between his castles and the tombs of his illegitimate children, we find reminders of this king's work all over Portugal!) and a Carmelite convent with a good classical cloister. Houses here are colorful and the chimneys begin to hint of the unusual styles of the Algarve.

South of Beja, on the main road to the Algarve, is Mertola, with its badly ruined Moorish castle. The parish church here is also of Moorish origin, almost perfectly square and divided into five aisles.

Beja At A Glance

Agricultural center, 78 km south of Evora.

LODGING: *While it is tempting to say that there isn't any, that is of little service to the tired traveler who finds himself here late in the day, as we often have. There is the Residéncia S. Barbara (84/ 22028), with small rooms, but comfortable beds. Far from grand, but clean and only $25 for a double. The Residéncia Coelho (84/ 24032) is a bit noisy on the Praça da República, but clean and adequate in the same price range.*

The best plan is to stay in Serpa, about 25 km east. The Pousada S. Gens (84/ 90327) sits on a hilltop just south of town, overlooking the plain. A bit more informal than other pousadas, it offers 17 rooms at $40-60.

FOOD: *For all its lack of lodging, Beja offers several good places to eat. Luis da Rocha is our top choice at under $10, with Aficionado serving much the same menu at slightly higher prices. Esquina is good and in the $5 range, but it is not air-conditioned, which can be important in the Alentejo summer. Pousada guests should eat there.*

IF TIME IS SHORT: *Keep on driving, with a stop at the convent in Beja if you need to stretch your legs and revive your soul with a gold-lined church. It is also wise to plan on having lunch at Beja on the way south, since restaurants are widely scattered here.*

Santiago do Cacém

Some places linger in a traveler's memory for reasons quite remote from their attraction. So it is with us and Santiago do Cacém. One of the relatively few cities in the part of the Alentejo where distances are longer and towns further apart than in other regions, Santiago do Cacém would not be visited by many were it not on the best road from the Algarve to Lisbon.

That is how we happened to be there one gray and rainy day in March. We had been driving straight since Alzejur where we had stopped to slide about on the wet stones of its castle and then pressed on. We were hungry and road weary but stopping-places along the route are few.

Just as the commanding form of the castle of Santiago do Cacém hove in sight, the gray sky began to pour. It was definitely not the time to go strolling in search of a restaurant. We came to the Rua de Lisboa and there was a space by the curb just large enough to hold our car. We parked and Julie noticed that we were in front of a restaurant. Water was forming a small river down the street and our feet were soaked in the few steps to its door.

Inside it was warm and slightly steamy, probably from all of the wet people eating bowls of hot soup. Men at the next table were wolfing down a platter of the most delicious looking yellow tangle and we asked the owner/waiter what it was. Bacalau a Bras, and it was their specialty. It looked like saffron and it steamed invitingly, so we ordered a platter too. It was every bit as good as it looked. We've been back since, on better days, and a full meal with wine is still under $5 each.

While I realize that a good meal when you are wet and hungry is not a reason to give a town a star in your guidebook, it sure beats a bad meal or none at all as a reason to stop. And we are not the only travelers who find the route from the Algarve less than exciting.

Santiago do Cacém makes a good place to break the trip, with its nice little pousada, one of the first of these. The castle, which is planted with cypress trees and holds a cemetery now, went back and forth in the struggle to regain Portugal from the Moors. When it was finally secured, the king gave it to the Knights Templar who rebuilt it. On a clear day you can see to the Atlantic from its ramparts. The Praça do Conde de Bracial is filled with fine old houses.

About 1 km north of the Lisbon road is a right turn with a sign for Mirobriga. Following that road a dirt lane leads to a Roman road and thence to a Roman city on the road to the left. It is thought to have been built on a previous Celtic site, built in turn on a late neolithic settlement. Here is the only Roman Circus yet found in Portugal.

On the coast is Sines, which is no longer the remote little fishing village that Vasco da Gama knew. Those who have read the accounts of its deserted beaches, cliffs, castle and lighthouse are doomed to a nasty surprise, for it has been chosen as the location of a huge tanker port and oil terminal with tank fields and pipelines crawling all over the former farmlands. Since its construction has been carried on in fits and starts, it is alternately a bustle of activity and a ghost town with wide multi-lane highways ending abruptly, and the skeletons of half-finished buildings.

Go instead to Porto Covo, a little fishing village with painted houses and many good views of the island of Pessequeira with its ruined fortress. Farther south along the coast is Vila Nova de Milfontes, whose small seventeenth century castle, once sacked by Algerians, is now a delightful guest house. Look for the unusual large flowering variety of gorse growing by the roadside.

North of Santiago is Grandola, whose only claim to immortality is the song "Grandola Vila Morena" which was the prearranged signal that all systems were "go" for the 1974 coup. That old favorite tune rang out on radios across Portugal and a government fell.

Santiago do Cacém At A Glance

Stopover town 140 km south of Lisbon and an equal distance north of Lagos.

LODGING: The Pousada de S. Tiago (69/ 22459). It maintains the flavor of a country inn, with small rustic rooms done with locally carved furniture and good views. In Vila Nova de Milfontes, O Castelo is in a small restored castle overlooking the Mira estuary. Guests are served dinner and, if they wish, sent off with fine picnic lunches. Doubles with bath are in the $70 range.

FOOD: *Martins 17 Rua de Lisboa, described so warmly above, specializes in seafoods, lamb stew Alentejo and curry, and is closed Fridays in the winter. On Friday try Fragateira on the same street.*

IF TIME IS SHORT: *Stop for lunch and keep going, unless Roman ruins are a special interest.*

Sagres and the Western Algarve

Lagos, Silves and Portimão are the largest towns in the western Algarve, Albufeira and Alte the prettiest, but to us, the main goal of a visit to this corner of Portugal is Sagres. It is to the historian what Fátima is to the pious — a place of pilgrimage.

It is easy to understand, looking out at the sea from Sagres, why men thought the world ended there. Unlike a beach which spreads out beside and around and under your feet, a promontory leaves you isolated with the sea behind, beside and beneath. The waves pound to froth against the ragged rocks so far below and seem to tear at the cliff.

Surely the world does end here. The illusion is strongest when the sky is an overwhelming gray and the wind that perpetually tears at Cape S. Vincent is carrying with it sheets of rain. No one walks the outer path along the cliffs, around the wall of Prince Henry's fortifications, so you are alone here. Only the impatient pacing footsteps of Henry are echoing beside your own. Like him, you know there is land out there, but feel less certain of it here than at the sun-swept beach at Nazaré.

Sometimes it is history's cruel trick that the most clever and talented prince does not become king. But in the case of the sons of Philippa and João I, it was fortunate indeed that the talented and far-seeing Henry was not born first. For weighed down with the responsibilities of government, he would never have been able to pursue his work that altered the course of history.

His brother Duarte was more skilled in government, and his leadership and patronage made Henry's work possible. Together with their brother Pedro, a skilled foreign ambassador, these half-English brothers were the brightest and the best of their day.

Henry began his work in a world filled with eye-witness accounts of sea monsters devouring ships and of a line off the coast of West Africa where the sea began to run downhill. It was a largely unmapped world without navigational charts or even communication between the few men who held pieces of this great geographical puzzle.

He chose Sagres for his headquarters — a point of violent seas where three of the world's geological plates converge. Ships had to pass this point under the right wind and it sometimes took weeks for the weather to change. Henry offered a safe harbor, water and provisions, as well as hospitality to these waiting seamen, and while they waited, he extracted from them every scrap of information about their experiences at sea. Here too, the bedraggled remnants of ships and crews returned, with stories and experiences Henry was the first to hear.

He invited scholars, cartographers, and masters of every discipline and of every belief to work with him there. He sent his captains farther and farther, told them what to look for and supplied them with better ships and navigational instruments developed at Sagres. His captains pushed around the west coast of Africa and beyond. They discovered Madeira, which became an important source of timber for his new caravels.

Although Henry died before much of his work bore fruit, nearly sixty years later Vasco da Gama rounded the Cape of Good Hope under the flag of Portugal and sailed on to India. Neither he nor Magellan nor Columbus could have sailed without Prince Henry's work.

That is the legacy of the sparse stone fort on the windswept point at Sagres, which during the lifetime of one man was the nucleus of the world's geographical wisdom.

Near Raposeira, where Henry lived for a time, there is a little thirteenth century chapel, N.S. de Guadeloupe where Henry prayed. The shore to the east of Sagres is lined with beaches, many under steep cliffs. One by one these are being developed for tourism, but there are still beaches without hotels in sight.

Lagos, which sits near the magnificent promontory of Ponta da Piedade and its curious rock formations, retains few vestiges of its long past, having been severely damaged by the 1755 earthquake. Quite well restored is the baroque Igreja de S. Antonio with some of the Algarve's best gilded wood carving.

Retaining more of the character of the Algarve than most of the other beachside fishing villages is Portimão, a busy port and market town. Plenty of tourists enjoy its streets, but don't obscure its lived-in charm as the business of everyday life goes on. Between Portimão and Lagos, 5 km northeast of Mexilhoeira, is a neolithic tomb at Alcala. Also between these two towns is Estomar, a classic white town set around an enormous church with onion-domed towers.

Albufeira, despite its reputation as the St. Tropez of the Algarve, is still much the attractive town it always was. It is actually much nicer than St. Tropez — more like the St. Tropez of 30 years ago — smart enough to be fun, but not jet-setty or contrived. New development has been required to fit in with local architecture and with the terrain; high-rises have not been allowed to spoil the view. White houses still sit like stairs along the narrow streets, and the life of the town centers around its harbor.

Down at the fishing beach, the boats still come and go, and on days when the sea is too rough, fishermen work on their nets. Some mend and some make new ones, a fascinating art to watch. Long strings are tied to a horizontal railing, and the men walk along them, making knot after knot until a net takes shape.

Julie took out her camera and asked in careful Portuguese: "May I?" The men beamed, stood taller, worked in grander gestures, but were obviously amused that the little girl would find such an everyday activity interesting. They had been making and mending nets here since they were her age. That they were practicing and ancient art did not occur to them. "It's not an art," one told us. "It's just a net to catch fish." Would the fish notice if each knot were not exactly spaced and each loop not perfectly placed? "Ah, no, but I would. That is the way a net should be."

Inland, off the main beach road and up into the mountains that separate the Algarve from the rest of Portugal, is a different countryside, one most travelers see only as they pass through on their way to or from Lisbon. But this Algarve sans sea is a beautiful place.

Silves was the hub of the Muslim Algarve — a vibrant, thriving city and cultural center. It fell first to crusaders, then to the earthquake, but in spite of both, its castle remains the finest Moorish fortification in Portugal. Its giant cistern, which held enough water to last through the frequent sieges, still supplies the city.

It is a shame that there is not more Moorish architecture surviving in Portugal because, especially in this area, the Moors were so long a part of its history. But because the war was a holy one rather than political, the evidence of the occupation was quickly obliterated, the mosques turned into churches and their great works replaced. Only in domestic architecture does the feeling of North Africa survive here.

Farther north into the mountains is Monchique, only 24 km from the coast, but degrees cooler in the summer. It is green and wooded, with orange trees, pine and cork oak. There is a spa nearby, set in the woods. Above the town is the early Renaissance convent of N. S. do Desterro, lonely and beautiful in ruin, overlooking the valley. The views here are the best in February, when first the almond, then the mimosa bloom, and in April and May when it is covered with a profusion of wildflowers.

North of Albufeira is S. Bartolomeu de Messines, a whitewashed mountain town. Its parish church contains twisted columns of variegated local marble, one of the few remaining samples of this early Manueline form.

The little town of Alte, just to the east, was runner-up in the contest many years ago which chose Monsanto as the "most Portuguese village." It hasn't changed much since then, and the restorers haven't found its remarkable Igreja Matriz. Through its Manueline doorway appears an interior completely covered, even up into its vaulted ceiling, with blue and white azulejos. These eighteenth century tiles representing angelic musicians, are designed to fit even into the triangular panels between the vaulting, which is intersected by painted boisseries.

Before seeing this little church, we never fully understood what was meant when we read that azulejos had been removed from a church's vaulted roof. The effect of the tiles covering the ceiling, running into points separated by stone vaulting is stunning.

From Alte there is a hike of about an hour to the caves of Buraco dos Mouros. The road past Monchique leads out of the Algarve to nearby S. Clara-a-Velha, where there is a beautifully set pousada overlooking the lake.

Sagres And The Western Algarve At A Glance

Seashore resort area, 265 km south of Lisbon.

LODGING: Unlike many parts of Portugal, the Algarve has more hotels than it has places to visit. As with the eastern Algarve, we shall suggest only those which have particular interest to the traveler, leaving the self-contained resorts and self-catered apartments to the care of a travel agent.

The Pousada do Infante in Sagres (82/ 642 22) is a good example of the style of architecture that blends into and enhances a landscape. It is an arcaded white building with red tiled roof and Algarve chimneys, stretched along the rim of a cliff. Its warm fire is welcome after *a windy walk with Prince Henry on the point opposite. Doubles are $70 in low season, $110 in high.*

Also nicely placed in its setting is the Residéncia Dom Henrique (82/ 641 33), a very comfortable hotel right in Sagres. Rooms here have balconies overlooking the sea, and are bright and comfortable. The dining room is quite good; if you do not plan to eat there (even though you probably should), mention it at the desk or they will be likely to save a table for you. Doubles are $25 to $45, less than half the pousada rate and more than half as nice.

Although as yet the Algarve has no formal organization of private estates offering lodging, as the Minho does, a few such places do exist. The Casa de S. Gonealo de Lagos (82/ 621 71) on Rua Candido dos Reis has 13 antique-filled guest rooms to which they have added private baths. This fine eighteenth century town house is well located in the city, but rooms face the quiet flower-filled patio. We have to rate this not only more interesting, but a better value than the pousada, at $40 in low season and $60 in the summer. It is not open for guests from November through April.

Although not inexpensive, the Estralagem Abrigo de Montanha (82/ 921 31) in Monchique comes highly recommended. We haven't stayed there, but we know several who have and they give glowing reports. Doubles are about $75, a good choice in the summer when the Algarve can be very hot.

FOOD: The Algarve is an exception to our advice elsewhere about hotel dining rooms. Since most of the guests at the hotels here are northern Europeans, the menus at many of the hotels are that one-size-fits-all genre called "continental". This can be very boring and if you long for good local specialties you'd do better browsing near the beachfront area, particularly in towns such as Albufeira and Portimão.

In Albufeira, Ze' Bel is next to the fish market and has, as you might guess, the freshest of the day's catch, at prices in the $10 range. In Lagos try Antonio on the beach, or the slightly better Cacerola, both at $10 or less. Avozinha in Portimão is a good value at the same price.

SHOPPING: The Algarve towns are filled with shops selling local crafts such as carved spoons from Monchique, fishermen's sweaters and baskets. Albufeira has a Saturday morning market as well as one on the first and third Tuesdays of each month.

FESTIVALS: The S. Pedro market is in Albufeira on June 29; there is a fair in S. Bartolomeu on the fourth Sunday in January; May

1 is the Festa da Fonte Grande in Alte and Lagos has a fair on August 16 and 17. Silves celebrates All Saints Day on October 31 and November 1. There are many more with variable dates, so be sure to get the current listing from any tourist office in the area.

IF TIME IS SHORT: Stop to see one of the towns — our choice would be Albufeira — and go to Sagres.

Faro and the Eastern Algarve

If the traveler could be delivered directly to the center of Faro, the impression would be better. For inside the ring of highrise rent-by-the-week apartments, there is still a charming medieval core held in by thick walls. The Arco da Vila connects this quarter to the yacht basin and garden.

Home to the Phoenicians, Romans, Visigoths and Moors, it was the latter that made the most lasting impression, for its whiteness and rounded shapes and colored tiles give it a Moorish flavor still. The most recent tide of invasion has been from northern Europe, making the traditional beach season almost impossible, not only in Faro but in other areas of the Algarve as well. The rest of the year — October through May — is more leisurely, and you may even hear Portuguese spoken.

The Sé is a white Gothic church with an assortment of ornament inside that combines into a general impression of splendor. S. Francisco, although better known to tourists for its Capella d' Ossos lined in human skulls, has much more than this curiosity to offer. The walls are covered in very good baroque carving, all richly gilded. The Chagas nuns would have loved it! Setting off the gold are blue and white azulejos — even in the chancel ceiling. The notion of stripping churches of their gold and tile and wood carving doesn't seem to have caught on in the Algarve, so here we have some idea of the splendor that once filled many of the northern churches as well.

S. Pedro, although a bit less of a riot, is also filled with baroque gold work and blue pictorial azulejos. A pair of splendid pulpits are reached by curving stairs.

For many, the only reason to visit the Algarve is for its beaches. Faro's beach is actually an offshore island, where both road and boats carry sun-worshipers in a steady stream. The major beach to the west, Vale da Lobo, is now a major modern tourist complex, as is the once-charming fishing village of Praia de Quarteira, now brimful of northern Europeans who rent holiday apartments in the blocks of high-rises that choke the shore. Since Faro has the airport, the beaches nearest it are the most congested and developed.

To the east of Faro, along the coast, is Olhão. Once known for the almost cubist-painting appearance of its North African architecture, there is very little of this apparent today. It has a working street with mosaic pavement, and a still-busy waterfront with a fish market. This building is easy to spot on the beach — it looks as though it has washed ashore from Coney Island. A short boat ride away are two of the Algarve's least spoiled beaches on the islands of Armona and Fuzeta.

Four miles north of Olhão is Moncarapacho which has a remarkable church, S. Cristo. The local brochure describes it in English as "a temple of some sumptuousity." (Since everyone has such good sport over my sometimes original Portuguese-Italian, I don't mind relishing some of the interesting translations we find!) Its azulejos are seventeenth century polychrome and they form an overall pattern set off by borders.

Tavira, once the Algarve's largest city, and possibly still its prettiest, has survived severe damage by the 1755 earthquake as well as the silting up of its once-important harbor. Apart from the new resort areas which surround it — mostly low lying and attractive — it retains the air of a quiet Algarve town with its towers and cupolas. It is known as the city of churches, with thirty-seven of them, several worth visiting. But its main charm is its domestic architecture. Decorated chimneys, bright tiles and iron balconies break the overwhelming whiteness, and above is a ruined castle, whose vine-covered walls can be climbed for good views.

S. Maria do Castelo, like much of Tavira, was heavily damaged by the earthquake, but was rebuilt with eighteenth century azulejos and gilded wood. Also inside the old walled town is the Misericordia with a fine sixteenth century portal and good carving on the high altar. The Igreja Carmo is a baroque fantasy inside, well worth the trouble of seeking its key from the house to the left of it.

The last beach in this direction is among the Algarve's best, the broad sandy strip of Monte Gordo. We never visit these areas "in season," but in February and March they are lovely. The beaches are deserted and we wander along them gathering the tiny pink shells. The resorts look deserted and a little bleak without their summer finery and activity, but the cafes are still open and the sun feels good. The houses in the village here are blue and deep red instead of the usual white.

Vila Real de S. Antonio is the border station connecting Portugal with Spain by ferry boats. Pombal built the town of stone shipped there from Lisbon (despite the availability of local stone) to impress the Spanish. When he had finished, he ordered the residents of Monte Gordo to move there, since it was an empty city. Most responded to his order by moving across the river into Spain.

Castro Marim, just up the river, is best known historically as the "hiding place" headquarters of the newly formed Order of Christ, in the time of King Dinis. He didn't want them at the former Templar stronghold of Tomar, which he wisely felt would attract attention to their very real ties with the recently abolished Templars. So Castro Marim became their stronghold for a time. The huge castle was badly damaged in the 1755 earthquake, but it is still impressive with its four towers and ruined church. It houses an archaeological museum.

Also on the Spanish border, north of Castro Marim, is Alcoutim, its castle overlooking the Guardiana and a hillside of red tile roof tops.

The inland area of the eastern Algarve is, to us, far more attractive than its frenetic, overbuilt shore. San Bras de Alportel is set between two hills in a countryside covered with fig, almond, orange and pine trees. In late January and early February, it is unbelievably lovely, as is much of the Algarve, with its hillsides white in almond blossoms.

There is a local legend that a Moorish prince had brought his northern European bride home to the Algarve, but she grew homesick for the winter snows of her homeland. The prince ordered the land as far as she could see planted with almonds so she would have her familiar white landscape, at least briefly, each winter.

Nothing that the traveler "must" see, San Bras is simply a charming city full of flowers set against its white walls and intricately carved chimneys. These chimneys are not constructed on the house, but bought separately, and there are displays of them along the road, looking like whole villages buried to their ridgepoles.

Nearby Loule has even more of these chimneys, in amazing variety. Women sit on doorsteps here weaving hats and baskets. The castle retains its walls and towers, and the Igreja Matriz has a Manueline chapel with a fine gold altar and azulejos.

About halfway between San Bras and Faro, off a side road out of Estoi, is Milreu, a partially excavated Roman settlement. Rising above the foundations of villas and baths is the rounded apse ∩f a very early Christian church, built over a Roman temple. Its walls are of honey-colored stone which crumbles almost at a touch. There is a surprising amount of this church left, given its age and building materials. The baths here are especially interesting, lined in mosaic tiles. Until very recently, visitors could just wander in and around Milreu, open and forgotten. But it is now fenced and has regular visiting hours; we liked it better empty and lonely.

Some of the artifacts from Milreu are in the gardens of the Palace of the Condes de Carvalhal, an eighteenth century mansion in Estoi. It is the only important country house in the Algarve, where there are also fewer monasteries and noble homes. Although the house is not open, visitors are admitted to the gardens (after ringing the bell for the caretaker). These are terraced, with lakes, stairs, cascades, statuary, Roman mosaics and azulejos set among flowers, palms and orange trees.

Faro At A Glance

Algarve port city, 300 km south of Lisbon, with access by rail and air from Lisbon.

LODGING: There are so many places to stay in the eastern Algarve, that they have almost swallowed up the reason for wanting to go there. Any travel agent will know dozens of beach apartments for those who wish to spend a week in the sun, but we shall suggest those places that retain a bit of the old Algarve, often those set back a bit from the shore.

San Bras de Alportel, a good center for exploring the region, has the Pousada de S. Bras (89/ 423 05), set high above the tree-covered country-side. It is in a fine building of classic Algarve architecture, amid gardens. Rooms are simple and comfortable, and the temperature is pleasant even in the heat of summer. Doubles are between $40 and $60, depending on the season.

While we prefer to stay outside of Faro, there is a very nice small hotel, originally a ducal town house. Casa de Lumena (89/ 220 28) sits facing a tree-filled square and is furnished with some very nice antiques. It is run by a very hospitable English family, and double rooms are about $35.

Monte Gordo's das Caravelas (81/ 444 60) is pleasantly set in the pine groves that lie behind its wide beach, with attractive rooms in the $40 range. The Hotel Apolo (81/ 444 48) is our favorite in Vila Real, *a good stop when traveling in or out of Spain. Doubles with balconies are about $40.*

FOOD: *The problem with the fast-paced resort areas, especially those frequented by foreign tourists, is that restaurants change quickly. There is the element of fashion, and a place that was wonderful last year may be "found" the next, purchased from the family that owned it, and changed completely. Our suggestion in resort towns is that you shop around for restaurants as you travel, checking posted menus. Expect the prices to be higher than in the rest of Portugal. Our favorable comments on hotel restaurants in Portugal do not hold true here.*

In Faro, Cidade Velha is excellent, established, well known and expensive, with meals in the $20 range. Kappra is in the same range — both are closed on Sunday. On the beach, try Roque, with local specialties at about $10. Matos, also on the beach, is plain, pretty good and even less expensive. Bruno on Rua Alportel is another good choice.

In Loule, the Avenida is good, although expensive, and in Olhão, Ilidro or Aquario are good seafood restaurants. In Olhão, walk along the beachfront near the fish market and look into the little bars. Many of these have nice dining rooms behind the bar, but there is no sign to indicate it.

In Tavira, try the Floresta Vale Caranguejo (which locals may still call the Torralta), a fixed-price tavern that's very popular, or look around the waterfront for seafood restaurants. In Vila Real, we like the Joaquim Gomes for fresh fish at around $10.

SHOPPING: *Not only are there many local crafts in the Algarve, but the area is still rich in local fairs and markets where craftsmen come with their wares. Olhão has shops with prices below those in other cities; Loule is known for its copper, leather and basket work. Ask at the tourist office or your hotel for the published list of events and markets for the current month. At the end of April there is an annual craft fair in Loule.*

FESTIVALS: *On August 15, Castro Marim celebrates the feast of N. S. dos Martires. On the Sunday nearest April 15, there is a Romaria in Loule, and the last two weeks of July there is a fair near the Igreja Carmo in Faro. During August and September there are fairs all over the Algarve, many of which vary from year to year.*

IF TIME IS SHORT: *Skip this side of the Algarve, or if passing through, see Tavira and possibly old Faro, adding Milreu if you are interested in Roman sites.*

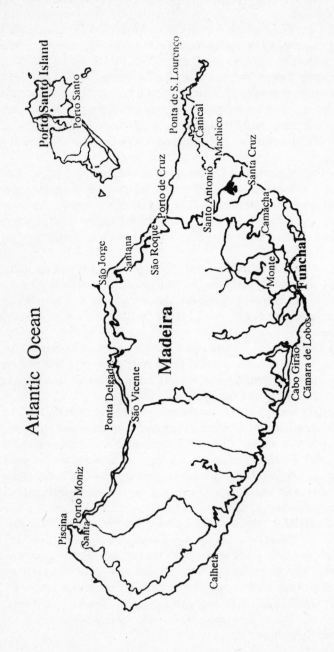

Porto Santo Island

Porto Santo

Ponta de S. Lourenço

Canical

Machico

Santa Cruz

Santo Antonio

Camacha

Porto de Cruz

São Roque

Santana

Funchal

São Jorge

Monte

Cabo Girão

Câmara de Lobos

Atlantic Ocean

Madeira

Ponta Delgada

São Vicente

Porto Moniz

Piscina

Santa

Calheta

Madeira

Even after the island of Porto Santo had been discovered by two of Prince Henry the Navigator's captains, having been driven off course and around the bulge of West Africa by a storm, the much larger main island remained a mystery shrouded in a cloud bank. They sailed back with reports of a cloud that hung constant over the southwest horizon.

The seamen feared that it was the perpetual overcast that covered the sea of darkness, that boiling sea of legend, from which no ship returned. But Prince Henry, and his Captains João Goncalves and Tristão Vaz Teixeira determined to find out what was under the cloud.

When the Captains broke through the mist they found themselves in an idyllic bay, backed by a tree covered mountain. The size and plenty of these trees, which were to provide timbers for Prince Henry's exploring caravels, led its discoverers to name it "Madeira," the Portuguese word for wood.

Its great forests are gone today, cut off for caravels, timber and firewood, burned over to clear land for farming. Unbelievably fertile and well protected by a climate of perpetual springtime, Madeira is one continuous garden today. Grape vines cover its precipitous slopes, and exotic flowers have found a home so favorable that many have escaped the gardens to wander wild.

Temperatures seldom fall below 50° Fahrenheit making it a pleasant environment for travelers escaping winter and providing an equally attractive environment for the gardens which cover the island with luxuriant foliage and an enormous variety of brilliant blossoms. They are at every level, from petunias and begonias, carnations and lilies at ground height, through the roses and dahlias which grow taller than people, the towering hedges of red poinsettias and the engulfing vines of the bougainvillaeas so brilliant one expects them to glow in the dark. As if this weren't enough, above are the flowering trees, the yellow bombax above the lavender puffs of the jacaranda, the red of the coral tree and the white of the magnolias. The senses are almost overcome with color and fragrance in the late spring, but all year round, it is a riot of bright blooms.

Known to Europeans (along with the Azores and the Canaries) as their islands in the sun, Madeira is best known in the New World for its extraordinary wine and its exquisite embroidery. Both of these occupations owe much to the English, whose ties to Madeira are long and several.

Although the first vines and sugar canes were brought by the original settlers in the fifteenth century, the wine industry there boomed during the days of the English colonization of America when the wines of Madeira and the Azores were the only ones allowed to be shipped to the colonies. English merchants quickly saw the profit in this arrangement and established the wine houses and the export trade.

These wine houses are still doing a thriving business and welcome visitors who are interested in touring the ancient lodges and learning about the history of the wines. Perhaps it is wise to begin exploration of the island here, since wine is so central to much that you will see.

Unlike the Canaries, Madeira has no prehistory. Prior to its 1419 discovery it was uninhabited, so there are no dolmen, no hill forts, no Roman settlements, nor even any Romanesque churches. It is about the only place in Portugal without a castle — or indeed any relic of the Middle Ages. The traveler looking only for early architectural or artistic wonders should remain on the mainland.

Madeira's attraction lies instead in its natural beauty — assured by its geology and setting. It is a 30 mile mountain chain of long ridges rising 6,000 feet and dropping abruptly to the ocean at its edges and to deep valleys in the interior. At 5,000 feet altitude lies a broad plateau, the strange and lonely Paul da Serra, rock-strewn and scrubby and often draped in cloud.

The rich deep green that covers most of the island is broken by cliffs of volcanic rock almost black in color and by a softer tufa. Steps and paths, and even buildings, are carved from it.

Architecture is mainly Gothic and baroque, and the most striking feature of the churches are the wooden ceilings and the carved gilt retables often framing fine paintings. Trade with Antwerp and Brussels brought both Flemish and Venetian artwork, especially the former, and excellent examples of both painting and statuary are found in the churches throughout Madeira.

The Sé has a particularly splendid ceiling carved of local wood with ivory inlay. The slender columns of the nave and the arcades of painted stone above them give them an added grace, their simplicity heightening the effect of the ceiling and of the paintings above the high altar. To the right of the chancel there is a rich baroque chapel in gilded wood and marble.

Be sure to see the carved stalls in the chancel with their painted and gilded niches housing statuary. The often humorous carvings depict scenes from fables, the Bible, and the imagination of the artist.

Down the broad Arriaga, past the tourist office, is the Jardim do S. Francisco, housing a botanical garden. All along this avenue jacarandas bloom in the spring. It leads eventually to the Parque de S. Catarina, a lovely public garden overlooking the Silore. The island's first church, the original S. Catarina, was built in 1425 by the wife of Zarco (João Gonçalves was nick-named Zarco for his blue eyes, after one of them was struck by an arrow in the battle of Ceuta in northern Africa).

The current chapel replaced a stone one in the seventeenth century which in turn had replaced the original wooden one in the fifteenth century. The date of the original is commemorated in stone above the door set in a porch of red stone pillars. The garden overlooks the harbor and gives a good view over the town.

Another overlook is from Zarco's residence, the Quinta das Cruzes, now a museum of decorative art set in a fine botanic garden. The house is furnished in sixteenth century Portuguese antiques, with collections of Chinese porcelain, Limoges enamels and ivories, Portuguese silver and lapidary, as well as English and French furniture. In the garden flowering plants grow amid carved stone pieces and there is an orchid house.

Below is the convent of S. Clara, inside whose azulejo covered church is Zarco's gothic tomb. In the convent itself, now a school, there is a cloister with the tombs of his two grand-daughters who founded the Order of S. Clara in Madeira. There is a very fine crucifix over the altar in the adjoining hall.

Just down from the convent is the mansion of the Count of Carvalhal, now the Municipal Museum, with a very nice facade. Inside, it has natural history exhibits including an aquarium and an excellent collection of the birds of the island, well labeled for those who wish to identify varieties seen there.

The Count's "new" Palace was not completed in time for him to live there, but it is now used as the town hall. It has an elegant staircase and is of almost pure baroque style. So is the Igreja do Colégio, which adjoins it. The white walls of these buildings contrast sharply with the basalt stonework at the corners, doors and windows.

The nave of the church is also in contrast to the austere exterior, with azulejos, and exuberant gold altars. The designs in these have been taken from native flora, and their use of the grape vine motifs is reminiscent of the churches north of Porto. The sacristy, to the left of the chancel, has an excellent ceiling, an ornate vestment chest and a frieze of azulejos.

The Museum of Sacred Art, also facing the Praça do Municipio, is in the former Bishop's Palace. Along with Portuguese and Flemish paintings on wood, there are some fine examples of sacred art taken from local churches and monasteries.

About 2 blocks from the harbor front and parallel to it is the Rua de Alfandega, narrow, cobbled, crowded and busy, lined with tiny shops. Following it away from the fortress of S. Lorenço, across the bridges spanning two of the cities three rivers, there is a square with the municipal market at the far end. Particularly busy in the morning, this is the center of commerce in fruit, vegetables, fish and other goods. In front are the colorful flower sellers, in their traditional costumes and black bonnets.

There are other places of interest in Funchal, and it is a city well worth strolling in. Visitors are continually cajoled to ride to Monte, about 4 miles away, and to take the toboggan ride back to town. The toboggans are baskets mounted on wooden runners which slide (none too gently) over the steep cobbled streets, held in check by two straw-hatted drivers who run along behind with the tether ropes. It is the main attraction touted to the thousands of cruise ship passengers who make day-stop at the island.

While we would prefer to walk back down and enjoy the steep streets and colorful gardens that line them, it is worth going to Monte for the view and to see the Igreja de N.S. do Monte and the iron tomb of the Emperor Karl I, the last of the Hapsburgs. Although he is memorialized here in a manner befitting royalty, those who have visited Vienna's Kaisergruft will feel a pang for this exiled king so far away from his homeland and his predecessors in that great line of monarchs. It makes the unusual gesture of

Portugal in bringing Manuel II back from exile to be buried in S. Vicente even more poignant.

For those who don't mind some extraordinary tests of nerve, renting a car in Funchal and driving around the rest of the island can be a series of unforgettably beautiful trips. The terrain is so steep that the roads have to be cut into the tufa and they ascend (and yet worse descend) in dizzying switchbacks. Twenty miles per hour is the absolute maximum speed, and it will likely feel too fast, especially if you look down.

Overlooking Funchal are some lovely quinta gardens: Palhiero Ferriero is only three miles from town and is open weekday mornings. The quinta itself is not open.

Camara de Lobos is a fishing village near Funchal, its harbor set on a stone beach beneath steep cliffs. Women gather at the communal laundry — a noisy place in the morning — on the same beach where the brightly painted fishing boats are hauled in. Looking down from the belvedere above, the laundry laid out on the rocks makes abstract mosaic patterns over the rocks on the beach.

Women, and even very small girls, sit on their doorsteps embroidering; it is a very pleasant village and only a short trip from Funchal, and the first stop in a tour along the south coast. Admirers of Winston Churchill's paintings will recognize the view from the terrace where he sat painting the white houses set in terraces of banana trees.

Beyond, the cliffs of Cabo Girão form a backdrop to the vineyards. Just off the coastal road is Estreito de Camara de Lobos, an attractive village in the wine producing area. It is set around its parish church. The rich baroque decoration and painting inside are worth stopping to see.

Cabo Girão rises almost 2,000 feet straight out of the crashing waves, striped by vineyards whose roots (and the feet of the workers who tend them) cling to an almost invisible terrace in the cliff face. At the top there is a lookout point with a dizzying prospect.

The road to Fonta do Sol is a bit rough, but the sea views open at every turn, with the sharp mountain face dropping in steep ravines — in one of these sits Porta do Sol, whose church has a tiled belfry and a Moorish painted ceiling. Nearby at Lombarda da Porta do Sol is the Capela do S. Espirito, originally built in the center of a plantation owned by a friend of Columbus. Now only the chapel remains, but its azulejos and baroque altars are among the island's richest.

The road continues along the coast, but don't be mislead by the short distance on the map. This circle around the more sparsely settled western end takes two days of traveling. Since the road passes too far inland to allow many shore views, it is probably better to go only as far as Calheta (see the church here for its ceiling and ebony and silver tabernacle, a gift from King Manuel I) and backtrack as far as the turn inland for Paul da Serra (about 8 km east of Loreto). This road climbs sharply away from the coast, through forests to a plateau on which sits a rather desolate moorland. This can be crossed via Lombo do Mouro or Caramula to reach the north-south road between Ribeira Brava and S. Vicente.

Alternatively it provides access through Rabacal to an old part of the levada system. This system of waterways, built before cement, provides needed water supply to much of the island, as well as delightful walks for visitors. Alongside these waterways are well kept paths, although at terrifying heights.

S. Vicente, on the north coast, sits a little apart from the sea, spread out along a deep ravine cut by the mouth of the S. Vicente River. To the west is Seixal, another wine growing area set on a promontory. Further on, past Ribeira da Janela, and the unusual rock formations of its offshore islands, is the north coast's only good harbor, Porto Moniz. At Ribeira da Janela there is a levada path to the Risco waterfall — a broad path without the sharp vertical drop-off on one side that many of the other paths have. Beyond, toward Senta, the road climbs up the face of a rock wall which overhangs the village. The drive is not for the timid but leads to spectacular views.

East of S. Vicente, the road to Boaventura lies under an impressive cliff, but vines still cling to the landscape, protected from the wind by rows of broom. Arco S. Jorge lies in a deeply eroded valley from which the road climbs to a belvedere where the driver can stop to look at the scenery. The road is such that there isn't much opportunity to glance away for the views while driving!

The church of S. Jorge is unusually rich for so small a town. The gold baroque altar is flanked by salomonic columns and the chancel has a very fine silver lamp and painted ceiling. The vestment chest in the sacristy is beautifully decorated as well.

Beyond is Santana, a village quite unlike the fishing harbors of the rest of the island. It is set in steep green slopes broken by waterfalls and flower-filled meadows. The houses are of wood with sharply pitched roofs covered in thatch. Gardens full of brilliant flowers are hedged in boxwood. The village is seen best from the road leading to the Parque das Queimadas. Although the road is unpaved, it is well kept and travels between the cottages and gardens to a lovely park at the foot of Pico Ruiva. This highest peak on the island is reached by a three hour climb beginning at the rest house at Queimadas, just to the southwest.

There are nice views beyond Santana as the road continues to San Roque, a tiny village on the crest of a long ridge separating two valleys. Beyond, the road turns inland to the mountains. From Ribeiro Frio there is a very nice levada path to Balcôes, where the view extends from the jagged mountain peaks into the deep valleys below.

At Flora da Madura is an excellent botanical garden and two belvederes with good views of unusual rock formations. These may be reached from Funchal via Terriero da Luta and the Poiso Pass, a rather desolate place of well over 4,000 feet altitude, only 8 km (most of them straight up!) from Funchal.

Another route out of Funchal leads along the coast to the east, through fishing villages and along a corniche road through uncultivated hillsides. Santa Cruz has the church of S. Salvador, considered the oldest remaining on the island, built in 1533. It has a painted chapel and fine Manueline features. Beyond is Machico, where there is a lovely rose window in the parish church and two fine doorways. At Caniçal is the only sandy beach on the island — the others are rock.

A road from Machico leads inland to Portela where there are dramatic views of the mountains from the pass. San Antonio da Serra is a resort village with views, a park and a very good golf course.

From San Antonio, a steep road passes through several tunnels into the islands deepest valley, the crater of an extinct volcano, and to the village of Curral das Freiras, the "corral of the nuns." The monastery here, away from the coast, was built by the S. Clara nuns to protect them from the ravages of marauding pirates. Their convent on the coast had suffered regularly from their attacks. For a spectacular view down into the crater go to Eira do Serrado on its rim.

Madeira At A Glance

A volcanic island, 550 miles from Lisbon, in the Atlantic, with dramatic landscapes, luxuriant vegetation and moderate year 'round climate. The island is reached by cruise ships or from Lisbon via TAP Airlines.

TRANSPORTATION: Is easiest by local buses which run on frequent schedule to all parts of the island, or by rented car. There are regular tours, but these are quite expensive, especially considering the ease and frequency of local bus travel. The tourist office at Avenida Arriaga 18 can arrange tours or give you bus schedules. Hertz and Avis both have car rental offices at the airport, but in busy seasons its best to reserve ahead. (Avis telex 72101P and Hertz telex 72136.) Taxis are another way of traveling, especially to Camara de Lobos. Arrange with your driver to return at a specific hour to pick you up.

LODGING: Top of the line here is Reid's Hotel (23001, telex 72139 Reids P), generally listed among the world's finest. Whether it is for the hotel itself or for its spectacular seacliff setting with acres of private gardens, Reid's does deserve its reputation. Most of its guest rooms have balconies overlooking the ocean. There are two heated seawater swimming pools as well as the full assortment of facilities expected at a resort hotel: several restaurants, health center, tennis courts, sauna, easy arrangements for fishing and all the water sports. Expensive by Portuguese standards, its $165 to $185 for a double in high season (winter) and $130 to $150 in the summer. It's very British in atmosphere and in clientele.

Our choice, however, would be the Hotel Savoy (22031, telex 72153), also overlooking the sea, but only a ten minute walk to the center of Funchal. It has as much of the old world elegance as Reid's, with a little more local charm. That does not mean that its service suffers in the least — it is also a superb hotel, with a full range of facilities, restaurants, nightclubs, pools, tennis courts, and its own jetty for sea bathing and water sports. The furnishings are traditional and well chosen; views are splendid. Rates are surprisingly low for such a world class hotel, $70 to $100 for a double in season.

The Hotel S. João (23343) is a little less elegant, but also very good with balconies for all guest rooms, two pools, fitness facilities, several restaurants and bars and resort activities. Guests here can take lessons in local handcrafts as well. It is not in central Funchal, but runs courtesy buses for its guests. Rates are in the $60-70 range for a double.

In the same price range but full of more local charm is the Quinta da Penha da Franca (290-87). It is a converted private estate, furnished in fine antiques. It has a swimming pool, lovely gardens with good views and the atmosphere of a private home. It is a short walk from the center of Funchal. Doubles range from $60-80.

Near Reid's is the small Quinta Lembranca, a seaside home with few rooms and less grand furnishings, but spacious and comfortable with a warm atmosphere. Doubles are under $40.

It is not essential to stay in Funchal, but if you want to have the city's wide choice of restaurants in the evening, it is the better choice. One or two nights elsewhere on a trip around the rest of the island makes sense, however, and makes traveling more leisurely.

The Pousada dos Vinhaticos is on the road between Funchal and San Vicente, at the top of a pass, with a full vista of mountain scenery. It is a well-run inn, with modern furniture and rates in the low $40s. There are some nice walking paths in the area and the climate is refreshing all year.

FOOD: The tropical fruits of the island are outstanding, from the Banana da Prata (found only here since it does not travel well), to the familiar mango and the annona, or "custard apple." Bife de Atum is tuna steak served with sauteed corn (milho frito). The Carne Vinho e Alho is a marinated pork with garlic. The local sweet is Bola de Mel, a honey cake a bit like gingerbread.

Reid's grill (where many guests still "dress" for dinner) and the Fleur-dy-Lys at the Savoy are the finest dining rooms in Funchal, in the $40 and $30 ranges respectively, each certainly well worth the price.

Romano, on Largo do Corpo Santo is our choice as the finest non-hotel restaurant with a full menu and good atmosphere at about $15 (closed Mondays). The best value, with excellent seafood but absolutely no atmosphere, is Gavinas just past the Lido swimming complex. It has a local air all its own and if your idea of a proper place to eat is a hotel dining room, you may not like it. But if you want fine seafood well prepared, you'll find it here and have trouble paying more than $8 for it.

If you want good dependable continental food without any new or unusual flavors, in a British atmosphere, try Casa da Carochinha near the tourist office. The roast beef and Yorkshire pudding will cost about $15, which is not unreasonable, if that is what you are looking for.

There are many other good restaurants, and we suggest that you use the same "browse and sniff" technique that we recommend on the mainland. A good pastry shop for an afternoon glass of Madeira and a "little bit of something" is Casa Minas Gerais on Avenida do Infante. The bar Marcelino has fado in the evening (as do several of the hotel night clubs, but not every night).

SHOPPING: There are two tourist shopping centers for locally made products, a good idea if time is short and also a good place to go first for an idea of quality, variety and price. Once you have seen the examples here you will have a better idea of what to look for in the shops and markets, as well as what to pay. Casa do Turista is behind the theater and Cayres Tourist Shopping Center is on Rua Dr. Fernão Ornelas. The Bazar do Povo on Rua Bettencourt has a general line of handwork, Artecouro in the Infante shopping center has good local leather work and Patricio and Gouveia have fine embroidery and needlework.

FESTIVALS: During Carnival season, Funchal is decorated and processions and parties fill its streets. In April there is a flower festival where every window is decorated in flowers and there are colorful parades and activities for three days. In September there is a wine festival — a fairly new event promoted by the Tourist Board, with tastings and folklore shows. We'd opt instead for one of the previously mentioned traditional festivals. On New Year's Eve, the harbor at Funchal is full of cruise ships for the huge fireworks display over the harbor.

IF TIME IS SHORT: A day will show you the best of Funchal and Camara do Lobos, then go inland — on a local bus or with a tour if you don't want to drive — to see the spectacular mountain scenery, or west along the coast to Ponta do Sol or Calheta for the sea cliffs and mountains.

Azores (Açores)

Visitors to the Azores invariably speak of the "other world" quality, a sort of detached atmosphere that combines with their tropical-volcanic geography to make them both lovely and interesting to visit. They have been compared in appearance to western Ireland, for their intense green landscapes and white cottages, but the bright tropical flowers, as well as the volcanic craters and rock foundations give them a character all their own.

There are nine islands from São Miguel, the largest at about 40 by 10 miles, to tiny Cavo, only about 8 square miles. From tip to tip, the archipelago is about 500 miles long. Like Madeira, the Azores are volcanic and have no prehistory. Their history is mostly a local one, except for an occasional sea battle and small roles in the vicissitudes of mainland royal politics: King Alfonso VI was imprisoned there after the restoration. There was an Allied air base there during World War II.

They were, of course, discovered by Prince Henry's ships and have remained Portuguese — loyal even during the years of the Spanish domination of Portugal in the early fifteenth century. An independent and resourceful lot, local residents fought off a Spanish attempt to land on Terceira by driving a herd of wild cattle into their landing force.

New Englanders planning to visit the Azores should first go to New Bedford, Massachusetts, since most of its Portuguese inhabitants have their origins in the Azores and have family ties there. Many of the emigrants returned to the Azores with their "fortunes" made in the new world, and you will find that a familiarity with New Bedford a great way to meet people in the Azores.

The climate makes the Azores attractive all year round, and the landscape, although different from Madeira, is just as lush and lovely. But mass tourism passed it by, much to the delight of those who have discovered it. Accommodations are comfortable and simple; there are no rows of high rise hotels. Its people are exceptionally hospitable, even for Portuguese, to whom hospitality seems second nature. You will be helped, guided and catered to as though you were a family guest.

São Miguel, first seen from above as the plane descends into Ponta Delgada's airport, appears as a solid bank of green in the sea. The impression stays. Once on land the lush vegetation is broken only by flowers — hydrangea bushes form hedgerows — and by trim white houses.

In Ponta Delgada, the capital, the gleaming white of the buildings is set against well-kept public gardens. Its architecture, like that of Madeira, dates from Portugal's golden age of exploration and uses stark white walls set off by black volcanic stone for corners, doors and windows. The geometric outlining is broken by the use of Manueline and baroque ornamentation, especially at the arches. The whole effect is stunning.

The most outstanding example of this architecture in Ponta Delgada is the Cathedral, which has a fine Manueline door and an ornate gold high altar. The convent of N.S. da Esperança houses a statue presented by the Pope in the sixteenth century. The jewels which surround the statue have been gifts over the centuries since then. The chapel, like most of the islands' churches, is lined with azulejos.

Other churches in Ponta Delgada worth seeing are S. José, with its azulejo lined walls and high relief carvings, and S. Sebastião with its carved choir. There is a natural history museum, with art and ethnology exhibits as well, in the Convento do S. Andre.

Ponta Delgada is small enough to get around in easily on foot. Set along the curve of a bay, its waterfront is a favorite place for strolling.

The one place in the Azores which has an international resort flavor, having been a favorite of Victorian British travelers, is Furnas. The thermal spa there is one of the most varied in Europe, offering over twenty different types: cold, hot, mud and effervescent, pouring forth in pools, springs, geysers and clouds of steam. It's a fascinating place to visit, even if you don't "take the waters," since the landscape alternates between bare black lava and luxuriant green plants of the adjoining botanic garden of Terra Nostra Park.

See the food section for a description of the meals cooked by the thermal heat at Lake Furnas. This entire long valley is surrounded by mountains and a waterfall drops from one of these directly into Lake Furnas.

Lakes dot the islands; in addition to Lake Furnas there is the Seven Cities, a double lake with one part blue and the other green.

Nearby is Jardim Pitoresco, a beautiful public garden. Logoa do Fogo fills an extinct crater, its slopes overgrown in tropical plants. Adjacent, inside the nature reserve, is the Lombades gorge.

The Ilheu da Vila Franco, just off the shore on the south, forms a circle around an enclosed lagoon-like area. Swimming here is the popular attraction, but the shapes of the surrounding rocks are worth the trip, even for those not of aquatic bent.

The towns of São Miguel — Vila Franca do Campo and Ribeira Grande — and other villages, are attractive and their churches well decorated. The church of S. Miguel in Vila Franca has an especially nice high altar and there is a pilgrimage church on the hill to the north of town.

Although one of the smaller islands of the archipelago, Faial is one of the best equipped to handle visitors, probably due to its large port. Like the others, it is a lush green garden, with blue hydrangea hedgerows, but its chief floral feature is its camellias. Small enough to be explored on foot, the island has good paths for hiking. In the center of Faial rises Caldeira, a perfectly circular crater with a lake at its floor and beautiful vegetation filling up its sides and streaming down its banks beside the little brooks that feed the lake.

Most of the island is agricultural. Its capital, Horta, still shows signs of its Flemish colonization in the fifteenth century. Its large harbor, built and equipped as a refueling station during the days of the great transatlantic liners, is now a haven for pleasure craft. Along with its churches and their stunning azulejo walls (see both S. Salvador and the Convento do S. Francisco) it has a fine museum of ecclesiastical art (the Museu do Arte Sacre). There is a fort, S. Cruz, on the island as well.

Terceira, so called because it was the third island to be discovered, has a major airport, where the "stopover" flights set down. It is well equipped for travelers, and its capital, Angra do Heroísmo, is perhaps the loveliest in the Azores, with flowering shrubs everywhere between its old white houses. Damage done by a 1980 earthquake has been substantially repaired.

Angra has a castle, rare on the islands, which contains the richly decorated Governor's Palace. King Alfonso VI was imprisoned in the castle. There is a museum covering a wide variety of subjects.

The churches are of sixteenth and seventeenth century origin: The Colégio church has good gold work and azulejos, while the

Sé's Chapter House contains an unusual set of portraits of its bishops and some excellent pieces of ecclesiastical art.

Caldeira is a crater nine miles in diameter and Algar do Carvão is a remarkable series of caverns with strange rock formations. Although the list of things to do here seems short, the island's natural beauty and its gardens, as well as the atmosphere of its old town, make it well worth visiting.

Graciosa is lined with white sandy beaches and is only about ten miles long. It is flatter and more gently rolling than the others, but has its own volcanic wonder, the Furno do Enxofre. This warm water lake is reached by a tunnel in the rocks surrounding it, so deep that the sun lights it only at mid-day. The landscapes are agricultural with windmills and vineyards.

In Santa Cruz, its capital, there is a museum of ethnology, and the parish church has nice rose windows.

Pico is well named for its mountain, nearly 8,000 feet in altitude. Black lava alternates with vineyards, orchards and beautiful flowers. The Furna da Malha is a 7,000 foot long tunnel formed by the sea and the volcano, and Furna de Frei Matias is an interesting cave.

Long a whaling port, Lajes, its capital, has an excellent whaling museum (Museo dos Baleiros), and whalers still put out from here. Small villages dot the island as do little churches. Keys to these, if they are locked, are at nearby houses — it is sort of pot luck as to which ones you will be able to get into, but well worth the effort. Most have lovely altars or, at the very least, good examples of primitive decoration.

São Jorge's central mountain is only half the height of Pico's, rising to a high plateau used to pasture the dairy stock from which is derived the island's major product: cheese. Velas, its capital, is still a little town, but has one of the Azores' oldest churches, built in 1460. Its carving is particularly fine.

Santa Maria was the first island discovered, and is of particular interest to those travelers who, like us, "collect" places associated with Christopher Columbus's voyages. He anchored the Nina here so that his men could attend Mass at the church. Its Pico Alto is under 2,000 feet high and is a pleasant climb for its view.

Santa Maria is a fossil hunter's paradise, particularly near the village of Figueival. Vila do Porto's parish church contains a Manueline ceiling in its chapel, which is the only remnant of the original church. The Convento do S. Francisco is not the original structure, either, but contains fine carvings and azulejos.

Considered to be the oldest church in the Azores, the Anjos chapel escaped the frequent pirate raids that ravaged most of the others. Its triptych, woodcarving and azulejos are excellent.

The hardest island to reach is tiny Corvo, with its toylike village, Vila Nova. Its volcano, Monte Gordo, rises with a secondary crater, inside of which is a lake with tiny islands. Everything here seems to be in miniature, even its own breed of cream-colored cattle.

We have saved our favorite for last, Flores, the island of flowers, was the last discovered, along with tiny Corvo next door. It is the outermost of the archipelago and absolutely covered with flowers. Its steep coastline has a natural amphitheatre scooped out at one side, with long waterfalls dropping from the cliffs.

It is difficult to find a scene on the entire island which is not framed in hydrangeas. These shrubs, along with other lush tropical plants grow in banks everywhere. The terrain is dramatic, with deep ravines and valleys, caves, craters, mountains and the surrounding sea beating against the cliffs of the deeply cut irregular coastline. Inland, cropping up between the shrubbery, are strange rock formations and several lakes. Lagoa Funda is surrounded by mountains rising from its sandy shore.

The capital, Santa Cruz, is filled with hydrangeas. Its sixteenth century church, S. Pedro, has a fine gilded high altar. The museum is well worth seeing for its excellent ivory work and local lace.

The caves at Enxaréus, not far from Santa Cruz, are fascinating for their rock formations, and there are several interesting churches, including the large pilgrimage church of N.S. dos Remédios on the western side. There is a road around the south coast and one across the center. One of the island's few taxis can be hired to take you on tour.

The Azores At A Glance

Archipelago consisting of nine islands in the Atlantic, 760 miles from Lisbon.

GETTING THERE: *The Azores are a common stopover point for travel between Lisbon and the U.S. Once there, inter-island travel is best done via SATA, the local airline which connects all but Corvo. Reservations on SATA can be made through TAP (1-800-221-7370).*

Inter-island boat travel, except between Pico, S. Jorge, and Faial, is almost non-existent. If you are connecting to a mainland flight, allow an extra day if a storm is expected. These are fierce, especially at Flores, where the winds meet violently, so local flights may be cancelled.

LODGING: *On São Miguel, our first choice in Ponta Delgada is the Hotel S. Pedro (96/ 2223 telex 83550), the former town house of the Bostonian, Thomas Hickling, who made his fortune here exporting oranges. Surrounded by gardens and overlooking the sea, it is furnished with antiques and filled with fresh flowers. Relaxing and surprisingly informal, the S. Pedro's top priority is in making its guests comfortable and at home. Doubles are $35 to $50.*

The Albergaria Casa das Palmeiras (96/ 22621) is an old villa of unique architecture with nine guest rooms, each with private bath. Comfortable doubles are $25 to $40, depending on the season (winter is high season here).

If you insist on a modern hotel, the Avenida (96/ 27331 telex 82352) offers 80 small rooms with color TV; doubles are in the $45 to $50 range.

Hotel Terra Nostra at Furnas sits alongside the botanical gardens, a stone villa in the art deco style. It is exactly what you expect at an elegant old spa, with large rooms, lovely gardens and good service. Doubles are in the $30 range and provide a good opportunity to stay in one of these classic old resorts without stretching the budget.

On Faial we like the Estralagem de S. Cruz (92/ 23021 telex 82255), built in the foundation of an old fort overlooking the water. With its modern inn architecture and use of local furnishing styles it reminds us of the Pousada at Valença set into the old fortification walls. Doubles are about $40.

On Terceira, the Albergaria Cruzeiro (95/ 24071 telex 82313) in Angra is a modern attractive hotel with doubles at $25 to $30 but the Hotel de Angra (95/ 24041 telex 82304) has more character and balconies for every room. Doubles here are $35.

Graciosa offers less choice, but the Residéntial S. Cruz is clean, hospitable and near the airport. All of its rooms have private bath and its doubles are about $20.

On Flores there is the Estralagem das Flores (92/ 52496) at $15; advance reservations are a must. On some of these smaller islands there are private homes which offer pleasant rooms. The best way to find these is to ask at your lodging on the larger islands. They will know of places and will usually make the phone call for you as well.

FOOD: *Seafood is king here, with tropical fruits, and fine local wines. Look for lapas (limpets), caranguejo (crab), and Masa Sovada (a pasta) and Bolo de Serta (corn bread).*

At Furnas they do a caldeirada (fish stew) in a pot that they bury in the ground near the hot springs to be cooked by the steam. The Hotellocas Terra Nostra has a "Tea House" at the lake where this dish is prepared and served. The hotel itself has a good dining room with meals under $10. Retiro at Furnas is also good and in the same price range with regional dishes.

In Ponta Delgada, the Hotel S. Pedro's dining room is not only excellent by any standard, but is quite inexpensive with full meals in the $12 range. It is tops for service and atmosphere as well as for the food. It is significantly better, we think, than the Casa Velha which is in the same price group. The Nacional is very inexpensive, with dinners of island seafood and other regional specialties in the $5 range.

In Ribeira Grande, we like Fervedouro with regional dishes at about $7.50 for a full meal. Its food is every bit as good as the "nouvelle French" served at Fannie et Melanie for twice the price. Unfortunately Fervedouro is only open on weekends. Realejo is a good choice in Vila Franca.

On Faial, the Estralagem S. Cruz, mentioned under **LODGING** *above, has a very good dining room, almost as good as the S. Pedro, with full meals at about $12. Tripeiro is reliable with local dishes at about $5.*

On Pico, the Restaurant Pico is good at about $8 for dinner and Lagoa, while not quite as good, is about half the price, with a terrace open in good weather.

Terceira has the Beira-Mar for the top choice with regional and international dishes in the $12 range. Their grilled squid is especially good. Ladeira is a close second with Portuguese food and slightly lower prices. Ilha in S. Sebastião is good with local specialties at about $7.50.

SHOPPING: *Local crafts are the things to buy in the Azores. Baskets and wickerwork, pottery, handweaving, embroidered linens, woodcarving, wool sweaters, whale ivory scrimshaw and handmade laces are all good buys here. Look in little shops and sidewalk stalls for any of these, or go to Casa Regional da Ilha Verde in Ponta Delgada which carries the products of cottage industries from all of the islands.*

FESTIVALS: *The Whalers Festival (Festa dos Baleiros) on Pico is the last Sunday in August. On the fifth Sunday after Easter is the* colorful procession of Senhor Santo Christo when the route is carpeted with flowers. Near Ribeira Grande, at Riberira Seca, June 29 is the pilgrimage of S. Pedro called As Cavalhadas. During the spring and summer there are a number of local festivals with varying dates, so be sure to ask about these if you are there between April and July.

IF TIME IS SHORT: Choose one island and see it, rather than spending all of your time hopping from one to the other. It is possible to see the smaller ones in well-planned overnight stays, but be prepared to hire a taxi guide.

Glossary

Adega – a wine cellar or wine bar.

Atrium (pl. Atria) – a patio in the center of a building.

Azulejos – glazed tiles used to face walls and ceilings.

Belvedere – an overlook, a specially constructed terrace.

Boisserie – bosses, raised knob-like ornaments, often found at the intersections of groining in a ceiling.

Campo – a field or large park.

Castro – a Celtic or Roman hillfort.

Chagas – related to the Order of Santa Clara (St. Clair).

Cincture – a belt worn by those in holy orders.

Citânia – an ancient city.

Corbel – a bracket of stone used to support a cornice or the spring of an arch.

Corniche – a road or path cut into the side of a mountain or steep slope.

Crenellated – notched or toothed stone or brickwork atop a wall, battlement or tower.

Dolmen – a prehistoric monument of two or more upright stones supporting a horizontal stone slab.

Enceinte – the enclosure of a castle or fortress wall.

Espigueiro – a granary, usually set on stilts, common in the Minho.

Ex voto – an offering made in prayer or thanksgiving.

Fado – a style of singing peculiar to Portugal.

Garth – the center space in a cloister.

Intaglio – a design engraved or cut into the surface.

Jesse Tree – an artistic rendition of the family tree of the ancestry of Christ.

Largo – a small square.

Lavabo – a place for washing, a small decorative fountain.

Misericordia – Hospitals built by the church, now the name of the churches that were once attached to these.

Mudejar – Arabic or Moorish style.

Oast-house – a conical kiln used for drying hops, malt or tobacco.

Ogival – a reversing curve in an arch, ending in a point.

Pensão – a lodging house, similar to the French pension.

Poor Clares – Sisters of the Order of Santa Clara.

Pousada – an inn operated by the Portugal government.

Praça – a square or plaza.

Quinta – a country house, often a wine estate.

Romaria – a religious pilgrimage.

Rossio – the popular name for certain large squares which are the center of activity in a town or city, always The Rossio, replacing the official name.

Solar – manor house.

Senhorial – belonging to a titled family.

Tessellated – an intertwining and perfectly fitted repeating design.

Torre – a tower, belfry.

Varinhas – women who sell fish.

APPENDIX I

Cast of Characters

Very few travelers actually read the section on the history of a place — or remember its details if they do. More often it is a reference point, something to flip back through to answer a question. That is hard to do when the information is in paragraph form, so here is our answer, from the notebook we carry for our own reference. It is certainly not complete, but a framework on which to hang the details.

2000-1000 B.C. – Earliest sites (Zambugal) date from this period, when Mediterranean peoples came in search of metals.

1000-500 B.C. – The Phoenicians establish trading posts on the coast, Celts establish settlements and Lusitanian tribes inhabit the western regions.

400-100 B.C. – The Romans move in, building roads, bridges and cities, driving out the Celts and governing the Lusitanians.

400-500 – The Visigoths and Sueves take advantage of the disintegrating Roman political structure and move in.

700 – The Moors sweep in from North Africa.

800-1100 – Various leaders push the Moors back, but not out.

1139 – Alfonso Henriques wins a decisive victory over the Moors, securing northern Portugal, proclaiming himself king and the independence of Portugal.

1147 – Lisbon captured from the Moors with the help of English and Flemish crusaders.

1185-1211 – Sancho I drives the Moors back to the eastern Algarve and encourages foreign trade and Portuguese culture.

1248-1279 – Alfonso III captures the final Moorish stronghold in the Algarve and establishes the national boundaries that exist today.

1279-1325 – King Dinis promotes agriculture and education, establishes a single language, writes poetry and sires a number of illegitimate children, whilst his wife Isabel is busy with the philanthropies that will bring her sainthood.

1325-1357 – Alphonso IV reigns, still obsessed with the childhood fear that his father would turn over the succession to one of his illegitimate half-brothers. This paranoia leads him to arrange for the murder of his son Pedro's Castilian mistress (and possibly wife), Inez de Castro.

1357-67 – Pedro I, after extracting vengeance upon Inez's slayers, encourages commerce and justice.

1367-1383 – Fernando I, unpopular at best, leaves Portugal in the regency of his even more unpopular wife Leonor and her Italian lover. The Spanish immediately claim the throne and attack.

1385-1433 – João I, Pedro's illegitimate son, well liked by the people but badly outnumbered militarily, defeats the army of Spain at Aljubarota and is proclaimed king. He rules brilliantly, marries Philippa of Lancaster, daughter of John of Gaunt, cementing a long alliance with England. They are active, popular rulers and raise three sons, one of whom is Prince Henry the Navigator.

1433-1438 – Duarte I encouraged exploration and expansion of the empire, a policy continued by successive kings.

1495-1521 – Manuel I reaps the harvest as Portuguese explorers land in Brazil and discover a sea route to India. Building flourishes and the Manueline style is born.

1581-1640 – Philip II of Spain takes advantage of the death of Portugal's young king and annexes Portugal. Drawn into Spain's wars, Portugal loses much of her empire in the 60 years of Spanish rule.

1640-1668 – The Duke of Bragança, descendent of João I, is proclaimed King João IV and Spanish rule is thrown off.

1706-1750 – João V, builder of Mafra and the University of Coimbra spends vast sums of the wealth still flowing in from Brazil.

1750-1777 – José I is king, but leaves the business of government to the Marquês do Pombal, who quickly becomes a dictator. The great earthquake of 1755 devastates Lisbon and Pombal rebuilds it.

1807-1811 – French occupation during the Peninsular War.

1908 – Assassination of Carlos I and his heir.

1910 – Abdication of Manuel II, end of the monarchy and establishment of the Republic.

1928 – Salazar becomes Minister of Finance, then Prime Minister, then dictator.

1974 – The armed forces seize power and an elective government is established soon thereafter.

APPENDIX II

Menu Terms

Breakfast – Always included with lodging, Pequeno almoço.
Lunch – Almoço.
Dinner – Jantar.
Appetizers – Acepipes.
Soups – Sopas.
Meat – Carne.
Fish – Piexe.
Shellfish – Mariscos.

Dishes you will find on the menu:

Açorda – A hearty soup, often with bread in it, always delicious and always with garlic.
Ameijos – Clams, often served with pork as Porco da Alentejo.
Ameixas – Plums, particularly as preserved at Elvas.
Arroz – Rice.
Assado – Oven roasted or baked.
Aziete – Olive oil.
Bacalhau – Salted cod.
Batata – Potato.
Bife – Beef.
Cabrito – Kid.
Cafe – Coffee.
Caldeirada – A fish stew, much like those found all along the Mediterranean, not at all like a chowder, to which it is sometimes compared.
Caldo Verde – A reliably good soup made of kale and potatoes.
Camarões – Shrimp.
Cebolha – Onion.
Cha – Tea.
Cogumelos – Mushrooms.
Costeleta – A chop.
Cozidos – boiled.
Espadarte – Swordfish.
Figos – Figs.
Frango – Chicken.

Fritos – Fried.
Grelhada – Grilled.
Guisado – Stewed.
Indiana – Curried.
Lavagante – Lobster.
Leite – Milk.
Leitão – Roast suckling pig.
Linguado – Sole.
Lombo – A fillet.
Lula – Squid.
Morangos – Strawberries.
Nas Brasas – Charcoal grilled.
Ovos – Eggs.
Pão – Bread.
Pão Doce – Sweet rolls.
Piri-Piri – Hot sauce.
Porco – Pork.
Quentes – Hard boiled (as in eggs).
Salada – Salad.
Truta – Trout.
Vinagre – Vinegar.
Vitela – Veal.

Utensils you will need:

Knife – Faca.
Fork – Garfo.
Spoon – Colher.
Glass – Vidro, copo.
Napkin – Guardanapo.
Plate – Praca, prato.

To ask for more:

Another – Um outro, mais um.

APPENDIX III

The Anatomy of a Church
(With some general notes on architecture)

In describing churches and other buildings, we use terms of art, not to impress, but for better and shorter description. It is easier to say (and to read) "entablature" than "the stone pieces that run along the top of the columns." When it is not clearer and easier, we do not. It is just as easy to say "matching pulpits" as "ambones," so we do.

Here follows a layman's guide which we devised for ourselves as we traveled, so we'd know where to look when the brochure or guidebook said "note the niche to the left of the chancel arch." If architecture is your forte, skip this amateur rendition. Where it is helpful, we've given the name in Portuguese so you can ask directions.

Aisles – The sections to either side of the nave, separated from the nave by columns. Not present in all churches.

Apse – The architectural name for the part of the building, often rounded, in which the chancel is located.

Azulejos – Glazed tiles used to cover walls; earlier ones are polychrome, while the more frequently seen later ones are blue and white.

Chancel (Capela Mor) – The business part of the church, usually raised, containing the main altar, from which the Mass is said.

Chancel Arch – The large arch, usually flanked by pillars, which separates the chancel from the nave and frames the main altar.

Chapter House – A room, usually off the cloister (often off its upper story) which houses church treasures.

Cloister (Claustro) – The open arcaded area adjoining most cathedrals and monasteries, usually directly beside the nave and entered by a door from the transept or side of the nave.

Coro Alto – The upper choir, usually in a balcony to the rear of the nave, reached from stairs in the rear of the church or from the second floor of an adjoining cloister or building.

High Altar – The correct name for the main altar at the end of the chancel.

Nave – The main body of the church where the people sit.

Nuns' Choir – Usually on the main level of the nave, in the rear of the church, but separated by a grillwork.

Organ Loft – The balcony on which the organ sits, sometimes in the coro alto, often highly ornamented.

Retable (Retablo) – The altarpiece or back panel above the altar.

Sacristy – A room, usually rich in ornament, which is used for storage of vestments and other items. Often the highlight of a church, these are reached in several ways. If there is a cloister, look for a door at the corner nearest the chancel. Or look for a door off the transept on the chancel side or off the side of the chancel itself. Larger churches may have all three doors, leading to a passageway from which the sacristy is reached. Like the sacristies themselves, these passageways often have richly decorated ceilings.

Side altars – Little altars set along the outer walls of either the nave or side aisles.

Side Chapels (Capelas) – Side altars set in recessed areas, usually behind a wooden railing. Look for light switches below or beside these rails or inside the chapels just to either side. It is all right to step inside these to look for the light switches if there is no one to ask. Turn them off afterward.

Transept – In churches built in the shape of a cross, the arms, usually containing chapels, to the immediate sides of the chancel arch. Right and left transepts refer to their direction as you face the altar.

Vestibule – The little entryway, usually wooden, through which the church is entered.

Plan of Typical Church

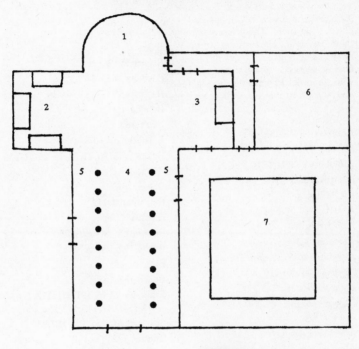

1. High altar
2. Transept and side altars
3. Transept and side altars
4. Nave
5. Aisles
6. Sacristy
7. Cloister

Index

During the course of preparing this index we have tried to keep in mind the primary purpose of this book. You probably won't will not look for the kings and queens here, but you will want quick access to information on towns as you approach or come upon them. The primary listings, therefore, are the city and town listings. We have also included an index of the *At A Glance* sections, by major city and town name, in order to make the lodging, food and other information of those sections even more readily available and useful.

xxi

Other Books Available From Mills and Sanderson

The Alaska Traveler: Year 'Round Vacation Adventures for Everyone, by Steven C. Levi. With maps and cartoons, this is a unique insider's guide to gold panning, stalking big game, windsurfing, dogsledding, etc. $9.95

The Portugal Traveler: Great Sights and Hidden Treasures, by Barbara Radcliffe Rogers and Stillman Rogers. A companion to fascinating places to eat and sleep, festivals and other events as well as insider tips to enrich your visit. Includes city maps. $9.95

The Cruise Answer Book - 1989: A Comprehensive Guide to the Ships and Ports of the Americas, by Charlanne Fields Herring. The premier guide to the cruise ships, itineraries, ports-of-call, and shore adventures awaiting vacationers. $9.95

Sicilian Walks: Exploring the History and Culture of the Two Sicilies, by William J. Bonville. Self-guided tours (with maps)of Sicily and the adjacent Italian mainland. $9.95

Bedtime Teaching Tales for Kids: A Parent's Storybook, by Gary Ludvigson, Ph. D. Eighteen engrossing stories to help children 5-11 work through problems such as fear of failure, sibling rivalry, bullies, divorce, death, child abuse, handicaps,etc. $9.95

Your Food-Allergic Child: A Parent's Guide, by Janet E. Meizel. How to shop and cook for children with allergies, plus nutrient and chemical reference charts of common foods, medications, and grocery brands. $9.95

There ARE Babies to Adopt: A Resource Guide for Prospective Parents, by Christine A. Adamec. "Dispels the baby shortage myth and teems about the choices available."- *Parents Adoption Pipeline*. $9.95 / $16.95 (hardcover)

Winning Tactics for Women Over Forty: How to Take Charge of Your Life and Have Fun Doing It, by Anne De Sola Cardoza and Mavis B. Sutton. For women left alone through separation, divorce or death, "this title presents many positive, concrete options for change." - *The Midwest Book Review* $9.95

Fifty and Fired: How to Prepare for it - What to do When it Happens, by Ed Brandt with Leonard Corwen. How to deal with getting forcefully "restructured" out of your job at the wrong time in your career. $9.95 / $16.95 (hardcover)

Aquacises: Restoring and Maintaining Mobility with Water Exercises, by Miriam Study Giles. Despite age, obesity or physical handicaps, anyone can improve their fitness with this instructive illustrated handbook. $9.95

60-Second Shiatzu: How to Energize, Erase Pain, and Conquer Tension in One Minute, by Eva Shaw. A helpfully illustrated, quick-results introduction to do-it-yourself acupressure. $7.95

Your Astrological Guide to Fitness by Eva Shaw. Ideal exercises, sports, menus, and related gifts for those born under each sign of the zodiac. $9.95

Bachelor in the Kitchen: Beyond Bologna and Cheese, by Gordon Haskett with Wendy Haskett. Fast and easy ways to make delectable meals, snacks, drinks from easily obtainable ingredients. $7.95

Order Form

If you are unable to find our books in your local bookstore, you may order them directly from us. Please enclose check or money order for amount of purchase and add $1.00 per book handling charge.

( ) Levi / *The Alaska Traveler* $9.95

( ) Rogers / *The Portugal Traveler* $9.95

( ) Herring / *The Cruise Answer Book - 1989* $9.95

( ) Bonville / *Sicilian Walks* $9.95

( ) Ludvigson / *Bedtime Teaching Tales for Kids* $9.95

( ) Meizel / *Your Food-Allergic Child* $9.95

( ) Adamec / *There ARE Babies to Adopt* $16.95 (cloth)

( ) Adamec / *There ARE Babies to Adopt* $9.95 (paper)

( ) Cardoza/Sutton / *Winning Tactics for Women* $9.95

( ) Brandt/Corwen / *Fifty and Fired* $16.95 (cloth)

( ) Brandt/Corwen / *Fifty and Fired* $9.95 (paper)

( ) Giles / *Aquacises* $9.95

( ) Shaw / *60-Second Shiatzu* $7.95

( ) Shaw / *Your Astrological Guide to Fitness* $9.95

( ) Haskett / *Bachelor in the Kitchen* $7.95

$1.00 per book handling charge _____

5% sales tax for MA residents _____

Total amount enclosed _____

Name: _____

Address: _____

City: _____ State: _____ Zip code: _____

Mail to: Mills & Sanderson, Publishers
442 Marrett Road, Suite 6
Lexington, MA 02173
617-861-0992

Our Toll-Free Order # is 1-800-441-6224